THE *Story* OF STORIES

K A R E N   L E E - T H O R P

NAVPRESS

BRINGING TRUTH TO LIFE
NavPress Publishing Group
P.O. Box 35001, Colorado Springs, Colorado 80935

The Navigators is an international Christian organization. Jesus Christ gave His followers the Great Commission to go and make disciples (Matthew 28:19). The aim of The Navigators is to help fulfill that commission by multiplying laborers for Christ in every nation.

NavPress is the publishing ministry of The Navigators. NavPress publications are tools to help Christians grow. Although publications alone cannot make disciples or change lives, they can help believers learn biblical discipleship, and apply what they learn to their lives and ministries.

Library of Congress Catalog Card Number: 91-61423
ISBN 08910-96701

Cover illustration: Marco Ventura

Printed in the United States of America

1 2 3 4 5 6 7 8 9 10 11 12 13 14 / 00 99 98 97 96 95

FOR A FREE CATALOG OF
NAVPRESS BOOKS & BIBLE STUDIES,
CALL TOLL FREE 1-800-366-7788 (USA)
or 1-416-499-4615 (CANADA)

Contents

What This Book Is About

Most of the Bible consists of stories. Why? Partly because God knew that people like and remember stories better than lists of abstract propositions. And even more important, the stories remind us that *life* is a story, and that God is not an abstract doctrine, but a Person.

The Bible is God's account of His love for a species of creatures who have consistently hesitated to return that love. It's been a rocky romance from the beginning. So the Bible ought to be treated as a story—a five-star drama rather than a legal treatise.

But many modern readers have trouble getting into the story because the style (in the literary tastes of two and three millennia ago) and content (according to ancient customs the original writers felt no need to explain) bewilder them. The purpose of *The Story of Stories* is to tear down those barriers and present the tale in a vivid and intelligible form for contemporary readers.

You can read this book cover to cover like a novel, or you can sample what it says about a specific section or book of the Bible. The table of contents in the front and the index in the back can both help you find particular passages.

There are many, many details that have been left out of this book—not because they're unimportant, but because this is not a scholarly reference book. And yet, it is thoroughly researched, and is *not* fictionalized. The technical work and theological reflections of many scholars—more than could possibly be listed—have gone into this book.

Certainly there are plenty of good reference texts available, but they often deal with debates that tend to leave ordinary mortals in the dust. So, for the sake of simplicity and read-ability, the story of God reaching down to man—which is truly the story of all stories—is told in a literary style, yet with the deepest respect for God and His Book.

The Story of Stories is certainly no substitute for the Bible itself. In fact, you'll want to investigate "the Original" often as you read. But this book will give you a sense of the flow, the drama, and the over-arching themes of the Bible, as well as a deeper appreciation for the Author of this compelling Story.

1

Beginnings

◆

Genesis 1–3

Inside most of us is a nagging feeling that things aren't going the way they were meant to go. We're not the people we were meant to be. And there's more to life than meets the eye. So we start asking questions:

What's going on?
Is there any point to this exercise?
Does anybody care?
How did we get into this mess, anyway?

Genesis is a Greek word meaning "beginning." The book of Genesis is the first book of the Bible, so it is (not surprisingly) about beginnings: of the earth, the human race, marriage, languages; and also of how we got into this mess. It launches the tale of the making, breaking, and restoring of the friendship between God and humans.

"God" is the name Genesis uses in its first sentence to name a Being with personality and aliveness, a Being who is communicating to us from beyond our world. Genesis doesn't argue for His existence; it assumes it. After all, the book was written by a man named Moses who had an intimate friendship with this God, so His existence seemed obvious.

The events of Genesis occurred long before Moses was born. Many of them were passed down orally in his family, some were probably written family records, and Moses got the straight story from God when God assigned him to write the book. Imagine penning a book by discussing the material with a Being whom you could not see but whose presence and personality you were constantly aware of! To Moses, this was not spooky stuff; God was his Boss and Comrade.

Moses was the leader of a motley rabble of fugitive slaves who wanted to know just what we want to know: How did we get into this situation? What's going on? And who is this God? So Moses wrote, *In the beginning . . .*

Creation

"In the beginning God created the heavens and the earth" (Genesis 1:1). God has always existed. He is perfectly, exuberantly content in Himself, but He enjoys expressing His personality in making things. For He is not a force like electricity, or a concept, but a Being with character and creativity and life. In fact, He is the very essence of those things.

That's why we refer to Him with capital letters. Moses wrote in Hebrew, and in Genesis his word for God is *Elohim*. In Hebrew, *el* means "god" and *elohim* means "gods." But God is a "he," not a "they." Moses used the plural to convey God's majesty, His endless potential. It's like spelling His name with capitals.

God's way of creating is to speak things into existence. His word is so powerful that He simply uttered, "Light!" and the whole spectrum of electromagnetic energy with all its intricate properties came into being.

God took six "days" to create the physical universe. (It's unclear how long a "day" was before the earth rotated and revolved around the sun.) He started with a formless, empty void. On the first three days He gave form to what was formless by organizing atoms into energy and matter, air and water and land. On the second three He filled what was empty: the universe with stars, moons, and planets; the earth with animals and a special creature called man. (Genesis describes the Creation from the perspective of our earth. The rest of the universe is not the point of the story, even though it is just as precious to its Creator.)

To manage all of His earthly creation, God made this creature called man in His own image. Not in His physical image (God isn't a material being), but with abilities to reason, to create, to make moral choices, and to love. The Hebrew for man—*adam*—means "dust," but this dust-creature was something with which God could relate person to person. Man would be His friend and the resident manager of His earth. Man had two sexes, male and female, and together they reflected the glory of their Creator.

God looked at the ordered and life-filled world He had made, and He pronounced it "very good" (Genesis 1:31). It was so splendid that He took another whole day and rested to enjoy it. (God is a dedicated artist, but He's no workaholic!)

Focus on Man
The story of creation pretty much ignored most of the universe and focused on earth. Thereafter the Bible zeros in on people and pays little attention to the rest of the earth. (Geology and botany are probably very important to the God who invented rocks and plants, but they are not what the Bible is about.)

The invention of man was a risk, the consequences of which the all-knowing God could already foresee. Sun, ocean, tree, and fish wouldn't give God any trouble; they would function according to the laws He had built into them. But a creature free to choose to obey and love could equally choose to betray and reject. And God had given that creature authority over the whole earthly creation. The One who uttered neutrons into existence was yielding much control over His masterpiece and exposing Himself to the pain of jilted love. Pain! He could have existed into eternity without pain, but He risked anguish in order to have something outside Himself to love that could love Him back.

This was the genius of God's invention. He had previously made creatures who were pure spirit: they could reason, make choices, and perceive qualities in God like His majesty. "Holy, holy, holy!" they cried as they worshiped Him unceasingly for His greatness and perfection. But His love was beyond their capacity to grasp. A being needed feelings—even passion— to understand what it would mean to offer oneself to another vulnerably and to share—well, to share love. God was a passionate, self-giving Being, and His angels were utterly unable to appreciate this side of Him. On the other side, animals had feelings but could not reason and make moral choices; their love lacked consciousness and maturity. Man was God's ingenious hybrid—spirit and soul, reason and passion, the finest reflection of Himself that God could produce.

So God put His first man in a garden where a mighty river and warm mist provided water for a lush array of fruit trees. To practice his Godlike qualities of creativity and authority, Adam/Man was to begin with gardening and naming the animals. To practice his ability to make moral choices, he received one restriction, so that he could choose whether to obey his Parent. In the middle of the garden grew "the tree of life" and "the tree of the knowledge of good and evil." Adam could eat from any tree except the tree of the knowledge of good and evil. Of the tree of life God said nothing.

When Genesis focuses on man, it adds a personal name for Elohim, *YHWH*. English Bibles render this word as "the LORD" with capital letters, or as "Jehovah" or "Yahweh." Modern scholars think "Yahweh" is the most probable original pronunciation, so we will use it (substituting "Yahweh" for "the LORD" in Scripture quotes). Adam knew God as Yahweh, but not for thousands of years did Yahweh disclose the meaning of that name.

Yahweh had made Adam need relationship the way he needed food and water. Most of all he needed relationship with Yahweh, but he also needed it with someone physical like himself. None of the animals would suffice because they didn't bear Yahweh's image. Adam needed a partner who could share his noble work. So Yahweh took part of Adam and made a second dust-creature like him. The two became man and woman, husband and wife. They were completely open to each other, emotionally and physically. They were an inseparable unity: "one flesh." Adam may have been the leader, but there was no dominating or manipulating.

Treason

Earth and its inhabitants were "very good." All but one—an invader from outside the physical universe, a spirit who camouflaged himself as a snake. He had been the highest of God's angelic servants until he rebelled. According to tradition, his name had been Lucifer ("lightbearer"), but it became Satan ("the adversary") and Abaddon ("the destroyer"). He simply did not care to spend eternity worshiping his Creator; he considered that boring and beneath him. So he declared his independence and set up a rival kingdom.

That meant war. A number of spirit beings joined with the rebel, while the rest fought for God. When his direct attack failed, Satan resolved to strike at God indirectly by corrupting His physical creation. He would smash the hopes of this foolish God who tied His own hands by giving choice to dust-creatures. He would claim earth for his own kingdom, reduce its inhabitants to slavery, and make them an eternal grief to their spurned Creator.

Most of this information is inferred from comments scattered later in the Bible (such as Isaiah 14:12-15, Ezekiel 28:11-19, Revelation 12:1-9). In Genesis we see only the Snake appearing to the woman as one of her harmless and loyal subjects. She was queen of her garden and feared nothing.

First the Serpent politely dropped a question: Did God

really ban you from eating fruit from these fine trees? (How unreasonable! Tyrannical!)

"No," said the woman, "only the one tree is off limits. We'll die if we even touch that one." Now God had said nothing about touching the tree; already God's instructions and character were blurring in her mind.

Into this tiny crack of doubt the Viper thrust a wedge. "You won't die," he declared. (God is a liar!) "For God knows that when you eat from that tree, your eyes will be opened, and you will be like God, knowing good and evil." (God doesn't love you. He wants to keep you in slavery and ignorance. Rebellion is the only rational course to protect yourself.)

Everything the woman knew about God's loving care, His desire for her and Adam to rule the earth, His wisdom and gentleness—all was forgotten as she considered the Snake's charges. The fruit's scent and color enticed her senses. And its deeper properties—its capacity to give her wisdom beyond what God had seen fit to grant—tantalized something else welling up within her. The Serpent knew its name, though she did not. The name belonged to the knowledge of evil she had not yet tasted. It was pride.

So this woman—who lived in unimaginable luxury as queen of virtually all she surveyed—chose to grab for yet more status and sensual pleasure. Had she waited, would God have given her the sweet fruit with the joy of knowledge in His own time? We can't say, for she elected what the Bible calls *sin*—falling short of God's best, rejecting His instructions, seeking to take by force what He would give by grace.

But the Snake hadn't won yet. The man was the senior partner in this marriage, and he might still have run to his Lord and begged pardon for his bride. We don't know what might have happened if the man had done that.

Because he didn't. The story tells us that Eve was deceived (maybe Adam didn't explain Yahweh's command to her properly), but Adam made a clear-eyed choice. Understanding the implications, he chose pride and sensuality over patience and trust. And when *both* of them had eaten the fruit, they understood evil from the inside. They felt guilty, exposed, shameful. They tried to cover their naked bodies. When Yahweh came to enjoy their company, what had before been delight was now sheer terror. Something in their minds had been twisted so that their perceptions of reality were distorted. They were paranoid—their beloved Friend seemed a grim enemy. They hid.

Yahweh knew what had happened. But in order to give every chance for a change of heart, He called out from a distance, "Where are you?" Are there any shreds of sanity that I can reach?

But instead of a gentle probe, the deluded man heard a harsh demand. Instead of crying out for forgiveness, he made excuses and blamed the woman—"the woman *you* gave me"—for the trouble. She blamed the Snake. The diagnosis was clear: acute paranoid psychosis. No signs of remission.

Heaven wept. The ache of rejection touched the Infinite One, and He embraced it. A spurned Lover, a betrayed Parent, He could have battered these rebels back into submission.

But Yahweh had foreseen this tragedy long before He formed these choosing creatures. He already had a plan to deal with their loss of mental and moral health, a plan that would astonish not only the fallen spirits who thought Him mad, but also the loyal ones who knew only the cool obedience of pure rationality. When He wooed these renegades back with love instead of power, the cosmos would marvel and understand.

Yahweh's first step was to curse the Snake. It would eat dust for the rest of its existence—a hint of degradation, but also an ominous sign since man was made of dust. Furthermore, the battle for the earth was not over. There would be permanent war between the descendants of the woman who served Yahweh and the descendants of the Serpent who served him. And one day a Descendant of this woman would finally crush that Snake, even though He would be bitten in the contest.

Next Yahweh turned to the woman. The price of choosing

pride and delusion was the warping of womanhood: child-bearing would be agony, and marital partnership would degenerate into lust, futile craving for intimacy, and fearful domination.

The man's cost was a curse upon his beloved earth. He would still have the dignity of tending it, but his labor would be bitter toil ending in the futility of death and dust.

There was no cruelty in these judgments. The joys of marriage and childbearing and fruitful labor were not wholly taken away, and Yahweh was merely declaring the natural consequences of the humans' choice. He had warned that stealing the fruit would bring death, and so it had: moral death, the death of friendship with God and intimacy between man and wife, the death of clear thinking and feeling—with a scent of corruption permeating every aspect of life.

Physical death would come, too. Yahweh banished the humans from the garden so that they would not also steal from the tree of life. For as much as it grieved Him to see His beloved ones decay and die, it would be far worse for them to live forever physically in moral and relational death. He planned to use physical death to restore real life.

As a sign of this, He killed an animal for the first time and used its skin to clothe His humans. Innocent blood was shed to cover their shame. It would not be the last time.

2

The Descent of Man

Genesis 5–11

The Sons of the Woman and the Sons of the Snake

In one day, Adam and Eve fell from lords of a garden paradise to subsistence farmers struggling to eke out a crop using stone tools and sweat. They could no longer chat with Yahweh familiarly, but had to learn formal rites by which to worship Him. They were helpless to shake off the serpentine smog that had infected their minds, hearts, and wills. Their one hope was the promise that a child of Eve would break the Viper's corrupting power.

That promise was on the Snake-spirit's mind, too, no doubt. When Eve bore her first two sons, he conceived a plan to foil God's intent. He easily seduced the older son, Cain, into pride, jealousy of his brother's favor with God, and eventually murder. That got rid of the younger son, who might have become the Devil's foe.

Yahweh might have killed Cain for his crime, but He didn't. In mercy, He only banished Cain from His presence and predicted that he would pass his life as a restless, dissatisfied wanderer. Yahweh even marked Cain in some way to protect him from vengeance by any of Adam's future children.

Well, Cain married someone (a sister?) and had children, and his children had children. But it was always "like father, like son." Cain's great-great-great-grandson was Lamech, a wanton prince who boasted that he would kill a man even for injuring him. He raised some ingenious sons dedicated to mastering nature and raising a civilization. (One son invented nomadic shepherding, a second musical instruments, and a third metalsmithing.) These men were making it without God, and proud of it.

Fortunately, Cain was not the only son of Adam left. Adam fathered a herd of children, but the Bible focuses on just one—Seth. Seth's descendants were a bit better than Cain's; they did their best to humbly acknowledge their dependence on God. But none became the promised Deliverer; each one fell in the end to death. The one exception, Enoch, lived such an exemplary life of love for God that he was taken to God without dying. It was a whisper of hope in a weary age.

For the Serpent was still at work behind the scenes. The Bible doesn't mention him, but his fingerprints are all over the data. The line of Seth was pure; these were the true sons of the woman. But the line of Cain became more and more a viper's brood with every generation. What if the two were blended? When you mix water and poison, which overcomes the other? If the only pure line of humans were tainted, then perhaps the Deliverer could never be born. Snakish reasoning.

By this time the Devil knew that even the noble sons of Seth were vulnerable to sexual seduction, and the brazen daughters of Cain knew how to seduce. The Bible says with its usual understatement, "the sons of God saw that the daughters of men were beautiful, and they married any of them they chose" (Genesis 6:2). Thus the line in which the character of God still shone mixed with the one whose traits were mere debased humanness. The result was a race whom people considered "heroes . . . men of renown," but whom God named the Nephilim, "the fallen ones."

He mourned. "[Yahweh] saw how great man's wickedness on the earth had become, and that every inclination of the thoughts of his heart was only evil all the time" (Genesis 6:5). Pride, lust, violence, exploitation—it was disgusting. Yahweh decided to wipe out the human race. (Did the Devil chuckle when he heard this?)

The Flood
But Satan hadn't won yet. There remained one descendant of the pure line of Seth. Noah was not the promised Deliverer, but he did honor Yahweh and try to live His way as much as possible.

He probably prayed to Yahweh regularly for guidance, and one day he got more than he bargained for. Yahweh informed Noah that He planned to destroy all human and animal life on the earth with a massive flood. When Noah recovered from the shock, Yahweh gave him detailed instructions for building a wooden ship the size of an ocean liner. He was to bring two of every kind of animal (plus extras of certain species) with him and his family into the vessel, so that the earth could be repopulated afterward.[1]

So in a landlocked region hundreds of miles from the sea, Noah built his ocean vessel. His wife must have spent weeks trying not to notice the neighbors whispering. Imagine pairs of animals beginning to line up in your backyard. Then hauling them and their fodder into the dark wooden box shaped alarmingly like a casket. These people had some gutsy trust in their God. It was vindicated when the rain began to fall and fall and fall.

For forty days, eight humans and a lot of animals listened to rain pelt the ceiling of their ship. For another 110 days, they floated aimlessly. Maybe they wondered as the months passed whether God had forgotten them. "But God remembered" (Genesis 8:1).

The waters receded, and at last the ship landed on a mountaintop in what is now Turkey. Seven months later, the waters were low enough for the whole crowd to emerge into the sunlight. After more than a year in a floating box, solid ground must have felt like Heaven.

The Rainbow Covenant

Upon landing, almost the first thing Noah did was to sacrifice some of the extra animals as a gesture of thanks to Yahweh. It seems like a grisly thing to do, but Yahweh had commanded the practice to sear a lesson into His people's minds. Human selfishness is ugly. Not only is it treason against the rightful King, but it smashes every relationship and stains the whole creation. It therefore merits the death penalty, and somebody has to pay the price. In His mercy, Yahweh accepted the blood of animals in exchange for that of humans. It was not a permanent solution.

In response to Noah's obedience, Yahweh covenanted in the sunlight of a freshly scrubbed world never again to deal with human evil through annihilation.[2] The sign of that commitment was light fragmenting through rain clouds into the full spectrum of the first rainbow. Sheer force had failed to achieve Yahweh's goal: freely chosen love from His people. He had a better plan.

Furthermore, Yahweh granted humans the right to eat meat (before this they were vegetarians) as long as they didn't drink blood. To humans, blood symbolized the mysterious power of life, and they had devised magical rituals of drinking blood to try to preserve or increase their life force. However, life was Yahweh's gift, and it was rebellion for people to try to take it against God's will. Magic was the epitome of Adam's sin: humanity's attempt to control power so that it need not depend on Yahweh's generosity.

The Nations

So Yahweh sent the humans and animals off to repopulate the earth. It was just as well that He had sworn not to engulf the world again, for it didn't take long for human perversity to reassert itself. Noah grew grapes and got drunk on wine; his youngest son, Ham, invited his brothers to mock the sot lying unconscious and mostly naked in his tent. Noah was livid when he awoke, and in his rage he prophesied the fates of all his descendants.

He cursed the line of Ham's son Canaan to be the slaves of his other sons' offspring. The Canaanites became a wicked Caucasian people who lived in Palestine. (We'll see what happened to them in chapter 9.) The rest of Ham's descendants filled southwestern Asia and northeastern Africa. God chose not to include them in their father's curse. One of them, Nimrod, founded the first "kingdom"—a state in which someone ruled not just a clan but a group of unrelated people—in Mesopotamia (modern Iraq). He did this by being the first to conquer subjects by force of arms. Nimrod was the first military dictator.

Unlike Ham, Noah's eldest son, Shem, loved Yahweh. To him Noah passed on the ancient hope of fathering the Deliverer. To his third son, Japheth, Noah prophesied that his territory would be great and that one day his offspring would share Shem's blessing of being God's chosen ones. The Japhethites became Europeans and Asians. The Shemites became the people we call Semitic: Arabs, some Mesopotamians, and Jews.

Babel

The descendants of Shem, Ham, and Japheth bred prolificly. By 7000 BC (archaeologists tell us) there were a few little farming communities with stone-walled cities and rock-hewn wells. By 4000 BC there were a lot of them. Many communities developed their own cults and dedicated themselves to their cultic gods. In rituals timed to the cycle of seasons, the people worshiped gods of rain, sun, and fertility. The community's chief was usually its priest.

Eventually, communities began to unite under one cult with one priest-king and one temple. The cult ran the kingdom. Those early religious states invented arithmetic to record economic transactions and astrological observations, and writing for legends, songs, poems, laws, and ethics.

Naturally, the descendants of Noah all spoke the same language. This made the gathering of communities into kingdoms easier. The people of Nimrod's kingdom believed they could control human destiny by reading the movement of the stars. To this end they invented the zodiac and horoscope. Their gods were the sun, moon, and the five planets known to them. They decided to build an immense temple-tower as a staircase from earth to the heavens.

On the same site we can still see the ruins of a tower called *Birs Nimroud*, perhaps a later attempted reconstruction. The base was built of mud bricks and tar in seven stages, like a staircase-hill. Each stage was painted a color that corresponded to one of the gods—black for Saturn, orange for Jupiter, and so on. On top was a tower painted with the signs of the zodiac, in which the priests sought to reach the heavens by magical rites. This tower was 153 feet high and covered nearly four acres.

The goal of the enormous tower was to win fame for its builders. They hated the idea that one day they would die and be forgotten, so they assuaged their wounded pride by striving for an immortal reputation (Genesis 11:4).

Now, Yahweh intended to one day unite all humankind in love of each other and of Him. But here they were uniting in honor of human pride and false gods (behind whom He saw spirit beings allied with Satan). Through their star magic, aided by their demon gods, they hoped to wrest control of human destiny from Yahweh. This was clearly another plan of that Snake to rule the world through evil people.

Yahweh had no intention of allowing a united world government on those terms. Unruffled, He simply touched the people's minds so that they could no longer understand each other. That put a stop to this project. The builders had called their city *Babel* (Babylon), which meant "gateway to a god," but Yahweh punned that it was really *balal* (translated "confused" in Genesis 11:9). A divine chuckle.

Then Yahweh scattered the people over the earth. They carried with them their false worship and their pride, but they were no longer powerful enough to hinder Yahweh's plan. It was an intricate strategy that set up His next critical move.

NOTES

1. Calculations have proven it would actually have been possible to fit representatives of all land species into a ship of the size the Bible specifies, along with enough food and water to sustain them.

2. A covenant is an agreement between two parties: a marriage, a business contract, a political treaty, a friendship pact. Many covenants are two-sided agreements between equals. But the Bible records a series of covenants that God freely bestowed on people as acts of love and grace. These covenants tied God and people together like a marriage bond, a legal adoption into a family, or a king's agreement to rule a group of people with justice. The covenants were solemnly sealed with legal ceremonies.

   The two big divisions of the Bible are the Old Testament and the New Testament. In modern English, a "testament" is a document that declares what people want to do with their property when they die. But in the Bible it is an old English rendering of the Hebrew word for "covenant." So the two divisions of the Bible are the Old Covenant and the New Covenant. The Old Testament could correctly be called "The Books of the Old Covenant"—books about the old agreement between God and a certain nation of humans. Because the humans found it impossible to live up to their commitments in that covenant, God promised to make a new one. The New Testament records how God made that New Covenant and what life is like under that agreement between God and people.

3

God Chooses a Family

◆

Genesis 11:10–50:26

Abram

As Noah predicted, the line of Shem was the focus of Yahweh's plan. Generations passed into centuries, wars flared here and there, the Babel debacle was dealt with, and inconspicuously a Shemite named Terah fathered three sons: Abram, Nahor, and Haran.

Terah was a herdsman near the prosperous and sophisticated city of Ur. It was a splendid site in Terah's youth, until a horde of barbarians called Guti conquered the region. They squandered Ur's wealth, let commerce and culture decline, and exploited the local population. Still, Terah managed to raise his three sons and get all of them married.

But eventually Terah decided he'd had enough of Ur and the Guti. (See map, page 360.) So he set off with his family for the land of Canaan, a thousand miles away. However, after covering six hundred miles, Terah called a halt in the town of Haran. Perhaps he'd heard that beyond Haran travel was a thirsty, risky business, and both the customs and climate of Canaan would be hard for an old man to adjust to.

Haran, though, was more or less like Ur. Both towns were watered by the Euphrates River so they didn't have to worry about rainfall, and in both towns the people worshiped the moon god Nannar and other astral deities. Terah's family were probably also moon worshipers. But there was also a family memory of a god named Yahweh. Back in Ur, Abram had had a strange encounter with Yahweh.

Was it a dream? A vision? An audible voice? It was a sevenfold promise out of the blue:

♦ "I will make you into a great nation."
♦ "I will bless you."
♦ "I will make your name great."
♦ "You will be a blessing [to others]."
♦ "I will bless those who bless you."
♦ "Whoever curses you I will curse."
♦ "All peoples on earth will be blessed through you" (Genesis 12:2-3).

All peoples. Even now, as Yahweh focused on a single family, He had all earth's families on His heart. Most of them, from Peru to China, had forgotten He existed and went on with their lives as though no world-shattering promise had come to a herdsman in Iraq. But the Snake knew. From this one would come the Son of Eve.

Greatness! Fame! Protection! And all Yahweh told Abram to do (at this point) was go to Canaan.

To Canaan

Abram didn't actually manage to obey this instruction until Terah had died in Haran. By that time, Abram was seventy-five years old—but better late than never.

So after burying Terah, Abram set out on the four-hundred-mile trek. With him went his wife Sarai, his nephew Lot, and all of the animals and hired or purchased workers

Terah had acquired in Haran. They would have had to find a caravan driver who knew the ropes, for between Haran and Egypt water was available only at closely guarded wells and springs. The driver had to know where those wells were, what route would assure that the animals could reach a well every evening, and how to negotiate payment for the water according to the local customs. At fifteen miles a day on foot, the trip would have taken about a month.

Eventually the family arrived at Shechem in the very center of Canaan. From one of the two hills nearby, Abram could have overlooked the whole country. There Yahweh appeared to him and added an eighth promise: "To your offspring I will give this land." This must have been the most staggering promise yet from Abram's point of view, especially since the land was already teeming with thousands of Canaanites.

They were a proud and unruly bunch. Each city was independent, and they constantly feuded over land and trading rights. Strangers planning to settle down among them were not always safe. So Abram led his caravan of family, servants, retainers, sheep, goats, and donkeys south to the rugged land near the semidesert Negev. This region sufficed for grazing, but not for growing crops, so only a few herdsmen used it. Their life included watching for lions, jackals, and bears; calling wandering sheep; carrying young lambs and kids; milking and shearing; mending tents; and searching endlessly for grass and water.

Faith and Obedience

Yahweh's great plan focused on a ragged nomad in the middle of nowhere. Not even an especially honest nomad: early on Abram fled Canaan during a drought and actually told his wife to say she was his sister so that Egypt's ruler wouldn't kill him to take her for his harem. And anyway, Abram reasoned, it wasn't *exactly* a lie—Sarai was his *half*-sister.

But Abram was strong raw material: perhaps he was fed up with the ritualized appeasement of vague and arbitrary gods, and was ready for a forthright give-and-take with a God with moral fiber. With a little coaching he could become the progenitor of a prime family through which he would bless the nations.

So Abram lived a hundred years after he left Haran, and Yahweh spent the first forty leading him through a course designed to teach him one basic lesson: *Trust and obey Me, no matter what the situation looks like.* The course went like this. On the one hand, Yahweh repeatedly got Abram out of messes and turned everything he touched to gold. But on the other hand, He kept dangling that promise before Abram's nose—"Your offspring will be countless and will possess this land"—and never so much as let Sarai get pregnant or allowed Abram to own even a bucketful of real estate. Three decades of this drove Abram crazy. But when he tried to handle matters himself, such as seeking a surrogate mother in Sarai's handmaid, he only ended up with a domestic nightmare. Slowly he learned that the only thing worse than waiting on Yahweh was not waiting on Yahweh.

And in his better moments, even though he ranted about the raw deal he was getting, Abram was convinced deep down that he could trust Yahweh. The evidence of his Friend's character outweighed that of the "laws" of nature. After all, who made the laws? This quality of faith was what Yahweh was striving for, the one criterion for the kind of friendship He longed to have with His human inventions.

So Yahweh let Abram and Sarai endure thirty years of silence with only rare promises to hang onto. Why wasn't He quicker? Because love trusts. Love waits because it knows the beloved's character. Yahweh didn't want to be loved because He always showed up on cue to grant wishes. He wanted to be trusted in the dark.

Then suddenly, after a thirteen-year silence, Yahweh appeared in some kind of physical form on Abram's doorstep. Over lunch, as though they were old buddies who hadn't seen each other for awhile, He announced that Sarai would have a son the following year. He put a letter from His own name (the Hebrew "H") into Abram's and renamed him Abraham, "father of many." He renamed Sarai as Sarah—"princess"—mother of nations and kings. (Renaming was an ancient way of claiming authority over someone, as well as a way of declaring something essential about the person.) To Abraham's male descendants He gave an unforgettable mark of loyalty: circumcision. It symbolized a self-cursing oath: "If I am not faithful to Yahweh, may He cut off me and my offspring as I have cut off my foreskin." And to top it all off, He named the long-promised son Isaac ("he laughs"). Giving sons to ninety-year-old women in answer to thirty years of prayer was Yahweh's idea of a joke—albeit a happy joke for Abraham and Sarah.

Final Exam
Abraham's final test came when Isaac had grown to adolescence. One day Yahweh ordered him to take Isaac to a certain mountain, slit his throat, and burn the body. What? But "Trust Me" had been engraved into Abraham's gut. The one non-negotiable fact on which he had bet his life was that Yahweh would keep His promises, even if it meant raising Isaac from the dead. So Abraham didn't have to lie awake at night worrying, or try to put the ugly order out of his mind. He simply obeyed. When Isaac asked him why they weren't bringing an animal to sacrifice, Abraham was able to reply that God Himself would provide it. He didn't know how, but he knew his Friend.

And Isaac trusted his father and his God. He didn't resist when Abraham tied him and laid him on the altar. And at the last instant, when Abraham was about to plunge the knife into his son's throat, an angel stopped him. Abraham had demonstrated that nothing—not even his beloved son or his dreams of greatness—meant more to him than Yahweh. So because they were not idols, he could keep both son and dreams.

Still, Abraham went to his grave with no evidence that Yahweh would fulfill His promises—other than Isaac himself.

He still had one childless son and owned nothing but a field for a family burial plot (for which he paid an exorbitant sum). Yet he died content.

Isaac

Considering all the agony Abraham went through to get Isaac, you might think the Bible would say a lot about him. But it doesn't. Isaac's role in Yahweh's plan was to raise his sons to be like his dad.

Isaac and Rebekah more or less relived Abraham and Sarah's life. Isaac became extremely rich; Rebekah was barren; Isaac even lied to a powerful prince that Rebekah was his sister, for fear that the man might kill him to take her. Where have we heard that one before?

Jacob's Transformation

When at last Rebekah became pregnant with twins, Yahweh selected the one who would be born second, the younger one, to carry on the plan.[1] Rivals from the start, the twins even came out of the womb competing to see who would be born first. Because the younger appeared grasping the older's heel, he was named Jacob, "heel-grasper." The name suggested a man who would hold fast to his goals and duties, but it also implied "deceiver," "supplanter." Jacob was the true son and grandson of men who had lied more than once to save their own necks.

So while Abraham's training in trust was a matter of endless waiting, Yahweh had to put Jacob through an obstacle course to fairly beat out of him his bent to use guile to get what Yahweh would give by grace.

Jacob was barely a teenager when he had to flee from home to escape his brother Esau's wrath; he had swindled Esau out of the firstborn's rights (a double portion of the inheritance, leadership of the family, and the father's blessing). He was scared as he began hiking northward five hundred miles from Isaac's camp in Beersheba to his relatives' place in Haran. In those days, a person was a fool to travel without a caravan of food, water, and companions to discourage robbers. Jacob had neither a map nor a guide. And like most people of his day, he probably believed that his father's God had power only in a particular locality—in this case, Canaan. Jacob had great confidence in his wits, but he was out of his depth.

On his first night out, Yahweh appeared to him at a spot called Bethel and repeated the covenant promises He made to Abraham and Isaac. Land and descendants meant little to teenage Jacob, but he clung to one assurance: "I am with you and will watch over you wherever you go, and I will bring you back to this land. I will not leave you until I have done what I have promised you" (Genesis 28:15). Here was a God who claimed power anywhere in the world! Jacob made a deal with Yahweh: You take care of me, and I'll worship you. It was not quite the arrangement Yahweh had with Abraham, but it would do as a beginning.

The Wrestler
It took Yahweh twenty years to break Jacob. It took an uncle who was a worse cheater than he was and two wives who treated him like a stud stallion to fuel their childbearing competition. It took twenty years of backbreaking work and endless bickering in his burgeoning tents. He became as rich as his dad and supported two wives, two concubines (slave semi-wives), thirteen children, and a lot of servants. He thought he owed his success to his own cleverness, even though Yahweh really deserved the credit. Yet in the end Jacob's uncle was mad enough at his good fortune to seize his family, so he tried to run again.

But this time his uncle caught up with him, and even Jacob could see that only divine intervention, not his own cunning, saved his skin. He also finally faced the fact that running from broken relationships was futile. So although he was heading to Bethel and would pass nowhere near Esau's land southeast of Canaan, Jacob sent a message to his brother that he was returning and wanted to be reconciled.

Jacob spent the night before their meeting alone, having it out with Yahweh. He wasn't so much concerned that Esau was coming with four hundred armed men who might slaughter his family. For the first time, he didn't want something from God, he wanted God. In the night a man appeared to him and wrestled with him until dawn. In the morning, his hip was injured so that he limped, and he had a new name: Israel, "he struggles with God." Like a proud stallion, Jacob had been broken to God's hand over twenty years of wrestling. Though he limped from the struggle, he was transformed. No more "Jacob the deceiver," cunning as a serpent; he was now a true son of the promise.

Sibling Rivalry

So Jacob-Israel[2] settled down in Canaan and became a responsible patriarch over a large household and thriving livestock business. Everything was going smoothly except that his twelve sons were a delinquent gang, capable of inflicting revenge on a whole town when one citizen raped their sister. Yahweh had slated Jacob's sons to father the twelve tribes of Israel, the bearers of His plan, and they needed more of Yahweh's discipline than Abraham, Isaac, and Jacob put together.

To mold the brothers for this role, Yahweh selected for special treatment number eleven, the adolescent Joseph, whose ten older siblings detested him for two reasons. First, he was Jacob's pet. Second, he dreamed about his family bowing down to him as their master. So one day the ten sold Joseph as a slave to some merchants traveling to Egypt, then went home weeping that a wild animal ate him.

As Joseph's dreams attested, Yahweh had grand intentions for him, but the road to greatness in Yahweh's service is rarely without its potholes. As a slave, Joseph rose to become the household manager for the captain of the Egyptian pharaoh's guard. Then for insulting the captain's wife by resisting her sexual advances, Joseph found himself in Pharaoh's dungeon charged with attempted rape.

By contrast, consider Joseph's brothers back in Canaan. Reuben, the eldest, was disinherited for seducing one of his dad's concubines. Son number four, Judah, had two of his sons killed by Yahweh for their depravity, but Judah blamed their widow, Tamar. He refused to marry his one remaining son to her, even though custom demanded it, and condemned her to childless widowhood. Desperate, she disguised herself as a prostitute and waited along a road she knew Judah was traveling. He hired her services and in pledge of payment gave her his staff and signature seal. When he got home, he tried to send payment, but no one had ever heard of this prostitute. But three months later, Tamar turned up pregnant, and when brought out to be executed for adultery, she virtually threw the staff and seal in Judah's face. Ashamed, he took her back into his house and took responsibility for her. She bore twin sons, Perez and Zerah, who became Judah's sole heirs.

Yet while Reuben and Judah dallied, Joseph languished in Pharaoh's jail until word reached Pharaoh that a certain Hebrew rotting in his prison was a master of dream interpretation. In the time it took Yahweh to give Joseph the meaning of Pharaoh's latest dream and a strategy for handling the agricultural disaster it portended, Joseph went from dungeon rat to prime minister.

Seven years later, famine hit the whole Middle East. But news spread that Egypt had grain because the prime minister had been stockpiling it. People began to stream from everywhere to buy food.

Jacob dispatched his ten older sons, but inexplicably, the prime minister had them jailed as spies. (Joseph had recognized them immediately, but it never dawned on them that this thirty-eight-year-old, clean-shaven Egyptian lord might be the obnoxious teenager they sold some twenty years earlier.) After three days he released all but one and declared that until they brought to Egypt the youngest brother whom they claimed to have, brother Simeon would rot in Pharaoh's jail.

The nine were aghast. They knew their God well enough

to recognize His hand somewhere in all of this, punishing their cruelty to Joseph. And Jacob was beside himself when they returned without yet another of his sons. He wouldn't hear of sending his youngest, Benjamin, to Egypt. But when the grain ran out and the children began to cry, he gave in. Reuben and Judah pledged their lives if they didn't bring both Simeon and Benjamin home safely.

Upon their return Joseph played some more mind games with them until they were convinced that Yahweh was destroying them for betraying their brother. When it was obvious that all of them had cracked under pressure, Joseph burst into tears and told them the whole story. It took several reassurances before they grasped that he was not about to execute them for their past malice. But Joseph had come to see that although they were responsible for their freely chosen crime, Yahweh had used it to save the whole Middle East from a desolating famine and especially to protect His chosen family from extinction.

Out of gratitude to Joseph, Pharaoh invited his whole family to come and live in some of Egypt's best land. Yahweh told Jacob to go. It so happened that the Egyptians considered herdsmen disgusting, so Pharaoh selected the fertile but out-of-the-way region of Goshen for Jacob's clan to settle in. There would be no temptation to intermingle with the Egyptians and lose their family traditions.

Into the Future
On his deathbed, Jacob's mind was on the all-important divine promises. He made Joseph promise to bury him with Abraham and Isaac in Canaan, as a sign of faith that the land would one day be theirs. He also pronounced prophetic fatherly blessings upon each of his sons, as well as upon Joseph's two sons. In these blessings, he declared how the family inheritance would be distributed and foresaw what would happen in future centuries as his sons' families became tribes of the great nation God had promised.

First was the matter of the firstborn. Reuben had forfeited the eldest son's rights. His tribe, therefore, would never fulfill its hope of greatness, and Reuben himself would inherit neither the headship of the family nor the double portion of property.

Simeon and Levi, the next two eldest, had instigated the massacre to avenge their raped sister. Therefore, Jacob passed them over for the firstborn's rights and said their tribes would be scattered among their brothers' tribes.

The fourth eldest was Judah. He received the right of headship. Jacob declared that Judah would be the ruling tribe of Israel "until he comes to whom it [the scepter of kingship] belongs" (Genesis 49:10). Whatever that meant. Did Jacob and sons think of the Son of Eve? Surely the Serpent did.

The next six sons received their blessings in their turns— all double-edged, foreseeing both their greatness and their weakness. Then came Joseph, the eldest son of Jacob's favorite wife. To him Jacob bequeathed the firstborn's double portion. He adopted Joseph's two sons, Ephraim and Manasseh, and gave each a full inheritance equal to that of Joseph's brothers. Ironically, Ephraim was the younger of the two, but Jacob saw from Yahweh that what he himself had stolen from Esau, Yahweh was giving to Ephraim with no need for human scheming.

Joseph ruled in Egypt about another sixty years after Jacob's death, raised his grandchildren, and kept his heart on the covenant between his father and his God. His last words to his family reassured them that Yahweh would one day bring them home to Canaan to take possession of it. Trusting in that conviction, he asked to be put in a coffin but not buried until the family could return to bury him with his ancestors in their promised home.

NOTES
1. It was not out of cruelty that Yahweh kept setting aside whole populations and choosing others who were in no way superior. On the contrary, by grooming the chosen branch in each generation (Abraham, then Isaac instead of Ishmael, then Jacob instead of Esau), Yahweh planned ultimately to bring blessing and deliverance to all the other peoples.To make the point that the nonchosen branches of the family are not forgotten, Genesis always includes short genealogies for them.

Yahweh was also underscoring the fact that He had the right to choose whomever He wished, and that He thought little of human criteria. He had selected an insignificant nomadic family—not sophisticated aristocrats or philosophers—out of all the families of the earth. He had closed Sarah's womb and then opened it when she was ninety. And now He selected Isaac's younger son when the human custom was to honor the firstborn.

2. The man Israel became the founding father of a nation by the same name. It was common practice in the Middle East for tribes or nations to be named after a noteworthy patriarch. Jacob's brother Esau, nicknamed Edom ("red"), gave his name to a nation southeast of Israel. Two nations east of Israel, Ammon and Moab, were named after two great-grandnephews of Abraham.

4

Liberation

◆

Exodus 1:1–15:21

Slavery

For two centuries, the family of Jacob-Israel herded sheep and goats in the fertile Nile delta. After the arid pastures of southern Canaan, this was sheep heaven. The flocks were prolific, and so were the humans.

The Egyptians left the filthy Hebrew shepherds alone with their animals and their strange uncivilized customs. In two hundred years the children of Israel picked up very little from the art, literature, religion, science and social life of the culture only miles away. They simply milked their goats, sheared their sheep, clung stubbornly to their one God, and multiplied. Soon there were thousands of them.

Meanwhile, Joseph was forgotten in the Egyptian court. The dynasties of the Middle Kingdom were overrun by Hyksos, a Semitic people who regarded their fellow Semites as rivals. And the Egyptian lords who finally rooted the Hyksos out of their country were in no mood to be harboring huge enclaves of Semitic foreigners. After all (reasoned Pharaoh

Ahmose, the founder of the eighteenth Egyptian dynasty and the man who finally expelled the Hyksos), if war breaks out, these Israelites might side with our enemies and then leave when we are overwhelmed again.

Ahmose was not about to let that happen. And since he wanted to build some fine cities for his glorious new dynasty, he enslaved all the Israelites, appointed slave masters to keep them in line, and assigned them to forced labor in his fields and brickworks. But the more the Egyptians drove the Israelites, the more they seemed to breed like rabbits. Exasperated, the pharaoh decreed that all Hebrew boys must be killed at birth.

A Savior Is Born?
But Jochebed, a descendant of Jacob's son Levi, resolved to protect her son from the slave masters. When he was three months old, she put him in a basket and floated it in the Nile. Pharaoh's daughter came down to bathe, found the baby, and on a whim decided to raise him. Not even Ahmose could dissuade his daughter, so a Hebrew joined the royal family. The princess named him Moses, which meant "is born" in Egyptian (her father's name meant "[the god] Ah is born"), but which happened to sound like the Hebrew for "to draw out."

Moses was raised as an Egyptian noble, studying astronomy and astrology, music, history, literature, and the practical wisdom of a sophisticated society. But while on the outside he was a smooth-chinned Egyptian aristocrat, on the inside he became a Hebrew hothead. He would go out to the fields and construction sites to watch his kinsmen and grind his teeth when a slave driver abused one of them.

One day when Moses was about forty, he lost his cool and killed an Egyptian who was brutalizing an Israelite. The next day he saw two Hebrews fighting and intervened. One of the men shot back, "Who made you ruler and judge over us? Are you thinking of killing me as you killed the Egyptian?"

His crime was known! Soon the current pharaoh (probably

Thutmose III) was out to arrest and execute him. Moses fled to Midian, southeastern Sinai. (See map, page 360.) The semidesert and its tribes of wandering shepherds were a sharp change for a man raised in the luxurious Egyptian court, but Moses was safe from retribution. He married the daughter of a pagan priest and bore a son. For forty years he followed his father-in-law's flocks from summer to winter pasture and back again.

The Emissary Commissioned
Meanwhile, Thutmose died and another pharaoh took the throne. The Israelites began to cry out to their God for freedom. That was what He was waiting for. He had not forgotten His covenant with Abraham, Isaac, and Jacob. He had told Abraham that the chosen family would become slaves in a foreign land. The whole thing was a scheme to get the Israelites out of Canaan and off by themselves for a few hundred years. There they could multiply numerically without attracting hostile attention in Canaan. At the same time, the Canaanites could become thoroughly depraved and deserving of judgment. And the Israelites could get enough of a taste of bondage to make them sick of authoritarian rule and desperate for a strong and merciful God.

For as long as they were sleek and happy in Goshen, they were not desperate. They remembered the God of Jacob, but they forgot both His awesome majesty and His desire for the kind of friendship He'd had with Abraham. They rarely, if ever, used His name, Yahweh. He was just their tribal god.

That attitude was going to end. Yahweh grieved to put His children through the anguish of bondage, but they had needed the discipline. And now He was about to liberate them.

His grand plan centered around a certain broken-down, eighty-year-old shepherd in the wastes of Sinai. Moses was a long way from the refined gentleman he had been. Windburned and sun-darkened, his beard long and his hair wild, he was typecast to play the desert prophet marching into the Egyptian court. But Moses didn't see it that way at all.

One dusty day in the shadow of Mount Sinai, the shepherd caught sight of a bush on fire but not being consumed. As he drew near, a voice from within the flames called his name. "Do not come any closer," said the voice. "Take off your sandals, for the place where you are standing is holy ground. I am the God of your father, the God of Abraham, the God of Isaac, and the God of Jacob." Moses was terrified.

"I have indeed seen the misery of My people in Egypt," God went on. "So I have come down to rescue them. So I am sending you to Pharaoh to bring My people the Israelites out of Egypt."

What? thought Moses. *Me?* "Who am I?" *Do You know me? I'm the murderer who ran for his life forty years ago. I tried to help my people then, and look where it got me.*

"I will be with you," God replied. So it doesn't matter who you are.

Moses was thinking fast. Not having been raised among his Hebrew kin, he knew rather little about the God of Abraham. *What if the Israelites ask for Your name? What should I say?* he wanted to know.

"I AM WHO I AM" declared the voice in the flame. I am Yahweh, the God of Abraham.

I AM. In Hebrew not just, "I exist," but "I am actively present." I am with you. Abraham, Isaac, and Jacob called this God *Yahweh*, "He is," but now the significance of the name began to become clear. Unlike the gods of Mesopotamia, Canaan, and Egypt, this God intended to be intimately present in the affairs of His people, no matter where they sojourned and what they suffered. He had been "I am with you" to childless Abraham, to Jacob fleeing alone to an unknown land, and to Joseph in the dungeon. And He was "I will be with you" to Moses facing Pharaoh and to the Israelites journeying back to Canaan.

Trust me, the wind whispered. But as Yahweh unfolded His plan—the elders of Israel will listen to you, but Pharaoh will laugh in your face until I do works of supernatural power to convince him—Moses grew more and more alarmed.

"What if they don't believe me?" I could lose my neck!

Yahweh gave him a couple of minor supernatural feats to impress his audience, but Moses was not comforted. *I'm a lousy preacher*, he protested. *I'm definitely not Your man for addressing the Egyptian court.*

Yahweh was losing His temper. *I made you with your mouth and your brains, didn't I? Do you think I don't know what I'm doing?* Cutting the argument short, Yahweh stated that Moses' brother Aaron was a fine speaker and would be Moses' mouthpiece to Pharaoh. The debate was over. Moses was left speechless before the smoldering bush wishing he had never been born.

Yahweh Versus Egypt

The elders of Israel were delighted when Moses told them Yahweh was about to liberate them and turned his staff into a snake to prove it. But the meeting with Pharaoh fulfilled Moses' worst fears. The lord of Egypt sat haughtily on his throne, flanked by his counselors and sorcerers, wearing his high royal headdress with its golden cobra on the front. The king was a veritable serpent himself. Not only did he deny Israel the right to go to the desert for a three day worship festival (he regarded it as a flimsy ruse), but he decreed that since the Hebrews had time to sit around fomenting rebellion, they had time to gather their own straw to make bricks for the city they were building. That was the end of the interview. And later, when the Hebrews failed to meet their brick quota because they were out gathering straw, they were flogged. The Israelite foremen vented their fury at Moses and Aaron, who had caused this impossible situation.

Moses, in turn, let Yahweh have it: "Why have you brought trouble upon this people? Is this why you sent me? Ever since I went to Pharaoh to speak in your name, he has brought trouble upon this people, and you have not rescued your people at all."

Yahweh told Moses to relax. I have a covenant with Abraham, He said. I am He Who Is With You, and when I get through with Pharaoh, you and all Egypt and Israel will know what that means.

Reluctantly, Moses went back to Pharaoh. The staff-into-snake stunt did not impress him; his own magicians were able to do the same thing by the power of the Egyptian gods (who were really servants of the Snake himself). So the next morning, Yahweh sent Moses to meet Pharaoh by the Nile after his bath and tell him, "By this you will know that I am Yahweh, He Who Is Present: With the staff that is in my hand I will strike the water of the Nile, and it will be changed into blood. The fish in the Nile will die, and the river will stink; the Egyptians will not be able to drink the water."

That failed to move Pharaoh, so the next week Yahweh caused the Nile's frogs to multiply rapidly and infest Egypt's houses, the beds, even the ovens and kneading troughs. Frogs everywhere! It was revolting. Pharaoh's sorcerers were helpless to get rid of the critters.

Yahweh was ridiculing two of Egypt's chief gods. Ha'pi, the Nile god, was supposed to make sure that the river stayed life-giving and not destructive. The frog goddess Heqit supposedly governed human fertility and assisted women in childbirth. But Yahweh mocked, *So you like frogs in your beds, ladies? Okay, I'll give you frogs!*

Pharaoh gave in to Moses just long enough for the frogs to die, then reneged. This business of repent and unrepent became a pattern as Yahweh sent in turn gnats, biting flies, a livestock disease carried by the flies, a related human skin disease, and the worst hailstorm in Egyptian history. The Egyptian gods in charge of animals, crops, and health did nothing. Pharaoh's officials (financially ruined in the loss of herds and crops) urged him to give in before the eighth plague hit. But Pharaoh just could not bring himself to lose so many excellent slaves.

Yahweh had selected this particular man to be king of Egypt at this time because He knew this pharaoh would harden his heart against Moses' pleas. Indeed, the Bible goes so far as to also say that Yahweh Himself hardened Pharaoh's heart. To people trained in Western logic, these two statements may seem to contradict each other. But the biblical writers were Orientals, and to them it was not only possible but necessary to hold certain apparent opposites in tension. "Both/and," not "either/or," was their approach. Yahweh had chosen and formed this pharaoh in order that His "name might be proclaimed in all the earth" (Exodus 9:16). It was all part of Yahweh's plan to reveal Himself to the nations who had turned their back on Him and no longer knew anything about Him. Yet Pharaoh was still free to choose—he was not Yahweh's puppet—so he remained morally responsible for his choices. Yahweh was able to turn even His enemies' choices to serve His plans.

So the wheat, spelt, and fruit trees that had survived the hail were devoured by locusts in plague number eight. When that didn't move Pharaoh, a sandstorm blew in so thick that the sun was obscured and the whole land, except Goshen, was reduced to darkness for three days. This was an insult to Egypt's greatest god: Ra, the sun.

By now Pharaoh was ready to bargain, but Moses' position remained all or nothing. "Just as you say," Moses retorted as he walked out. "But tomorrow you will be begging us to leave Egypt, because at midnight tonight every firstborn son of man and beast in this country will die."

Escape
He left Pharaoh and his officials to chew on that one, and returned to prepare the Israelites for the final plague. It was spring; the goats and sheep were giving birth. Yahweh had decreed that from now on, this month (Abib) would be the first month of the year. And tonight, and each year on the fourteenth of Abib, each Israelite household must slaughter a year-old, flawless male lamb at twilight. They must smear some of its blood on the doorframes of their houses, then roast the meat and eat it with bitter herbs and unleavened bread while

being dressed and ready to leave home. For tonight Yahweh would pass through Egypt, and in every home not marked with lamb's blood He would strike the firstborn dead. The blood would warn death to pass over the house that believed in Yahweh, so the annual commemoration would be called Passover. Once again, the blood of a substitute stood between Yahweh's people and death.

At midnight, wailing could be heard from every non-Israelite home in Egypt. From Pharaoh to the least slave to the cattle—every family lost its firstborn. Pharaoh ordered Moses and Aaron to get out of Egypt, they and their people. The Egyptians, who by this time held Moses and Israel in high respect, were glad to give the Israelites their silver, gold, and fine clothing, if only they would leave immediately. Thousands of Israelites set out east, and not a few Egyptians joined them, having been convinced that Yahweh was greater than the gods of Egypt. Many of the joiners were probably slaves and laborers hoping for a better life with these impressive Hebrews.

Moses led the throng, carrying with him the bones of Joseph. Leading the fugitives was a glowing cloud that shaded them from the intense sun during the day and lit their way by night. The cloud was called the "glory" of Yahweh, a physical manifestation of His presence.

Across the Reed Sea
Following Yahweh's instructions, Moses led the people by the desert road to the "Sea of Reeds" (Exodus 13:18, Hebrew).[1] Moses told the crowd to camp by the sea. For Pharaoh had changed his mind yet again and was in hot pursuit with his whole army in chariots. Yahweh wanted Pharaoh to think he had Israel helplessly pinned against the sea.

The Israelites were certainly convinced. "Was it because there were no graves in Egypt that you brought us to the desert to die?" they wailed at Moses. This was not the last time they would wail at Moses. But Moses told them that if they would just shut up, Yahweh would fight for them. Yahweh wanted Egypt to remember that He was the God Who Is Present. So all night long a strong east wind blew back the waters of the sea. Toward morning, the whole Israelite cavalcade was able to walk across the deep lake bed. When the Egyptians pursued, Yahweh jammed their chariot wheels in the mud. As horses reared and men cursed, the water swept back into the sea bed and swallowed all of them up. The Israelites stood wide-eyed on the opposite side watching the bodies wash up onto the shore. They were starting to take Yahweh and His envoy Moses seriously.

For a while the crowd was silent as the cries of the dying faded into the breeze. Then Aaron's sister Miriam, a prophetess, began to lead the women in a dance. They shook their tambourines, sang, and shouted their thanks to Yahweh:

> Who among the gods is like you, O [Yahweh]?
> Who is like you—
>   majestic in holiness,
>   awesome in glory,
>   working wonders?
> You stretched out your right hand
>   and the earth swallowed them. (Exodus 15:11-12)

NOTE
1. This was probably one of the large freshwater lakes between the Gulf of Suez and the Mediterranean Sea. The Hebrew name *Yam Suph*, "Sea of Reeds," included what we now call the Red Sea, the gulfs of Suez and Aqabah, and these lakes. Greek translators rendered Yam Suph as "Red Sea," and some modern commentators think the Israelites crossed that large saltwater body. But the Hebrew name in Exodus could mean one of the gulfs or lakes, and most scholars lean toward the latter.

5

Israel Makes a Treaty

♦

Exodus 15:22–23:33

The Training Course Begins

The next day, Moses led the still exultant mob eastward into the desert. But for three days they traveled without finding water. They were used to hard work and poor rations, but not this grinding thirst and endless walking in the heat and glare. Moses' formerly awed fans began to grumble. When at last they found water but it proved to be undrinkable, the crowd's mood grew ugly.

In desperation, Moses cried to Yahweh for help. Yahweh showed him a piece of wood and told him that if he threw it into the water, it would become safe to drink. That seemed ridiculous, but no more so than anything else that had happened during the last couple of months. So Moses obeyed, and it worked. While the people were drinking and watering their fainting herds, Yahweh gave Moses another message:

"If you listen carefully to the voice of [Yahweh] your God and do what is right in his eyes, if you pay attention to his commands and keep all his decrees, I will not bring on you any of the diseases I brought on the Egyptians, for I am [Yahweh], who heals you." (Exodus 15:26)

Trust Me, obey Me, and I will take care of your physical needs. Ignore Me, and you are at the mercy of the climate, the food supply, and of things called germs that you know nothing about. Yahweh must have felt like the parent of two million two-year-olds, with only one eighty-year-old nurse to commiserate with.

What Is It?
The travelers recouped at a large oasis beyond which lay the foreboding Desert of Sin. Two weeks had passed since the Reed Sea, and the people were getting tired of hiking. The kids were crying, everybody had sore feet, and there was little to drink and less to eat. They were forgetting how bad it had been to make bricks for the Egyptians; all they could remember were the stews they had cooked. A riot was brewing. Once again, Moses and Aaron faced the rabble and said, "You're not grumbling against us, but against Yahweh." They pointed toward the huge glowing cloud hovering near the camp.

Patiently, Yahweh appealed to His squalling toddlers on their level. At twilight a vast flock of quail flew in, and the people feasted. In the morning, dew lay on everything. When the dew burned off, thin flakes like frost covered the desert floor. *Manna?* people asked each other. What is it?

"It is the bread Yahweh has given you to eat," Moses explained. "Everyone is to gather as much as he or she needs, about two quarts for each person in your tent. No one is to keep any until morning."

The people did as they were told. The stuff was white and tasted like wafers made with honey. Not too bad. They called it "what-is-it?"

Slaves into Servants
This whole desert journey was the beginning of a school. Yahweh had trained Abraham, Isaac, Jacob, and Jacob's sons as

individuals; now He had to put more than a million people through the same course. Some of them weren't even Jacob's descendants and had only heard of Yahweh a few months earlier. Nearly all of them had grown up as slaves and children of slaves.

This stage in Yahweh's plan was about transformation. First, Yahweh had multiplied Israel from a clan of seventy to a mob of some two million people. But they were an unruly rabble, and Yahweh intended to make them a tight-knit, disciplined army and a united nation who saw themselves as family. At the same time, He was moving them geographically from Egypt to Canaan. And third, He was going to transform them socially and spiritually from slaves of men into servants of God.

To change from slaves into servants, the people had to learn to fear—and at the same time trust—Yahweh more than any other god or human. One might expect that the plagues, the Reed Sea miracle, and the constant physical presence of the cloud would have convinced them, but dry mouths and growling stomachs proved otherwise. Hence, Yahweh deprived them of the sources of their basic necessities to force them to depend on Him. Then each day He provided just what they needed, so as to reinforce an attitude of daily dependence. They were going to need this attitude sorely when they reached Canaan and ceased to get so many dramatic physical signs of Yahweh's presence and power.

At this point, they still fell far short. As soon as water ran scarce, the mob was ready to riot. "Is Yahweh really among us or not?" they demanded. Moses panicked, but Yahweh continually came through. *I am really the God who is there.*

The next test of faith for the Israelites came when some desert tribesmen called Amalekites attacked. They normally occupied the southern approach to Canaan, but having heard that a horde was approaching their territory, they sent a contingent to cut them off.

Now the Israelites had left Egypt armed for battle, but so

far they hadn't had to fight. Moses instructed his young aide, Joshua, to array the troops. Moses himself stood on a hill over-looking the field and prayed to Yahweh all day while the armies clashed. In the end, Israel was victorious and saw yet another side of Yahweh: He was their Deliverer, their Healer, their Provider, and now their War Standard. And Yahweh declared that there would be a permanent feud between Israel and Amalek. Why? Because just as He saw the Serpent behind the throne of Egypt, so He knew His ancient Enemy was in this attempt to crush Israel before it could be fully born.

Covenant
So far, freedom seemed to spell nothing but deprivation. For while Yahweh cared about His people's empty stomachs, He was more concerned about their empty hearts. So day passed into weary day as the cavalcade followed the golden cloud through the desert.

Exactly three months from the day they left Egypt, the Israelites came to a mountain jutting 2,200 feet above the desert floor. Moses ordered them to camp, then climbed a short way alone to receive Yahweh's instructions. Yahweh told him to tell the people,

> "You yourselves have seen what I did to Egypt, and
> how I carried you on eagles' wings and brought you to
> myself. Now if you obey me fully and keep my
> covenant, then out of all nations you will be my treas-
> ured possession. Although the whole earth is mine, you
> will be for me a kingdom of priests and a holy nation."
> (Exodus 19:4-6)

Moses took this message back to the elders of Israel—the heads of each clan in each tribe—and they recognized what Yahweh was offering. He was using the form of a treaty between a sovereign and a vassal (dependent) people that was used throughout the Near East. Yahweh claimed to be the rightful King over all the nations of the world, even though they were in rebellion against Him. So, if Israel would commit to recognizing Yahweh as King, He would give them an honored place as the first nation in His eventual world kingdom. They would be His priests in that they would mediate between Him and the rest of the earth's peoples.

Two key words in this treaty proposal are *obey* and *holy*. *Holy* means "set apart from the commonplace." Ancient Near Eastern peoples recognized two categories of things. On one side of a chasm were common things, including humans and animals. On the other were holy beings and everything that belonged to them. As priests, the Israelites would be wholly set apart from pursuing their own ends, wholly dedicated to Yahweh's agenda.

Most ancient people thought of the holy in terms of power and inscrutability. All the divine beings were holy, from the least tree spirit to the father of the gods. Holiness did not imply morality or love at all. But Yahweh's holiness was drastically different. Since holiness was one of His chief qualities and would have to be a primary trait of His people, one of His tasks in training Israel would be to change the nation's idea of holiness. First, He had to get across that only He was holy, not the gods and spirits of the pagans. Second, what belonged to Him was untouchably, radically holy and its separation had to be taken seriously. Third, because morality was an essential trait of Yahweh, it was an essential trait of His holiness. Anyone who violated moral rules was therefore unholy and could not approach the Holy God. Such a violator was "unrighteous"—out of right covenant relationship with the King because of lawbreaking. Everyone set apart for Yahweh had to be righteous or face His wrath.

The elders of Israel did not yet grasp the implications of what they were getting into, so they readily agreed to make a treaty with Yahweh. They began to get an inkling when Moses ordered them to wash and abstain from sex for three days as outward signs of inward purification and separation from earthly activities. They got nervous when Moses told them to bar the people from touching the mountain, lest they die. Then on the third day the mountain began to quake, smoke and fire poured forth, thunder crashed, lightning flashed, and a loud trumpet blared out of nowhere. Suddenly it did not seem so appealing to be the priests who could be familiar with this Holy God; the people were content to let Moses receive Yahweh's instructions and bring them back.

The Ten Commandments
So Moses climbed into the smoke and returned a short time later with a pronouncement that followed the treaty form of the day. First the Great King identified Himself and described the gracious deeds He had done for His subjects: "I am [Yahweh] your God, who brought you out of Egypt, out of the land of slavery" (Exodus 20:2). Israel had done nothing to earn this relationship. On the contrary, by liberating Israel, Yahweh should have earned the people's gratitude and loyalty.

Israel was supposed to express that gratitude by keeping the ten basic treaty stipulations that followed. The first four dealt with how the people would relate to Yahweh:

♦ You shall have no other gods before Me.
♦ You shall not make for yourself an idol.
♦ You shall not misuse the name of Yahweh.
♦ Remember the Sabbath day by keeping it holy.

A subject could have only one king, and a wife but one husband. Yahweh wanted this relationship to have the intimacy of a marriage. He was dealing with Middle Eastern peasants, former slaves, some of whom had grown up worshiping the forces of nature depicted as beings in wood and stone. His goal was to draw them each into personal companionship with Him, but they weren't ready for that yet. He was bringing them as fast and as far as they could come.

The first step was to wean them from worshiping natural

forces and demons. The next was to convince them not to make idols, neither of Him nor anything else. Human thinking is so concrete; we're not comfortable unless we can have a thing we can see and touch to adore. And we are so impressed with the energies of the earth. Above all, we long for control over our world. So Yahweh said, I—the Creator of the earth and all its powers—am the only one worthy of worship. Do not bow to anything else, material or spiritual. Don't confuse the Maker with the made. Don't use My name in magic or casual swearing, as though you could use Me to get what you want. Don't say, "God told me" when I didn't. And one day out of your week must be devoted to resting and enjoying Me, so that making a living won't shrivel your spirits and make you deaf to divinity.

Yahweh's last six commands described how His subjects should relate to each other. These were intended to safeguard individuals and communities so that everyone could prosper. For instance, He told them to prize, respect, and care for their parents. He knew how quickly a society would fragment when children harbored resentment against their parents and denied them care in their old age. Bitterness against parents would shackle a person to forever seeking approval or revenge in relationships. And the person who ignored elderly parents would one day find his or her own children doing the same. To honor and forgive parents—even those who had failed— was a key to inner freedom.

Similarly, in forbidding murder, Yahweh wanted to instill a value for life. No culture could long survive if its people accepted the blithe killing of unwanted children, the aged and infirm, unloved wives, and personal enemies. Yahweh banned adultery in order to protect lifelong commitments between husband and wife. He knew how adultery destroyed everyone involved, leaving spouse and children feeling abandoned, and numbing the adulterer's ability to commit the deep levels of his or her heart to anyone.

Yahweh forbade theft to protect property rights, but he

also prohibited coveting other people's property. Like unforgiveness and unfaithfulness, coveting was a cancer in the heart, robbing a person of joy and contentment, poisoning relationships. Yahweh cared not just about His people's outward behavior, but also about their inner health and character.

In addition, Yahweh banned lying, especially in court. Legal corruption, He knew, would rot the nation. Truth had to be a fundamental value.

The King's Law
After these ten basic commandments, Yahweh gave an assortment of examples of how they would apply in the daily life of peasant farmers. He elaborated on property rights and on how to show the value of a human life in the way one treated one's servants. He discussed penalties for violent crime and extolled generosity to the poor. He said a bit about how to worship Him and explicitly forbade consorting with other spirits for power. More legislation would come later; this was just enough to show His subjects what He was getting at.

In short, Yahweh was setting Himself up as the King and sole Lawmaker of the nation. This was unheard of in the ancient world. No other nation's law code claimed that a god gave it or was its authority for justice. Babylonian and Assyrian law codes recorded what some judges had done in the past, but judges were free to decide by their own opinion. Kings made and unmade laws and in many states they decided justice according to their whims, not permanent laws. Egypt's pharaoh was considered a god on earth, so his every decree supposedly embodied truth and justice, whether or not people were treated justly, alike, or in proportion to their deeds. Thus, there was no Egyptian law code at all.

But in Israel neither Moses, nor the elders, nor judges, nor even later kings would have the right to make laws. They could administer and execute laws, collect taxes, keep the peace, and make judicial rulings, but Yahweh was the legislative branch of the government.

We might fear this would lead to chaos, but in fact Israel had the most fair and humane laws of its day. Many of the legal principles Yahweh laid down underlie the codes of modern nations. For instance, when Yahweh gave sample cases, He repeatedly gave motives or reasons for the just decisions to show the logic or moral value behind the decree. Justice was to be reasonable and compassionate, not arbitrary. Again, Israel's law commanded the death penalty for crimes against God and against the holiness of life, but it was strikingly humane compared to other codes. Only Deuteronomy 25:11-12 mentions bodily mutilation, in contrast to many places in Babylonian, Hittite, and other codes. Flogging was limited to forty lashes in Israel.

Other codes treated commoners' lives as less valuable than noblemen's. They regarded harm done to a woman, a slave, or an ox all as harm to a man's property. For instance, if a nobleman caused the death of a noblewoman, the Babylonian code of Hammurabi said that the killer's *daughter* had to die. If a nobleman caused a slavewoman's death, he paid a sum of silver to her owner. By contrast, Israel's law protected women and slaves explicitly from being used as property, and made justice the same for all social classes. Physical discipline of slaves was limited, though not forbidden, and killing a slave was punished the same way as killing a freeman.

"An eye for an eye" is a well-known principle from Israel's law code. Many people suppose it was a harsh, vengeful standard, but in fact Yahweh was limiting the sternness of tribal justice. Ancient tribal custom demanded that if a man killed someone in your tribe, you killed at least him, if not his whole family. If he injured you, your family tried to kill him. But Yahweh said no, a punishment must not exceed the crime. It must also not be too lenient, as in many countries where noblemen received preference. In practice, "eye for eye, tooth for tooth" was a figure of speech. If a man blinded his slave's eye, he did not lose his own eye, but he did have to free the slave (Exodus 21:23-27). Property damage, personal injury, and accidental killing were covered by fines, not retaliation. Only with premeditated murder did "eye for eye" apply literally because Yahweh took human life extremely seriously.

Social justice was one of Yahweh's passions. Yahweh warned judges not to show favoritism to either rich or poor, nor to let a crowd's opinion sway a decision. He forbade bribes. He warned His people not to oppress foreigners who would come to live in Israel: "You yourselves know how it feels to be aliens, because you were aliens in Egypt" (Exodus 23:9). He even banned the lending of money at interest to fellow Israelites. People didn't borrow money to set up businesses or buy houses in those days; they borrowed only when they were broke. Yahweh wanted His subjects to treat each other like family, lending without interest out of love. He repeatedly warned that if poor or defenseless people cried to Him for help against the rich and powerful, He would avenge them.

Indeed, when Moses said, "What other nation is so great as to have such righteous decrees and laws as this body of laws I am setting before you today?" (Deuteronomy 4:8), he was telling the truth.

6

A Court for the King

Exodus 24:1–40:38

The Treaty Is Sealed

When Moses returned from the smoking mountain and recounted the covenant stipulations, the people responded enthusiastically. Yahweh's pyrotechnics had impressed them, and they were back in their Reed Sea mood. So Moses wrote down the whole treaty and called the document "the Book of the Covenant."

The next day he held a covenant ratification ceremony in which men from each of the tribes sacrificed bulls to express their commitment. Moses sprinkled half of the blood on the altar he had built to symbolize that Yahweh forgave any past wrongdoing and accepted the offering. Then when he had reread the Book of the Covenant and the people had sworn allegiance, he sprinkled the rest of the blood on them. "This is the blood of the covenant," Moses pronounced solemnly. It was a tangible expression that this commitment was sacred and serious. To break faith after being sprinkled with the sacrificial blood would mean incurring bloodguilt (equivalent to murder) and Yahweh's judgment.

After that, Moses took Aaron, Aaron's two oldest sons, and seventy clan elders partway up the mountain. It was customary for the parties of a covenant to seal it with a meal, so the seventy-four men ate and drank the covenant meal in Yahweh's presence. Then Moses took Joshua and climbed farther up the mountain, leaving Aaron and an elder named Hur in charge until they returned. The cloud of glory settled over the mountain, looking like a consuming fire from the Israelite camp. Moses and Joshua disappeared into the cloud for forty days.

A Royal Tent

Yahweh spent most of this forty days giving Moses minute instructions for constructing, furnishing, and staffing a royal tent for Himself. To get His people used to the idea that He was their King, He Who Is Actively Present, He would have a dwelling in the center of their camp like that of a great sheikh. The tent was called a "tabernacle" (dwelling place) and a "sanctuary" (holy place).

It was an elaborate affair, as befitted royalty. It stood about forty-five feet long by fifteen feet wide by fifteen feet high. It consisted of a sectionalized wooden framework covered by four layers of curtains (embroidered linen on the inside, then woven goat hair, then ramskin leather, then sea-cow hide). On the inside it was divided into two compartments: the Holy Place (about thirty feet by fifteen feet) and the Most Holy Place (about fifteen feet by fifteen feet). The Most Holy Place was thus a perfect cube.

Linen, ramskin, and sea-cow hide were all precious fabrics. Likewise, the embroidery and even the loops to hang the curtains were of blue, purple, and scarlet thread; these were royal colors because the dyes were extremely expensive (they came from shellfish and the eggs and carcasses of a special kind of worm). The tent frame was covered with gold, which was considered a perfect, royal metal because it was uncontaminated by other metals. The furnishings inside the tabernacle were also of gold.

The bases that supported the structure were of silver, made from the money that ransomed each firstborn male Israelite. Yahweh had declared that each firstborn in Israel belonged to Him because He had spared them in the last plague on Egypt. Rather than sacrificing the firstborn, the Israelites had to ransom them with silver money. Thus Yahweh's tent stood on the people's ransom price.

Beginning with the base of the tabernacle's entrance, the furnishings outside the holy tent were of bronze. This is a harder metal, more suited for heavy use. It is also an alloy, so it is by definition not pure. It symbolized judgment for sin.

The tabernacle was erected on the west side of a surrounding courtyard measuring about one hundred and fifty feet by seventy-five feet. All around this courtyard, except for an entryway some fifteen feet wide on the eastern side, was a curtain almost eight feet high.

The furnishings of Yahweh's tent all symbolized important truths He wanted to impress on His people. In the Most Holy Place was a hardwood chest covered in gold called the "ark [chest] of the covenant." Its pure gold lid was flanked with two golden cherubim (angels) like the winged sphinxes that often adorned the arms of Near Eastern thrones. For this "atonement cover" was the throne of Yahweh. The ark was fitted with rings so that it could be carried on poles like a litter when the camp moved.

The Holy Place contained a table upon which bread would be laid as an offering of Israel's produce, a seven-branched lampstand to represent Yahweh's glory reflected in the people's holy lives, and an incense altar where the burning fragrance would symbolize the people's prayers going up to God. All this was of gold.

In the courtyard stood an altar of bronze-covered wood seven and a half feet square and four and a half feet high—large enough to burn whole bulls and rams. There was also a bronze basin in which one had to wash before entering the tent or offering a sacrifice.

The people were supposed to supply the fabric, wood, and metal to construct all of this out of their own love for Yahweh. They would also continually provide the bread, oil, incense, and animals as their gifts.

To staff this royal residence, Aaron and his sons would be set apart as priests—Yahweh's personal servants. They would offer the sacrifices, fill the lamp, bake the bread, and so on. No one but a priest would be allowed in the tabernacle, and a priest had to be of the prescribed family, consecrated with certain intricate rites, and dressed in precisely defined garments. All of this had just one point: to impress on Israel Yahweh's utter holiness.

Yahweh spelled all of this out to the last detail, including the names of the men who would oversee the construction. In some mysterious way, the tabernacle reflected the spiritual realities of Heaven.

Then He sent Moses back down the mountain with these instructions plus two tablets of stone. On each tablet, Yahweh had inscribed a copy of the ten basic covenant commands. It was customary to make two copies of a covenant document, one for each party. Each party usually put his copy in the presence of his god. Therefore, both copies of Israel's covenant with Yahweh were going to be kept in the ark of the covenant.

The Price of Impatience
Meanwhile, the Israelites were getting bored and concerned waiting for Moses. They finally decided that he had disappeared forever and that they would have to choose another leader and invoke another god to get them from Sinai to Canaan. So they persuaded Aaron to melt down the gold jewelry they had taken from the Egyptians and cast it into an idol in the form of a calf. (To stockbreeders, young bulls represented strength and virility, so they were standard fare for idols.) Then the people held a typical pagan festival: animal sacrifices, food and alcohol, dancing, and debauchery.

Moses was at that very moment on his way down the

mountain. Yahweh warned him what was going on and said, "These people are like stiff-necked oxen who won't respond to a pull on their yoke. I'm going to wipe them out and let you father a nation who will plow my way."

Moses blanched. He had been serving as mediator between the King and His subjects in liberating them and giving them their laws. Now he found himself having to beg the Sovereign to forgive their treason. He reminded Yahweh of His great plan and His promises to Abraham, Isaac, and Jacob, and he implored the Lord to relent.

This was just the response Yahweh wanted from Moses. The covenant mediator was supposed to stand between Him and His people to seek mercy when the people broke the agreement. Yahweh's justice demanded that He punish rebels, but He always preferred to be merciful. (His children were no worse than their warped father Adam, and He loved them.) There was something—as yet secret—about a mediator's intercession (standing between) that satisfied the required justice and allowed mercy.

Moses sighed his relief, then set off to find Joshua and get back to camp. But when he saw the orgy, he lost his temper, smashed the tablets, and threw the calf into the fire. He could get nothing out of Aaron but excuses, so he waved him away and shouted, "Whoever is for Yahweh, come to me." His kinsmen, the Levites, rallied to him. He ordered them to start killing revelers until the party stopped.

The next day Moses interceded again, offering to give up his own life if Yahweh would forgive Israel. But not even Moses' life was a sufficient substitute. Yahweh had to send a plague through the camp because the price of rebellion had to be proportional to the nearness of the Holy One. But in His mercy He spared as many people as possible. Then He ordered them to set out for Canaan without Him.

The people were stunned. Abandoned by Yahweh? They wept while Moses strode into the temporary meeting tent, where he and the King had a frank exchange.

"If You're not going to go with us," Moses stated bluntly, "then don't send us. How will we be any different from any of the dozens of roving tribes? We can't accomplish Your plan without You, and it's doubtful we'll survive."

Yahweh liked the way Moses never minced words. He and Abraham had been friends like that; Abraham had respected Him, but he was never afraid to say what he felt and ask for what he cared about (see Genesis 18:16-33). For friendship's sake, Yahweh granted Moses' plea.

Moses followed with a personal request: he wanted to really see Yahweh. So the next day found Moses on the mountain again with a replacement pair of stone tablets. The glory descended on the peak, and Yahweh let Moses see His "back" (whatever that meant), for no one could see Yahweh's "face" and survive. As He passed by, Yahweh proclaimed His identity:

> "[Yahweh, Yahweh], the compassionate and gracious God, slow to anger, abounding in love and faithfulness, maintaining love to thousands, and forgiving wickedness, rebellion and sin. Yet he does not leave the guilty unpunished; he punishes the children and their children for the sin of the fathers to the third and fourth generation." (Exodus 34:6-7)

Moses fell on his face and worshiped. Yahweh reaffirmed that He had forgiven Israel by restating the covenant terms, but He warned emphatically that the people must not make treaties with the Canaanites but must obliterate their debauched religion. If Israel compromised, she would be sucked into the seductive cults and commit spiritual adultery against her Husband. And Yahweh, "whose name is Jealous, is a jealous God" (Exodus 34:14).

When Moses descended this time, his face shone with the reflection of God's glory. It was so bright that people could not look at him unless he wore a veil.

Chastened by the plague, the Israelites were only too glad to contribute their wealth and their time to construct Yahweh's dwelling. When it was finished, the glory enveloped and filled the tent so that not even Moses could enter it. From then on, when the cloud lifted off the tabernacle and began to move across the desert, Israel knew it was time to pack up and move out. And when the glory halted, they made camp, set up the tent, and watched in awe as the cloud settled in. Everything— their diet, their moving and stopping, their whole lifestyle— was dictated to them as infants by the awesome Parent who hovered nearby, eager to see them grow up.

C·H·A·P·T·E·R

7

A Generation Lost

◆

Leviticus, Numbers, Deuteronomy

Living with a King

Yahweh was now enthroned right in the midst of His subjects. But He still could not wander among them as He had in Eden; He had to confine His undiluted presence behind four layers of curtains and a screened courtyard. His holiness would scorch such polluted people if He lowered the barriers. Yahweh wanted them to be holy with Him—set apart from the world order that years of the Serpent's influence had perverted—so that He and they could enjoy each other face to face.

But their haste to lapse into religious lechery, greed, and power-lust showed they still had only the vaguest idea of the true God's character, values, and expectations. Even at their current distance, Yahweh would continually have to send plagues to satisfy the requirements of His holiness. So besides the laws that governed what we might call "secular" life, Yahweh gave Israel a detailed system of rituals to illustrate graphically what holiness meant. The message was that as citizens of Yahweh's Kingdom, they had no secular life; all of life was sacred, set apart for His service.

The main act of worship was animal sacrifice at the tabernacle. Daily, endless blood sacrifices had to be brought to the King to maintain His approval. Why? To modern ears this sounds like senseless waste and cruelty, but Yahweh demanded it to make a point: *Evil costs dearly.* Whenever someone offered an animal, he laid his hands on it to identify himself with it. When he watched it butchered and burnt, he knew that Yahweh was accepting its death in his place. He was the son of Adam who, like his father, repeatedly rebelled against his Lord no matter how hard he tried not to. Yahweh's holiness demanded that a price be paid for treason, and the price for treason was death. But knowing His people were incapable of living up to perfection, He graciously accepted an animal to substitute for the human. In fact, he abhorred the human sacrifice practiced by other Near Eastern peoples.

The sacrificial system was a tableau, a piece of shocking theater to teach shocking truths. Every morning and evening the priests would burn a whole, perfect animal to symbolize Israel offering herself wholly to Yahweh and to atone for (cover) unintentional sin (rebellion, lawbreaking) in general. As the animal was wholly consumed in fire, so the offerers were wholly surrendered to God. When people committed some specific unintentional sin, they offered a perfect animal as their sign of confession; it paid the price and allowed Yahweh to forgive and cleanse the defilement. When restitution could be made for the sin (such as theft or cheating), they had to repay the debt plus twenty percent and also sacrifice the animal. Finally, to express thanksgiving a person would give a "fellowship offering" (or "peace offering"). Only the fat of this animal would be burnt; the priests and offerers would feast on the rest to celebrate peace and friendship with Yahweh.

The typical procedure on a high holy day would be to sacrifice sin offerings to deal with the people's inner corruption, then whole burnt offerings to demonstrate total devotion to Yahweh, then finally fellowship offerings to express the bond between Yahweh and His children-friends. The whole thing was accompanied by offerings of grain, wine, and oil to represent gratitude for Yahweh's abundant provision.

Hence, holy days were feast days, set apart for celebrating Yahweh's goodness. When Israel reached Canaan and scattered, the people were supposed to gather three times a year to commemorate how He had liberated them and brought them to their land and to rejoice over their unity in Yahweh's Kingdom. Celebrating these feasts with joy was so important that better-off Israelites were supposed to finance the feasts for their servants, the poor, and even nonIsraelites living nearby.

Yahweh wanted His people to enjoy living in His Kingdom. It was customary at that time for the king of a land to receive a tenth of each family's produce as a tithe, a royal tax. Two out of three years, Israel's tithe would fund the sacrificial system and the festivals. The third year's tithe would be set aside for those unable to make decent livings: widows, orphans, and poor nonIsraelites.

One holy day was not a feast day. On the Day of Atonement—the Day of the Covering of Sin—the nation fasted as a sign of mourning. In addition to regular sacrifices, two goats were offered for the wickedness of the nation. One was sacrificed, its blood brought all the way into the Most Holy Place to be sprinkled on Yahweh's throne, and its body burnt outside the camp. The other was driven into the desert to symbolize that the people were driving sin from their lives. This was the only day of the year on which anyone could approach Yahweh's throne, and only the high priest could do it, bringing blood.

Thus were joy and grief intermingled in a constant rhythm in Yahweh's relationship with Israel. Evil was paid for, but the price was endless because the people never fundamentally changed. Joy was sweet in Yahweh's great mercy, but death was ever final.

Holy and Common

We might be tempted to describe these rites as Israel's "religion," as opposed to her secular life. But the line of holy and common ran through every aspect of life, just as it ran through every heart. "You must distinguish between holy and common, between the unclean and the clean," Yahweh commanded.

Food was divided into clean and unclean; unclean foods like pork, shellfish, and most insects were forbidden possibly because they tended to be unhealthy, but more importantly because Yahweh was teaching His children about distinctions. (Dietary laws would also help separate Israel from casually socializing with pagans.)

The blood from menstruation and childbirth made a woman temporarily unclean, just as bodily discharges or contact with a corpse made anyone unclean. A person had to wash and abstain from sacrifices and sex for periods of time to regain cleanness. Skin diseases symbolized corruption, so they made a person unclean. Even mildew in a house, representing rot and decay, made the house unclean. Bodily fluids, death, and skin diseases all represented the natural world that Yahweh wanted to distinguish from the perfect, holy, eternal, divine.

The rules of holy and common even descended to the most apparently absurd distinctions: do not plant two kinds of seed in your vineyard; do not plow with an ox and a donkey yoked together; do not weave wool and linen together for clothes!

In dividing the earthly from the holy, was Yahweh saying that the physical world was evil while the spiritual world was good? No. To understand these laws, we have to understand what Yahweh was working against. He was talking to a civilization that worshiped nature and used things like blood and corpses for earth-magic.

The Canaanites did not believe that one Person created the world and was in charge of nature and human relations. Instead, they thought that myriad *baalim* and *elohim* (lords, geniuses, spirits) governed sun, rain, harvest, animal fertility, the planets, and so on. All these "holy ones" belonged to a clan. El—the gods' father and the world's creator—had delegated control of the world to his sons and daughters, so although he was formally acknowledged, he received little worship. His son Baal, lord of sky and storm, was much more involved in human affairs. Humans could solicit his favor by feeding him with sacrifices and performing magical rituals.

Three goddesses, or three faces of one goddess, were also highly esteemed in Canaan. The Mother, Asherah, ruled the home; Astarte, the Lover, ruled fertility; and the Virgin, Anath, ruled war and hunting. These three are also known by pagans around the world as the virgin-mother-crone, birth-life-death, the new-full-old moon, and other magical trinities.[1] (They even appear in tarot cards, modern goddess worship, and witchcraft.)

Other deities abounded: Grain, Sun, Moon, Dawn, Sunset, Sea, and Death. All were called "holy," but the word meant chiefly "other, beyond human." The gods did not act according to moral laws, nor were they interested in human goodness or justice. They supposedly could be persuaded to act for good or ill by flattery, begging, sacrifice, or magic. However, because they cared nothing for humans and had no morality, they were unpredictable and fearful. Personal intimacy and covenant love between human and god was out of the question.

Canaan's climate was erratic, so religion's chief goal was to influence the divine forces of nature to give sunshine, rain, and fertility in desirable times and amounts. The primary method was "sympathetic magic." That is, the Canaanites acted out rituals that they wanted the deities to imitate. For instance, men performed sex acts with women holy to Baal so that Baal would water the earth. Rites with menstrual blood tapped Astarte's fertility for the land. The blood of sacrificed animals was eaten or sprinkled on the earth because blood carried the power of life. People would even put their babies into ovens shaped like the mouths of the god Molech and watch as the screaming infants burned to death. Substances that symbolized the great forces of life and death—blood, semen, corpses, etc.—were mainstays of religious magic.

Hence, Yahweh made these substances "unclean" ritually so that Israel would blanch at such magic. Fertility, sex, and food were all good, but Yahweh alone ruled nature and He could not be manipulated by magic. Israel needed to learn to distinguish between Creator and created, and between humble petition to a loving Parent and attempts to control life. So Yahweh banned all activities associated with tapping into the god-forces or natural energies of the earth or the cosmos.

Besides sympathetic magic, Yahweh also forbade what is now called "channeling." Israelites must not consult spirits, whether those of dead people or discarnate beings. They could not seek His or any other god's will, nor peer into the future, by interpreting leaves, fire, birds, rain, clouds, or anything else. Incantations were forbidden. Why? First, because the spirits were not the helpful informants they pretended to be. They were really servants of the Snake, luring those lusting for wealth, sex, power, knowledge, or sensation into deception, bondage, and death. The price for their information was too high, and Yahweh knew it. And second, any knowledge, prosperity, or power that Israel needed, Yahweh was happy to provide. To seek those things elsewhere was to say to their Dad, "We don't need You, we don't want You, we don't trust You, we don't love You." It was to repeat Adam and Eve's insult, attempting to take by force what Yahweh would give by grace.

Israel would not need channelers because she would have Yahweh's written word and His living spokespersons, His prophets. These men and women were called by Yahweh and gifted to see the truth in events and the mind of God because of their intimate relationship with Him. If Israel needed to know the future, Yahweh would tell the prophets and they would tell the people. If Israel needed to know God's will these spokespersons would tell them that, too. (Moses wrote down everything Yahweh told him, the priests interpreted those writings, and the prophets spoke God's current will to each generation.) Israel could tell a true prophet from a false one because a true one would speak nothing that contradicted what Yahweh had already told Moses or what actually happened in the world.

With a Holy God in their midst, holiness touched every aspect of these people's lives. But with the advantages of having a God next door went the drawbacks of having even the textile composition of one's clothes turned into an object lesson. The book of Leviticus (the holiness manual of the tribe of Levi) underscores the message with these refrains:

Be holy because I, [Yahweh] your God, am holy. . . . I am [Yahweh] your God.

NOTE
1. Concepts of the triple goddess overlapped in the Middle East, so exact beliefs about each goddess varied from city to city.

8

March
to the Promised Land

◆

Numbers, Deuteronomy

Yahweh Musters His Army

Yahweh gave most of this legislation while Israel remained camped at the base of Mount Sinai. For eleven months Sinai was a tent city, as populous as many ancient capitals, while craftsmen constructed Yahweh's tabernacle, the priests learned their duties, and Moses wrote down the King's instructions.

At the end of that time, Yahweh ordered Moses to take a military census of all men over twenty years old. The 600,000 troops were organized in divisions according to their clans and tribes. The tribe of Levi was set aside to assist the priests in caring for the tabernacle and its furnishings (mending, cleaning, polishing) and cleaning up the unimaginable mess of slaughtering and burning several large animals each day.[1] The tribe of Joseph was divided in two according to his sons, Ephraim and Manasseh, to bring the total tribal military divisions back to twelve.

Yahweh dictated the order in which the tribes would trek through the desert and how they would camp. On a march, the Levites led carrying the ark, God's throne. In camp, the tribes were arranged in a square surrounding the tabernacle in the center. In this manner Israel would march to Canaan like the conquering army of God that she was. The rabble sorely needed such discipline; they were on display before all the nations.

After almost a year at Sinai, the Israelites set out to finish the journey to Canaan. They began in high spirits, singing as they tramped, but as before they soon grew bored. It was the same old complaining: manna is dull, water is scarce, walking is tedious, wouldn't it be nice to be eating lamb and garlic in Egypt? So Yahweh sent quail again, but He also sent fire and plague to snap the mob into line. It seemed that nothing but strong discipline made a dent in these people's hard hearts.

Cowardice

Despite all the grumbling, Moses managed to lead his ragtag outfit several more hundred miles to somewhere just south of Canaan. There he appointed a man from each tribe to a reconnaissance team. It would scout the land and bring back a thorough report: population, fortifications, soil quality, land features, agricultural produce. The people needed some encouragement to begin their conquest, and also some military intelligence.

When the spies returned forty days later, they brought a glowing report of the land and a depressing assessment of the foe. Two of the scouts—Joshua and Caleb—were hot to move into this rich land, but the other ten were scared. While Joshua and Caleb saw what Yahweh could do, the others focused on what they could not do.

Cowardice prevailed. The people swore at Moses for leading them into this mess and debated stoning him, choosing a new leader, and trying to go back to Egypt. Better to be live slaves than dead soldiers. Moses begged them to reconsider, but the complaints grew louder until suddenly the cloud of glory blazed out from the tabernacle. Yahweh thundered:

"How long will these people treat me with contempt? How long will they refuse to believe in me, in spite of all the miraculous signs I have performed among them? I will strike them down with a plague and destroy them, but I will make you into a nation greater and stronger than they." (Numbers 14:11-12)

Moses had to intercede again. He based his plea on two facts: Yahweh's character ("slow to anger, abounding in love, forgiving sin and rebellion") and His plan to demonstrate that character to the nations by liberating and caring for Israel ("If You put these people to death all at one time, the nations . . . will say, 'Yahweh was not able to bring these people into the land He promised them on oath'").

Yahweh was pleased. He always responded when people showed they were betting their lives that Yahweh's word and character could be counted on. So instead of wiping out the whole people, He decreed that the generation of faithless cowards would die in the wilderness, and that forty years hence, when a new generation had grown up, He would lead them into the Promised Land. Only Joshua and Caleb would survive to see Canaan, because they trusted Yahweh.

The Israelites mourned bitterly when Moses conveyed this to them. The glowing cloud terrified them, and they decided they would rather die quickly invading Canaan than spend the rest of their lives wandering through this desert. So they determined to attack the Canaanites after all.

Moses begged them not to try it without Yahweh's help. But they ignored him, and the Canaanites trounced them soundly. Sadly the survivors returned to the camp, and the cavalcade set off for the deep desert.

Wandering
It must have been miserable trudging aimlessly through the desert for forty years. Children were born and raised on manna. The flocks were used for sacrifice, so the people may

have tasted the meat of fellowship offerings and perhaps some milk, but there were no spices, no vegetables, no bread. Manna kept one healthy, but it was insipid. It was a major feat to keep idle men from brawling.

When revolt brewed, Moses never bothered to defend his authority. He always knew it was really Yahweh who was being rejected, so he left it to Yahweh to defend His own honor. Two hundred fifty upstart Levites were consumed by fire in one rebellion, 14,700 people died in another.

In all, Moses was a wise and humble leader. Yahweh loved him dearly. But with great honor and gifting went great responsibility. Moses, above everyone else, had to treat Yahweh's commands with respect. One day another of the perennial quarrels over water shortage was simmering. As usual, the people shouted abuse while Moses and Aaron fell on their faces before Yahweh, who told Moses to speak to a certain rock and water would gush out. But Moses lost his temper and shouted to the gathered community, "Listen, you rebels, must we bring you water out of this rock?" Then he struck the rock twice with his staff. Water gushed out, but Yahweh was mad. Moses had publicly dishonored Him by disobeying His order and acting rashly, as though his action, not Yahweh's word, were providing the water. The cost was severe: both Moses and Aaron (who had supported the offense) would die before they reached Canaan.

Three Attacks
As the time of wandering drew to an end, Moses began to lead the people toward Canaan. (See map, page 360.) The Edomites denied passage through their land, so Moses circled around and approached from the east, through Moab. The Moabites let Israel pass through peacefully, but then the Amorites and, after them, the people of Bashan blocked the way. Yahweh enabled Israel to defeat both of these groups and take their land. It was fertile, well-watered real estate, especially good for livestock, so two and a half of the tribes (the tribe of Man-

naseh split) asked Moses if they could claim this as their promised land. Moses agreed on the condition that while the women and children could settle there, the fighting men must help the rest of Israel take their territory.

After securing these northern areas, Moses led the people south again to the plains of Moab, just east of the Jordan River. Right across the river was the Canaanite fortress of Jericho, strategically situated as the doorway to Canaan and the first target of the Israelite assault.

But Balak, king of Moab, did not believe Israel intended to use his land only as a staging area for an attack westward. He had heard of the easy victories over Bashan and the Amorites, and feared Moab was next. Convinced that he could not defeat Israel by force of arms, he resorted to sorcery. He summoned a certain Mesopotamian prophet-for-hire named Balaam to put a curse on Israel.

Balaam did his best. But every time he tried to accommodate his client, Yahweh threatened to kill him, so Balaam kept pronouncing blessing over Israel.

Balaam was essentially a sorcerer. As such, he ultimately served Satan. The biblical account does not name him, but it was the Snake who stood behind both attacks on Israel: the military and the occult. Both had failed, yet the Serpent had one more strategy. At his prompting, Balaam suggested to Balak that Israel might be neutralized if some local women could seduce the Israelite men into pagan orgies. This ploy met with splendid success: Yahweh had to kill 24,000 of His men with a plague before the Israelites turned away from the allure of paganism.

It was an omen of things to come. What force and sorcery could not do, seduction and the Israelites' own senseless moral choices could, and did. Yahweh could protect them from external attack, but His whole plan depended on humans making free choices either for or against Him. In this intent, so foreign to Satan's notions of domination and subjugation, the Viper thought he saw Yahweh's defeat. But Yahweh's plan had a facet so incredible, so unspeakable, that Satan never for an instant foresaw it or could scheme against it.

Moses' Farewell

As it happened, despite all the rebellions and debacles, 600,000 men of fighting age survived to enter Canaan when Yahweh finally declared that the moment had come. On the plains of Moab overlooking the Promised Land, Moses gathered the people to hear his final words. During the desert sojourn he had recorded for them their history (Genesis, Exodus, Numbers) and the royal law by which they were to live (Exodus, Leviticus, Numbers). Now he delivered three long speeches that together formed an impassioned exposition of Yahweh's covenant. He even used the traditional treaty format. After all, only Moses, Joshua, and Caleb, and a few people who had been children forty years earlier, survived of all those who had seen the plagues of Egypt and the miracle at the Reed Sea. Most of this generation had been born in the desert.

The book of Deuteronomy records Moses' three sermons. He recounted Israel's failures and Yahweh's faithfulness. He reiterated the basic stipulations of the covenant and preached on the meanings of many specific laws of economics, social justice, and worship. He set before the people a choice: life and blessing if they obeyed their King; death and cursing if they rebelled.

> Observe [these laws] carefully, for this will show your wisdom and understanding to the nations, who will hear about all these decrees and say, "Surely this great nation is a wise and understanding people." What other nation is so great as to have their gods near them the way [Yahweh] our God is near us whenever we pray to him? And what other nation is so great as to have such righteous decrees and laws as this body of laws I am setting before you today? (4:6-8)

Hear, O Israel: [Yahweh] our God, [Yahweh] is one. Love [Yahweh] your God with all your heart and with all your soul and with all your strength. (6:4-5) He humbled you, causing you to hunger and then feeding you with manna, which neither you nor your fathers had known, to teach you that man does not live on bread alone but on every word that comes from the mouth of [Yahweh]. (8:3)

This day I call heaven and earth as witnesses against you that I have set before you life and death, blessings and curses. Now choose life, so that you and your children may live and that you may love [Yahweh] your God, listen to his voice, and hold fast to him. For [Yahweh] is your life, and he will give you many years in the land he swore to give to your fathers, Abraham, Isaac and Jacob. (30:19-20)

"Who is like you, O Israel, a people saved by [Yahweh]?" Moses concluded. Then he climbed nearby Mount Nebo and looked across the Jordan at the rich land Yahweh was giving them. He wished that after all this he could have crossed that river, but to see the land was enough. Now he was going home.

Yahweh buried him, and the nation mourned him for thirty days. But Moses had laid his hands on Joshua before his death, and the Spirit of God that had given Moses his wisdom to lead the people had fallen upon Moses' aide. Moses had been Israel's shepherd, now Joshua would be her general. And Joshua turned his face toward Jericho.

NOTE
1. God's dealings with Levi is a good example of His mercy. Both Simeon and Levi had been sentenced to be dispersed among the other tribes because of their forefathers' crime of massacring Shechem. But God turned Levi's punishment to blessing because it was the only tribe that resisted the idolatry at Sinai. Yahweh's justice was drastic and irrevocable, but He could transmute it to mercy in the most amazing ways.

9

A Taste of Conquest and Defeat

◆

Joshua, Judges

Rahab

The fortress of Jericho stood on a large and fertile plain just west of the Jordan and guarded the foot of the road that climbed steeply up the Judean hills. In order to gain control of Canaan, an army had first to take Jericho to reach the road, then to conquer several more fortresses that guarded the high ground at the top of the road. From there an army could launch strikes to the south and north of Canaan while leaving a safe camp on the plains of Jericho.

Joshua knew all of this from his reconnaissance mission forty years earlier. But he didn't know how things stood in Jericho now, so he dispatched a pair of spies to reconnoiter. They slipped into the city during business hours, gathered some information, then (when it became clear that the city officials were on to them) convinced a prostitute named Rahab to hide them. A brothel was a good place for unfamiliar men to enter without attracting the neighbors' attention, and a prostitute was unlikely to be a fan of the city rulers.

The spies had guessed right: Rahab was happy to betray her city into Israel's hands. Her attitude doesn't seem callous when we understand what she was rejecting and what she was choosing. Canaanite society was divided into sharp classes. At the top were "kings," actually lords of individual walled fortresses like Jericho. The kings owed allegiance to the Egyptian pharaoh, but Egypt was having internal troubles, so in practice Egypt left the kings free to run their territories ruthlessly.

Under each king was a class of nobles and another class of priests. In exchange for their support, the king gave them lands and status. Below these was about ninety-eight percent of the population. Slaves and tenant farmers worked the lands owned by the king, nobles, and priests. They lived in villages near the city. Free farmers and shepherds lived in villages farther from the city, but they paid taxes to the king and were subject to conscription for wars or building projects without pay. Crop failures might drive a family to sell its land or some of its children to the king or nobles, or a poor family might supplement its income by making its daughters prostitutes for the wealthy. Rahab probably sold her body because it was the only way for her family to survive in that system.

No wonder the Israelites considered her a good bet. Jericho was buzzing with the news that the God of these invaders had freed them from Egypt, led them through the desert, and defeated the Amorite kings. The upper classes were cringing in fear, but to Rahab, what she heard about the God of Israel inspired her with hope. She saw her chance to join a society whose God cared about oppressed slaves enough to liberate them and do mighty deeds for them. So she risked her life to save the spies in exchange for a promise that Israel would spare her family when they took the city.

Another Dry Crossing
In Joshua's whole army, only he and Caleb had walked across the Reed Sea bed and seen the waters piled up on either side. So to prove to this new generation that He was the real God

and able to keep His promises, Yahweh repeated that miracle at the Jordan River.

When the cavalcade halted at the edge of the gorge, they saw the green, fertile upper level at the other side. But the leaders could see that below stretched a belt of lifeless gray clay, and below that was a thick jungle. At the bottom, a thousand yards down, the river tumbled by. It was early April, and the winter rains and melting mountain snows had swollen the Jordan to a torrent.

Alone, the priests picked up the poles carrying the ark of the covenant and trekked down through the jungle to the water's edge. As their feet touched the water, the river stopped flowing from somewhere upstream. Soon the riverbed was dry, and the priests carried the ark to the middle. Joshua signaled for the people to follow. It must have taken the rest of the day to get all of the children, donkeys, and flocks across.

This exercise proved two things. First, Yahweh was demonstrating that He had more power than Canaan's chief god, Baal, who was supposed to have more power than the god of sea and river. Second, Yahweh was showing that He, not Baal, had the rightful claim on the land. According to Near Eastern custom, one could tell if an accused person was guilty by throwing him into a river. If he didn't drown, the gods had declared him innocent. Anyone in Canaan or Israel would have understood Yahweh's jest: His throne was not drowned even in the time it took for a whole army to pass through the riverbed. Yahweh was thumbing His divine nose at Baal, just as He had at Egypt's gods.

Jericho

Joshua still didn't know how he was going to take the fortress, so he hiked over to have a look for himself. As he approached, he met a man holding a drawn sword. Grimly, Joshua challenged him: "Are you for us or for our enemies?"

"Neither," the man retorted, "but as commander of the army of Yahweh I have now come."

Joshua's eyes widened. He had imagined that *he* was the commander of Yahweh's army, that this war was human against human. Israel was the good guys; everybody else was the bad guys. Sure, Yahweh was in charge, but . . .

And for the first time in more than forty years of involvement in this endeavor, Joshua's eyes were opened to the real situation. This was Yahweh's battle against the dark spiritual forces who had usurped His earth. He had humiliated them in Egypt; now He was taking on the ones in Canaan. The Israelites were the good guys only because Yahweh had chosen them as His human agents and only to the extent that they followed His orders. Joshua was the human commander, but this being (whoever or whatever he was) was evidently his commanding officer. Joshua's nose hit the dirt.

The commander outlined Yahweh's orders. Once a day for six days Joshua was to march his men around Jericho with trumpets blaring. On the seventh they would march around it seven times, then the people would shout and the walls would collapse. Every living thing in the city must be killed (except Rahab's family), and all booty would be holy to Yahweh. The strange tactics would display that this was Yahweh's battle from first to last, so He alone would receive the spoils. As the first of Canaan's cities to fall and a center of worship for the moon god, Jericho would be a symbol of Yahweh's judgment on the whole evil culture and the spirits behind it.

The attack went just as Yahweh commanded, except for one detail. One soldier couldn't resist taking just a little of the plunder for himself. To let Israel know what He thought of such infractions, Yahweh withdrew His support in the next battle against the city of Ai. After a humiliating defeat, Israel's courage melted to mush, and Joshua spent all day on his face complaining to Yahweh. Finally Yahweh responded: "Stand up! What are you doing down on your face?" He explained the trouble and ordered the culprit and his whole household (who were presumably accomplices) stoned to death. Because Israel was a community, the corruption of one man defiled the whole group. If Israel wanted a God who accompanied her at every step and gave detailed instructions for every battle, then she must pay the high price of such intimacy with a Holy God. He intended to be stern at this early stage to convince the mob to take His holiness seriously.

Almost Victory

For the next seven years, Israel did take this lesson seriously, and Joshua led Israel in a two-pronged strategy to break the northern and southern Canaanite power bases. King after degenerate king fell with his nobles to Israelite swords. Not a few local peoples decided to throw their lot in with the newcomers. The city of Gibeon, for instance, was ruled by elders who hoped the Israelites might be more pleasant masters than the Canaanite overlords. They tricked Joshua into making a treaty with them and later became loyal servants of Yahweh.

The Israelite system should have attracted most of the underclasses of Canaan. Instead of a system that drove poor people to becoming slaves of their creditors, Yahweh's law said that each extended family must have its own plot of land, and that clans (groups of families) were responsible to take care of their own so that land would never be sold outside the clan. It could be rented for a period, but every fifty years it reverted to the original family. Yahweh cared about the private needs of little people in a way Canaan's gods never did. He even cared about the land: every seven years the land had to be left uncultivated (Israel didn't know that land needs to be left fallow periodically to reaccumulate soil nutrients, but Yahweh did).

Yet the Israelites let their golden opportunity slip away. After seven campaigns, the first stage of conquest was solidified. Joshua was around ninety years old, and it was time for the tribes to divide up the land and claim their inheritances without their aging general. But the people were getting tired. Caleb's family requested its portion and set off enthusiastically to wrest it from the enemy. The rest of Judah showed up for its allotment, but those clans were much less successful in taking their property because they trusted Yahweh less, so they decided to cut their losses and settle down among the Canaanites. Live and let live. The tribes of Joseph took the same attitude and even grumbled about the measly portion they were getting. They didn't like having to clear forests in the rocky hills, and they were afraid of the Canaanites on the fertile plains who had iron-clad chariots while Israel didn't know how to work iron. The Israelites refused to listen when Joshua told them not to fear chariots, so they settled in the hills to eke out a living and left the Canaanites to enjoy the plains. Finally, Joshua practically had to drag the other tribes to allot and move into their lands. Conquest was just too much work, or too scary, and it was easier to tolerate Canaanite neighbors. One could even learn a few things from them.

This was just what Yahweh had warned against. Living as neighbors would lead soon enough to intermarriage, then intermingling of religions, and eventually to a debasing of Israel's morals. The drinking and whoring of Canaanite worship was attractive, and Israelite farmers would figure they could hedge their bets by placating Canaan's fertility gods *and* worshiping Yahweh. Pretty soon their kids wouldn't be sure whether Yahweh and Baal might not be different names for the same god.

It was this danger that had moved Yahweh to order the execution of all Canaanites and the destruction of all religious objects. When the Israelites faltered in this mission, Yahweh started leaving them to defeat. This was partly punishment and partly a test: if Israel wouldn't exterminate Canaan, could she resist its seduction?

This was Joshua's question just before his death. He held a spectacular covenant renewal ceremony at Shechem, a natural amphitheater flanked by two small mountains. Half the people stood on Mount Gerizim shouting the blessings for keeping the covenant, while the other half stood on Mount Ebal shouting the curses for breaking covenant. Joshua gave a stirring speech, exhorting the nation to choose whom it would serve: the pagan gods or Yahweh. The people swore to remain faithful to Yahweh and agreed that if they rebelled they deserved the curses. They cried, "Far be it from us to forsake [Yahweh] to serve other gods!" (Joshua 24:16).

But Joshua died, as did the leaders who had known him, and their successors were not cut from the same cloth. Less than fifty years after Joshua's death, Israel had degenerated so far that she looked very much like a poor imitation of Canaan huddling in the few pieces of land the Canaanites hadn't taken back.

Judges

So began a sordid cycle. The people's love for Yahweh grew cold, and they practiced fertility religion in order to take by manipulation the prosperity that Yahweh would have given freely. Like a cuckolded husband, Yahweh would withdraw His favor and let raiders plunder or enslave His people. When they saw they were losing every battle and were in danger of starving to death, they would cry out to Yahweh for help. Then Yahweh would forgive and raise up a military leader to liberate Israel. And when the people were comfortable again, they would forget Yahweh, go back to the debauched customs of their neighbors, and the cycle would repeat.

Moses had warned the people not to say when they grew rich, "My power and the strength of my hands have produced this wealth for me" (Deuteronomy 8:17). And three generations of Israelites had sworn they would never do this and had invited Yahweh to curse them if they did. So Yahweh held the children to the bargain.

The author of the book of Judges sums up the situation neatly: "In those days Israel had no king [not even Yahweh most of the time]; everyone did as he saw fit" (Judges 21:25). What everyone saw fit to do got pretty disgusting. For instance, a Levite took a concubine, but she ran away from his shack in the backwoods of Ephraim and returned to her father's house in Bethlehem, a nice little village in Judah. So the Levite traveled to Bethlehem to fetch her back. On their way home, they stopped for the night in Gibeah, a town in Benjamin. They sat in the city square for hours before an old man noticed them and offered them his hospitality. (Hospitality was a sacred duty throughout the Near East. It was a matter of honor to offer it to travelers.) Sometime later the scum of the town banged on the host's door, demanding that he give the Levite over to them for gang homosexual rape. The only defense the Levite and his host could think of was to send the concubine out to the men, who raped and abused her until she died on the doorstep. The Levite carried her corpse home, then cut it into pieces and sent them to the elders of the other tribes. The tribes were scandalized, so they attacked Benjamin. Three days of slaughter and pillage followed. In the end, there weren't enough women left in Benjamin to carry on the tribe, and the other tribes refused to give wives to Benjamin, but they agreed to let the Benjaminites kidnap women from an Israelite town who hadn't shown up for the battle when called (Judges 20:1–21:24).

This was the kind of degeneracy Yahweh was trying to drive out of His people by letting raiders oppress them. But even when He raised up a deliverer, He had poor material to work with. Ehud, for instance, was an assassin. Jephthah was an outlaw bandit of confused ethics; he even offered his daughter as a blood sacrifice to Yahweh. Samson was more interested in sex than national liberation. And Gideon was a coward who tried every way he could think of to get out of having to lead Israel. But as with Jacob and Moses, Yahweh enjoyed working with losers because it would be obvious to anyone that He, not the human leader, deserved credit for the victory. Yahweh even told Gideon to send home all but 300 of the 32,000 troops who had gathered to drive out countless thousands of bandits.

In fact, in an age where women were commonly treated like the Levite's concubine and Jephthah's daughter, Israel's only really noble leader in several centuries was a woman. Deborah was a prophetess in Ephraim, and people came from far and wide to put before her their legal disputes. When a Canaanite king was oppressing the northern tribes, she asked a man named Barak to lead troops against the invaders. But Barak was afraid to go without Deborah. Because of his cowardice, Yahweh showed what He thought of Israel's men by allowing a housewife (Jael) to kill the Canaanite general.

What About a King?
It was an impossible situation. The Canaanites were remultiplying, and new peoples were moving from across the Mediterranean and settling on the western shore of Palestine (Phoenicians in the north and Philistines in the south). While they raided from the west, nomads encroached from across the Jordan. Marauders made travel between tribes, and even between villages, perilous. Canaanites still held ground between tribal settlements. Even the geography was against Israel: hills and valleys dissected the region, especially cutting the northern tribes off from Judah and Simeon in the south. In theory Israel was a confederacy united under a common faith, gathering together three times a year around the tabernacle to celebrate their love for Yahweh. But in reality it was every clan for itself, with some villages so remote that they scarcely remembered their brethren. In particular, Judah (which contained Simeon) was rarely involved in the battles and interests of the rest of Israel.

What could be done? Some Israelites wanted a king to unite the nation against her enemies. Gideon had refused to become king, saying that Yahweh ought to be Israel's King (Judges 8:23). His son Abimelech tried to make himself king by murdering his brothers and staging a coup, but Yahweh dealt with him. Moses had warned that a human king would bring Israel nothing but trouble if he were not totally committed to Yahweh's justice (Deuteronomy 17:14-20). Kings were expensive; they tended to finance grandiose wars, building projects, and lifestyles by taxing their people. But although local elders, prophets, and occasional guerrilla freedom fighters were cheaper, they were not keeping Israel from chaos. Something had to change.

10

A Tale of Two Kings

◆

Ruth, 1 Samuel, Psalm 18 and 22

Ruth and Boaz

Something had to be done, and Yahweh was doing it. Quietly.

A famine in Judah drove a family to Moab from Bethlehem. (See map, page 361.) The two sons of the family married Moabite women. Later, the father and both sons died. The bereaved mother, Naomi, returned to Bethlehem, and one of her daughters-in-law was too loyal to let her go alone. Bitter Naomi and faithful Ruth survived several months by grit and grace—Ruth gathered the sheaves of grain the harvesters left behind in rich men's fields.

But Yahweh maneuvered things so that Ruth was working in the field of Boaz, an unmarried kinsman of Naomi's who was far more faithful to his God than most Israelites of the day. Boaz noticed that Ruth had more guts and more morals than the wealthier women he knew, so he was entirely willing to fulfill a kinsman's duty to take over Naomi's husband's property and marry Ruth to provide children for her late husband's line. He didn't care that Ruth was a

91

foreigner whom most Israelites would consider scum; she loved Yahweh and lived like it.

The book of Ruth calls Boaz and Ruth a man and woman of "excellence"—jewels of loyalty and generosity in the slimepit of vice and selfishness that was Israel in the late eleventh century BC. They were nobodies, just trying to live God's way. But because they made themselves available to Him, Yahweh let them play a key, if quiet, place in His design. Boaz was a descendant of Judah through Perez. His and Ruth's first son was named Obed. Obed had a son named Jesse. And Yahweh had plans for one of Jesse's sons.

Hannah and Samuel
About the time Ruth and Boaz were happily raising Obed, another wife was suffering the curse of barrenness less than thirty miles north. Her husband's other wife teased her to the point that Hannah was praying desperately for a baby. When Yahweh finally gave her a son, she was so grateful that she dedicated him to serve at the tabernacle as soon as he was about three years old. She gave him into the care of Eli, the priest in charge.

Eli was not a bad old guy, but his sons seduced the cleaning women and extorted from the people who brought sacrifices, and Eli did nothing but scold them. Yahweh was so incensed that He told Eli He was going to wipe out his family.

At this time, Israel's main threat was the Philistines. The fight was terribly uneven because the Philistines knew how to forge weapons from iron, while the Israelites knew how to make only bronze or stone weapons. Eli's sons tried to use the ark in battle like a talisman, but Yahweh turned His back. The ark was captured, Eli's sons died, and that evening Eli died of shock when he heard the news. Yahweh sent plagues until the Philistines sent the ark back to Israel, but the Israelites put it in a little town and ignored it for twenty years.

Meanwhile, Hannah's son Samuel grew up to be a priest and a prophet. Because they trusted his prophecies and legal decisions, the people began to rely on him as their unofficial leader. He managed to do what no judge before him had done: unite the unruly tribes under one religious and legal authority. Samuel led the nation back to being faithful to Yahweh, and the tide of war began to turn in Israel's favor. The prophet-priest was even willing to serve as military chieftain when the need pressed. In all, things went well for Israel as long as Samuel was traveling from town to town settling legal cases and exhorting the people to rely on Yahweh rather than Baal and Astarte. Samuel was preparing Israel for the next stage of her life in Yahweh's plan.

Saul

When Samuel grew old, the people grew nervous. Like Eli, he had spent so much time fathering Israel that he had failed to raise his own sons properly. When he appointed them as judges in his place, they took bribes and turned the legal system into a racket.

Israel's elders had had enough. The nation had been a mess for two centuries, and they wanted somebody they could trust to establish order. The Israelite population was outgrowing its crude villages huddled in the hills, Canaan's least farmable land. The people wanted to spread into the lush plains, and for that, they needed a battle chief who could unite the tribes. Under the current system, a good leader might arise, but when he died Israel was back to square one because there was no way to find a successor other than to see who turned up. The elders didn't trust Yahweh to lead them, so they demanded a human king.

Samuel was furious and warned that they would regret the decision. But Yahweh simply said, *You want a king? Okay— you see how you like it.* The people should have learned from Eli's and Samuel's sons that hereditary monarchy was not all it was cracked up to be.

The fact was, Yahweh had been planning to give Israel a king. But He didn't care for the people's motive: to be like the other nations. They were like eight-year-olds who just had to have what the other kids had.

Yahweh also wanted to put on record the difference between a good king and a bad one. He wanted to give Israel a taste of wise government so they would never settle for less, and He wanted to make them good and sick of rulers who cared more for themselves than for Yahweh or His people.

Now if it were up to you, would you choose a spiritual leader whose overdependence on people's approval led him to break a few instructions about ritual and holy war? Or a leader who committed adultery and murder, and who was such a lousy father that he let his eldest son get away with raping his daughter and his second son get away with killing the first?

Yahweh chose man number two, of course. Approval seeking cost Saul his kingdom, but Yahweh forgave David's crimes. Why? Because Yahweh looked deeper than the outward action, down to the motives and attitudes of the heart.

Saul was a tall, handsome warrior, a fine military commander, successful for years. But it became obvious that he did not possess the basic quality of leadership in Yahweh's kingdom: trust in the King of kings. Fear of losing his men's loyalty made Saul disobey Yahweh repeatedly. People's opinions and his own interests just meant more to him than Yahweh's instructions, so like Adam, Saul could not imagine letting Yahweh be in charge. Samuel eventually notified him that he was going to be replaced. Even then, Saul didn't actually grieve that he had disobeyed Yahweh but only begged Samuel to keep up appearances so the elders of Israel wouldn't know the two leaders were at odds.

David

Yahweh genuinely felt sorry that He had to put Israel through the misery of being led by Saul, even though the nation deserved him. Israel's Father sent Samuel to Bethlehem to anoint one of the sons of Jesse as king. This one, Yahweh assured Samuel, would remember that he was only vice-regent ruling under Yahweh's authority. (Anointing with oil signified conferring Yahweh's power and authority. Priests and kings were traditionally anointed.)

Samuel liked the looks of Jesse's seven older sons, but Yahweh commented, "Man looks at the outward appearance, but [Yahweh] looks at the heart" (1 Samuel 16:7). The chosen one turned out to be Jesse's youngest, David, a teenager whose whole life had been spent herding sheep and composing songs.

But Yahweh knew what He was doing. Adolescent David had guts that came not from self-confidence but from a matter-of-fact trust in Yahweh. One day Jesse sent him to take provisions to his brothers who were off soldiering with Saul. David found them all cowering in fear of a Philistine champion named Goliath, who had challenged Israel to settle the battle by single combat. Neither Saul nor his warriors dared face this hulk with the fifteen-pound iron point on his spear shaft. But David thought it was disgraceful for Yahweh's army to cringe in their tents. It never occurred to him to doubt his God, so he was sure Goliath was dead meat for insulting Yahweh. And true to His name, Yahweh was I Am There For David. The teenager felled Goliath with a well-aimed shot from his sling.

Everybody was more than impressed with David the shepherd warrior. But Saul, whose courage was crumbling, was also beginning to suffer fits of depression, irrational jealousy, and violence. He had rejected Yahweh, so Yahweh was allowing an evil spirit to torment him.[1] Saul's servants were getting frantic, but they remembered that young David was also known as a fine harpist. So David was summoned to Saul's court to play music when the king had one of his attacks. Saul liked the boy and made him an armor-bearer.

Fugitive Singer

David proved brilliant in battle, and soon the people were singing victory songs about Saul and David in the same breath.

That was the last straw for Saul. His paranoia attached

firmly to David; nothing anyone could do would shake it. He tried to get rid of David by sending him on suicide missions, but David always made it through. One of Saul's schemes backfired, and David ended up married to Saul's daughter. He now had a legitimate claim to the throne, and Saul was even more scared. At last he tried to run David through with his spear, but David fled.

So began a decade in which David fled from Saul, who became obsessed with chasing him down. The Philistine war languished. Saul murdered a cityful of priests for allegedly harboring David, so intent was he to foil Yahweh's plan to replace him. But David twice declined the chance to kill Saul; he was determined to let Yahweh deal with Saul and fulfill His promises in His own way. He refused to try to take by force what Yahweh promised by grace.

What kept David going through years as the fugitive captain of an outlaw band in the wastelands, for a while even working for the Philistines in order to stay alive? His secret was pouring out his fears, hopes, praises, and accusations to Yahweh in songs. He lived an intensely honest relationship with his God. He braved the truth about his own circumstances and feelings:

My God, my God, why have you forsaken me?
Why are you so far from saving me,
so far from the words of my groaning? (Psalm 22:1)

And about Yahweh's unshakable character:

Yet you are enthroned as the Holy One;
you are the praise of Israel.
In you our fathers put their trust;
they trusted and you delivered them. (Psalm 22:3-4)

It was the *Yet* that sustained David through years of terror and seemingly futile waiting.

David's trust was not in the rock caves and fortresses he hid in, but in Yahweh, his real refuge. He could write about Yahweh as an angry thundering God:

The earth trembled and quaked,
    and the foundations of the mountains shook;
    they trembled because he was angry.
Smoke rose from his nostrils;
    consuming fire came from his mouth,
    burning coals blazed out of it. (Psalm 18:7-8)

David knew that if this wrath were directed against him, he should slink in shame. But instead, it was directed against the spiritual and human forces arrayed against him:

The cords of death entangled me;
    the torrents of destruction overwhelmed me. . . .
In my distress I called to [Yahweh];
    I cried to my God for help.
From his temple he heard my voice;
    my cry came before him, into his ears.
[Then] the earth trembled and quaked. . . .
He reached down from on high and took hold of me;
    he drew me out of deep waters.
He rescued me from my powerful enemy,
    from my foes, who were too strong for me.
        (Psalm 18:4,6-7,16-17)

Yahweh was David's Dad; He would handle the bullies who picked on His kid, although He would let David go through just enough trouble to raise him into a man.

Saul's End
Yahweh did deal with Saul. Saul had killed or driven off his priests because they had aided David, his prophets had deserted him to join David in exile, and Yahweh wouldn't talk

to him directly, so he was at his wits' end when the Philistines amassed to attack Israel. David had Yahweh's constant guidance about where to go and what battles to fight, but Saul had only silence. Crazed with panic, he consulted a witch to call up the ghost of Samuel (who had been dead for some years by now) for counsel, but the spirit he met only promised that Saul and his sons would be carrion fodder the next day.

And so it was. The Philistines overwhelmed Israel, and in despair Saul took his own life. Yahweh had maneuvered David a hundred miles south of the battlefield to protect him. When news came of Saul's death, he could not rejoice in an enemy's defeat, but grieved for a man he had loved, who could have been great.

NOTE
1. It seems that while psychological problems can come from chemical imbalance, responses to childhood trauma, and other causes, evil spirits can also be involved. Yahweh lets them attack people who give them permission by choosing to reject Him. If people want to serve darkness, He lets them reap the results in hopes that they will come to their senses.

11

David's Glory and Shame

◆

2 Samuel, 1 Chronicles, Psalm 32 and 51

David's Righteousness

David knew his Holy Dad delighted in him because he was "righteous" and "blameless" (Psalm 18:20-24). But how could David say that about himself when his faults were so glaring that they nearly brought his hard-earned kingdom down around his ears? Simple. "Righteous" and "blameless" in Hebrew did not mean that David obeyed every one of a long list of rules flawlessly. They meant that David was living up to the terms of a covenant relationship. Those terms, expressed at length by Moses, boiled down to loving and serving Yahweh with a passion that consumed one's whole being, confessing failure and rebellion when they occurred, and desiring ardently to turn from and make amends for those wrongs. Even when he committed the most appalling crimes, David remained "righteous" in Yahweh's eyes because, unlike Saul, he never tried to rationalize or evade his guilt. He always felt more horror at offending his Beloved than at being found out.

Jerusalem

After Saul's death, David's own tribesmen were quick to welcome him back from Philistia to reign over Judah. But it took seven and a half years of civil war, allegations, treachery, and assassination until the ten northern tribes were ready to turn from Saul's family and accept David as king. However, while David ruled Judah as tribal chief by popular acclaim, he governed Israel (the northern tribes) only by treaty: he and the tribal elders made a covenant each to fulfill certain obligations.

The Philistines had left Israel alone as long as it was divided and weak, but once David (whom they knew all too well) was proclaimed king of a united nation, they attacked swiftly, hoping to neutralize him before he got his footing. But in two decades of leading armies, David had learned the same secret that had carried Joshua to victory: Yahweh was his commanding officer. David consulted Him before every battle. On occasion, Yahweh would even sketch the combat strategy.

Once he had subdued the Philistines, David faced his real challenge: governing his unruly people. Because Judah and Israel were rivals, it was difficult to choose a capital that would not make one or the other half of the nation feel slighted. So David cast his eye on a stronghold high in the mountains in the Canaanite territory between Judah and Benjamin. Because Jebus (also called Zion) belonged to neither Israel nor Judah, it would be a neutral site for a united kingdom. The only difficulties were: (1) it was held by about 3,500 Canaanites; (2) its walls were surrounded on three sides by sheer dropoff; and (3) it had a secret water supply that made it invulnerable to siege.

No problem. Yahweh disclosed the entrance to the water shaft, and the Israelite army poured through it.

So David established the fortress of Zion as his citadel and built up the land around it for a royal city. He called it Jerusalem—it was probably the Salem where a Canaanite priest-king, Melchizedek, had once reigned and won Abraham's homage. In the same vicinity was Mount Moriah, where Abraham had brought his promised son to be sacrificed.

Before long, the neighboring nations began to take the new kingdom seriously. The Phoenician city of Tyre was the main seaport of Palestine. Tyre depended on Israel for agricultural products and for the inland trade routes to the rich East, while Israel desired the cedar of Phoenicia and luxury products from the West. So Israel and Tyre became allies, and the king of Tyre helped David build a regal palace, the Near Eastern symbol of kingly status.

Yahweh's House and David's House

But David felt that if Yahweh was the real Lord of Israel and he himself was only vice-regent, then Yahweh needed a palace as grand as his. His first idea was to bring Yahweh's throne to Jerusalem. David really did mean well. He sulked for three months when one of his men died because he didn't know the ark shouldn't be touched (the writings of Moses had fallen into obscurity during the centuries of chaos). But he got over it and led the final procession that welcomed the ark into the city with shouts and trumpets. Wearing nothing but the skimpy undergarment of a priest, David cavorted with wild abandon to celebrate his King's arrival in His capital. David's wife was disgusted—her father Saul would never have displayed himself with such indignity. Exactly. David didn't care what people thought of him as long as Yahweh was delighted.

He really hoped to please Yahweh with a fine cedar house instead of a tattered tent. But Yahweh sent a message through the prophet Nathan that, far from David building Him a house, He was going to build David a house, as He had already begun to do. David would have a son who would build a palace for Yahweh, but Yahweh would build that son's lineage into a dynasty that would never fail to give Israel a king. Nathan, quoting Yahweh, prophesied, "I will be his father, and he will be my son. . . . Your house and your kingdom will endure forever before me; your throne will be established forever" (2 Samuel 7:14,16).

Alone with his King, David marveled: "Who am I, O Sovereign [Yahweh], and what is my family, that you have brought me this far? . . . Is this your usual way of dealing with man, O Sovereign [Yahweh]? . . . There is no one like you" (2 Samuel 7:18-19,22)!

That was an understatement. An unending dynasty? Here was a promise to rival Abraham's. But Yahweh had kept His promises to make Abraham's descendants numerous and to give them this land with rest from their enemies. David could hardly doubt Yahweh's word, since he was sitting here as king having defeated everybody from Syria to Edom and from the Mediterranean to well east of the Jordan. (See map, page 361.)

Lust and Murder
David was flying high. He had been reigning in Jerusalem for some years, he was well over forty, and he was beginning to enjoy palace cushions more than mats in a tent on the eve of battle. So "In the spring, at the time when kings go off to war" (2 Samuel 11:1), he didn't. He let his nephew quell an uprising out east, and stayed home to enjoy the cool evenings in his rooftop pavilion at the summit of Jerusalem.

One evening he noticed a woman—the wife of one of his captains—bathing in a courtyard below. The predictable happened to a bored leader in midlife: attraction, seduction, pregnancy. With uncharacteristic clay feet, David tried to cover up his crime by inviting the captain home for a little "R and R" with his wife. When the man refused to sleep with her out of loyalty to his men in the field (what a slap to David!), the king secretly ordered the commander-in-chief to send the captain to certain death on a frontline combat mission.

After a mourning period, David married the widow, Bathsheba. She had her son, and the gossip would have died down if Yahweh had only cooperated. But He had strong opinions about kings who used their power to get away with murder. So He sent Nathan to finger David. Because He loved him, He would not take away his throne. But so that no one would say that Yahweh's grace meant license to abuse other people, David's son would die, his family would be plagued by violence, and he would suffer the same shame he had inflicted: someone close to him would one day raid his harem. A stiff penalty, but in Yahweh's order, greater honor means greater responsibility and greater cost for rebellion.

David could have had Nathan executed. Or like Saul, he could have made excuses and asked the prophet to hush things up. But instead, he simply admitted with shame that he had held Yahweh up to contempt. Throughout his son's illness he fasted, slept on the ground, and begged Yahweh for mercy. When the child finally died, he got up. His servants were baffled. But all along David was betting on Yahweh's character: while the boy lived there was still time for the mercy David had received so often, and when the boy was dead, it was time to go on trusting his God as he always had.

Why was David righteous and blameless even though he was a seducer, liar, and murderer? Consider three verses of the song he wrote (Psalm 51) while watching his son die:

Have mercy on me, O God,
    according to your unfailing love;
according to your great compassion
    blot out my transgressions. (verse 1)

Against you, you only, have I sinned
    and done what is evil in your sight,
so that you are proved right when you speak
    and justified when you judge. (verse 4)

The sacrifices of God are a broken spirit;
    a broken and contrite heart,
O God, you will not despise. (verse 17)

This was not a morbid wallowing in guilt, but a frank facing of truth and a trusting pursuit of restored relationship. Forgiveness. The other nations had no concept of an intimacy with a god that evoked such feelings, nor that a god could forgive a person by accepting the pain of a wrong into his own heart. Forgiveness. Yahweh so obliterated the crime that He was willing to treat David as though nothing had happened. David was blameless. But not proud, not self-confident. He knew he owed a debt to his God payable only in gratitude.

> Blessed is he
>> whose transgressions are forgiven,
>> whose sins are covered. (Psalm 32:1)

David understood the sweet freedom of forgiveness that meant he could approach his God with confidence.

Consequences
The relationship was restored, but the effects of wrong choices could not be evaded. David's two oldest sons lost respect for him after the Bathsheba affair. Amnon, his eldest and heir, raped his half-sister Tamar. David would not discipline his son for doing what he himself had done; like Samuel and Eli, the man who had led Israel to a golden age was a failure as a father, and he would not face it. In disgust, Tamar's brother Absalom murdered Amnon.

And again David did nothing but refuse to see Absalom for five years so that he would not be reminded of his failures and poor example. Absalom matched David's rejection with contempt: he resolved to wrest the throne out from under his father's backside. The attempt nearly succeeded and left David broken with grief and disgrace: Absalom died miserably, but not until all Israel watched as the son violated his father's concubines on the palace roof.

David's Last Years
It did not bode well for a hereditary monarchy that healthy

fathering was such an unknown art. But at about fifty years old, David resolved to try again. He passed over his surviving sons in favor of a new baby of Bathsheba's named Solomon. In his fifties and sixties David could no longer travel to war, so he spent his time preparing for the palace-temple that Solomon was to build for Yahweh. He amassed absurd quantities of gold, silver, bronze, iron, cedar, stone, and workmen of all kinds. He had elaborate plans drawn up, detailing everything from the size of each portico to the weight of gold in the lampstand—all of which, like Moses, he received in consultation with Yahweh.

Since the tabernacle would no longer be used, he organized the Levites as to which would supervise various temple matters and which would serve as judges and officials in the towns of Israel. In particular, he appointed certain families of Levites as temple musicians: they would write and play all sorts of worship music on stringed instruments, trumpets, and cymbals. Our current book of Psalms traces its roots to these musicians, who collected songs written by and/or dedicated to David.[1] They and successive generations for some six hundred years wrote more songs that ranged from riotous celebration in praise of Yahweh to heartrending prayers for help. David's frank and passionate writing set the tone for the way Israel would worship her God.

At seventy years old, David managed to hand over his kingdom to his barely grown Solomon. Thanks to Nathan the prophet, a coup attempt by David's fourth son was crushed. David exhorted Solomon to do three things: tie up some political loose ends, build the temple, and above all, obey Yahweh. The first two Solomon accomplished superbly. The third, well . . .

NOTE

1. Scholars debate whether the label "of David" in the book of Psalms always means David wrote the psalm, or whether it sometimes means the psalm was dedicated to him. The Hebrew phrase leaves both possibilities open.

12

Two Kinds of Wisdom

◆

1 Kings 1–14, 2 Chronicles 1–12, Job,
Proverbs, Ecclesiastes, Song of Songs

Prophetic Silence

One thing about David's court: It was always full of prophets. The prophet Gad had joined David's outlaw band; Nathan turned up when David settled Jerusalem; David even assigned some of the temple musicians to train in prophetic music (whatever that meant).

When we think of prophets, we may imagine fortune-tellers, or thundering preachers, or wild-eyed desert ascetics. Pagan prophets were all of these, as well as magicians, ecstatic mediums, and plain frauds. A prophet of Yahweh, however, was a little different.

Yahweh was Israel's King, and judges, elders, generals, and human kings were his vice-regents. Their job was to lead the people according to Yahweh's covenant law given to Moses. They couldn't do whatever they wanted; they had to follow the guidelines laid down in the covenant.

In this system, the prophets were Yahweh's official emissaries to the kingdom. The kings and elders were not always gifted in hearing directly from Yahweh; instead, the King gave specific instructions through prophets. For instance, David— who was pretty good at listening to Yahweh by himself— often asked the prophets' advice when making decisions about whether and how to fight battles, what to do about the temple, and so on.

Besides instructions, the prophets also conveyed Yahweh's praise or rebuke. Praise came when the leaders or people were living up to the covenant; rebuke came when they were not. Nathan brought the good news that David must not build the temple but would have an eternal dynasty. He also had to bring the bad news that David was in hot water for abusing his royal power with adultery and murder. If Israel was a building under construction, David was the foreman and Nathan was the code inspector.

David liked to hear everything Yahweh had to say—even the bad news was better heeded than ignored. So prophets were welcomed at court, and Nathan was a trusted counselor. He and other prophets got David out of more than one political mess because of their wisdom and information from Yahweh.

There were probably other prophets in David's time who lived quietly, as they had during the time of the judges, listening to Yahweh and praying for the nation. In addition, the prophets established themselves as the record-keepers on the kingdom's ups and downs. The Bible mentions "the records of Samuel the seer, the records of Nathan the prophet and the records of Gad the seer" (1 Chronicles 29:29) on David's reign, as well as those of Ahijah, Iddo, Shemaiah, and Isaiah (2 Chronicles 9:29, 12:15, 26:22) on the reigns of later kings. In fact, the Jews call the biblical books of Joshua through 2 Kings "the Former Prophets" because all of those history books were written by prophets as Yahweh's official assessment of how well Israel did or didn't live up to the covenant in each generation.

Certain prophets—Moses, Samuel, Elijah—were later singled out by the Jews as especially great. They were called the *shaluchim*, the "sent ones," because they were Yahweh's special envoys to guide the nation through a transition. Moses presided as Yahweh changed Israel from slaves to servants, and Samuel oversaw the shift from confederacy to monarchy.

But all of the prophetic activity during David's reign echoes against the silence under Solomon. Nathan and Gad died, and they were not replaced. Evidently, Solomon did not care to hear Yahweh's ambassadors assess his rule.

King of Wisdom
Perhaps in the beginning he did not need to. Twenty-year-old Solomon prayed for the wisdom to govern the nation justly, and Yahweh granted the request. Solomon started off as a brilliant judge and administrator. In the international luxury trade, he launched some joint ventures with neighboring states that began to bring huge profits. The temple rose magnificently in seven years, and after it followed thirteen years of construction on an opulent palace. Solomon's court became known throughout the East as a center of "wisdom."

"Wisdom" was the art or skill of sensible living, an understanding of the right goals and the best means of reaching them. Attaining wisdom was the purpose of education throughout the East. Fathers or teachers imparted wisdom to pupils or sons by means of proverbs, pithy sayings that crystallized truth memorably through vivid figures of speech. Archaeologists have unearthed collections of wisdom from Egypt, Babylon, and elsewhere that date from around the time of Solomon.

But Solomon was the master of his day. He wrote three thousand proverbs himself, and collected many more from Israel and the surrounding nations. Learned men would come from all over to hear Solomon's ideas about wise government, family life, and even plants and animals.

Unlike his pagan neighbors, Solomon knew the essence of true wisdom:

The fear of [Yahweh] is the beginning of wisdom,
   and knowledge of the Holy One is understanding.
      (Proverbs 9:10)

This fear was not craven cowering before an angry God, but a realistic awareness that Yahweh was in charge. The right means and ends were those that came from Yahweh and conformed to His moral requirements. Humanity was not the measure. Human reason was not ultimate. Truth was not relative.

These perceptions led Solomon to others, such as the following from Proverbs 11:

When pride comes, then comes disgrace,
   but with humility comes wisdom. (verse 2)

Wealth is worthless in the day of wrath,
   but righteousness delivers from death. (verse 4)

From this foundation, Solomon accumulated insights into government, parenting, marriage, friendship, work, emotions, and every other arena of daily life. He also wrote 1,005 songs, one of which (Song of Songs) was inspired by Yahweh as His stamp of approval on passionate, erotic love within a committed marriage.

Place me like a seal over your heart,
   like a seal on your arm;
for love is as strong as death,
   its jealousy unyielding as the grave.
It burns like blazing fire,
   like a mighty flame.
Many waters cannot quench love;
   rivers cannot wash it away.
If one were to give
   all the wealth of his house for love,
      it would be utterly scorned. (Song of Songs 8:6-7)

Solomon wrote this poem, perhaps for one of his weddings.[1] It expands on his counsel to a young man in Proverbs 5:18-19—

> May your fountain be blessed,
> and may you rejoice in the wife of your youth.
> A loving doe, a graceful deer—
> may her breasts satisfy you always,
> may you ever be captivated by her love.

Pride and Disgrace

The trouble was, the more rich, powerful, and respected Solomon grew for his wisdom, the more he began to rely on it instead of on its source: his healthy respect for Yahweh. Forgetting the beginning of wisdom, he soon forgot what he knew about pride, wealth, and love.

It was a clever move on his part to divide Israel into twelve administrative districts for taxation and labor enlistment. In bypassing the tribal boundaries, he weakened the quarrelsome tribal leaders and strengthened his central government. He was shrewd to marry seven hundred royal wives to cement alliances with all of his neighbors, and to make a pharaoh's daughter his queen and build her a splendid palace of her own. It was astute of him to fortify strategic towns on major trade routes and to amass 1,400 chariots and 12,000 horses to protect his country's economic and security interests.

But all of this smart politicking proved to be his undoing. Even the wealth of international trade could not finance Solomon's lavish building projects and defense spending. He had to rely on work gangs conscripted from the common people, on high taxes from the same folk, and on royal bureaucrats to administer the increasingly complex system. Jerusalem was opulent, but Israel was remembering that Samuel had predicted all of this (1 Samuel 8:11-18).

Even more serious, as Solomon blossomed in the international sophisticate set, he was drawn to the exotic gods of his foreign wives. The man who wrote an ardent poem about monogamous love was ensnared by clever alliances and a weakness for romance. "Many roads lead to the divine" became the mentality in cosmopolitan Jerusalem, and why shouldn't the queens of Israel have altars for their gods? Soon children were being sacrificed to Molech on a hill east of the capitol, and all manner of rites were being performed within.

The king's example gave license to the people to dabble in Baal and Ashtoreth worship, spiritism, and whatever else they fancied. Israel was becoming like any other Near Eastern land. Solomon had forgotten what he had prayed when dedicating the temple, the whole reason Yahweh had wanted a glorious building in the first place:

> As for the foreigner who does not belong to your people Israel but has come from a distant land because of your name—for men will hear of your great name and your mighty hand and your outstretched arm— when he comes and prays toward this temple, then hear from heaven, your dwelling place, and do what- ever the foreigner asks of you, *so that all the peoples of the earth may know your name and fear you, as do your own people Israel,* and may know that this house I have built bears your Name. (1 Kings 8:41-43, emphasis added)

Solomon's temple and kingdom were supposed to be setting an example that would attract the nations to Yahweh, not con- forming to those nations' corrupt values.

Yahweh was not about to let Solomon wreck His plan. Because of His promise to David, He did not wrench the whole kingdom out from under Solomon and his heirs. But He did tell Solomon that the realm would be sundered after his death. He also sent a prophet to a man named Jeroboam, the head of Solomon's work gangs in Ephraim, to say that Yah- weh was going to put Jeroboam in charge of the northern tribes of Israel. Jeroboam jumped the gun, launched an abortive coup to fulfill the prophecy, and had to spend the last years of Solomon's reign hiding out in Egypt.

Rehoboam and Jeroboam

But after thirty-three golden years under David and forty under Solomon, the flower of the nation shriveled and fell in 931 BC. Solomon's son Rehoboam succeeded him in Jerusalem, and the elders of the people traveled there to renegotiate their covenant with Judah's tribal chief. The leader of this delegation was none other than Jeroboam. Rehoboam had been raised to be a haughty oriental monarch, not Yahweh's vice-regent and the elected leader of the twelve tribes. (Fathering failed again!) The elders could see that there would be nothing but more taxes, forced labor, and bureaucrats from this fool, so they thumbed their noses at him and walked out.

The people of Israel were quick to proclaim Jeroboam king to protect them from Rehoboam (who was prevented from invading them only by another prophet's warning that Yahweh wouldn't let him win). So now there were two nations with two kings: Judah (which included Simeon and Benjamin) and Israel (which included everybody else). (See map, page 361.)

Now the prophet had warned Jeroboam that his throne was only as secure as his loyalty to Yahweh. He was I Am With You only for those, like Joshua and David, who knew who was really in charge. But Jeroboam was like Saul. Instead of looking at the God who had made him, the son of an obscure widow, king in Israel, he looked at the impossible situation facing him. The people still venerated David and Yahweh, and they had gotten used to going to Jerusalem for the magnificent festivals Solomon had staged. Jeroboam was convinced that if they kept traveling to Jerusalem three times a year, they would soon return their allegiance to Rehoboam. So he devised a solution that seemed astute to human reason but proved foolish in the long run because it bypassed the wisdom from Yahweh.

Jeroboam's scheme was to set up two national cult centers in Bethel and Dan, in the north and south of his kingdom. (See map, page 361.) In each he placed a golden calf—Syrian and Canaanite gods were often depicted standing on calves as symbols of fertility. Thus, Israel's calves with no visible god riding them would represent Yahweh's throne, counterparts to the ark in Jerusalem. Jeroboam handpicked some loyal followers to be priests and scheduled festivals to substitute for the ones in Jerusalem. He dealt ruthlessly with rebel Yahwists but gave free rein to any sort of pagan worship. Jeroboam knew that religion was either the opiate or the amphetamine of the masses, and he wanted Israel addicted to his supply.

The whole contrivance was a mockery of what Yahweh had ordained. It reminded Him of Babel, and He knew who was behind it. He gave Jeroboam one chance to reconsider: He sent a prophet from Judah to denounce the new cult. To show He meant business, He split the altar at Bethel from top to bottom. When Jeroboam tried to assault Yahweh's emissary, He shriveled the king's hand until Jeroboam apologized. (But once again, great authority entailed great responsibility: this prophet lost his life the next day for disobeying one of Yahweh's orders while on an official mission.)

Still Jeroboam persisted in his rebellion, so Yahweh took his eldest son's life and decreed that not one of his other descendants would even receive a decent burial. Israel's spurned Parent had no choice but to play hardball with children who were willing to squander the hope of the human race for the sake of their own power and pleasure.

It was the same with Rehoboam. He kept up the state religion only because it supported his throne. He was glad to let Levites and other Yahweh-lovers flee from the north into his land, but he did nothing to discourage the spread of paganism that had begun in Solomon's time. Orgies and homosexual prostitution were added to child sacrifice. Rehoboam shaped up somewhat in his personal loyalty to Yahweh after Egypt overran Judah and looted Jerusalem. But in all, Rehoboam's C minus grade was not much better than Jeroboam's F. The prophets had gone underground while wisdom reigned in Solomon's court, but they were back in force in the divided kingdom as both halves teetered toward disaster.

Warnings on Wisdom

True wisdom is as much a gift from Yahweh as revelation, but the case of Solomon proves that abused wisdom is disastrous. As wisdom flourished in Judah and Israel for centuries after Solomon, later writers exposed and refuted the most dangerous abuses.

Ecclesiastes. One wise man looked around him at an increasingly secular culture. His people believed in God, of course, but they saw Him as a vague, far-off Creator, uninvolved in their lives. The real world was about getting and spending—eat, drink, and be merry, for tomorrow we die.

To shake his society to its senses, the wise man wrote a brilliant expression of its philosophy. He called it, "The words of the Teacher, son of David, king in Jerusalem." Here, he said in effect, is the way Solomon would have described life after he was seduced by secular wisdom into making sex, wealth, and power his gods:

> "Meaningless! Meaningless!"
>   says the Teacher.
> "Utterly meaningless!
>   Everything is meaningless." (1:2)

> "The fate of the fool [death] will overcome me also.
>   What then do I gain by being wise?" (2:15)

> "Man's fate is like that of the animals . . . man has no advantage over the animal. Everything is meaningless." (3:19)

This is the tenor of Ecclesiastes (the modern title is Latin for "Teacher"). Because death is final and God is uninvolved, life is pointless. It makes no ultimate difference whether we are selfish or generous, kind or wicked. Accumulate toys, do good, or get high—it's all a rat race to avoid facing the fact that we are worth zero.

That is the sensible way to look at things if God is irrelevant. But to the author of Ecclesiastes, God is Yahweh: I Am Actively Present. In the last two sentences of his book, the author gives his response to the cold wisdom of a secularized Solomon:

Fear God and keep his commandments,
　for this is the whole duty of man.
For God will bring every deed into judgment,
　including every hidden thing,
　whether it is good or evil. (12:13-14)

Work and wisdom and honesty are not futile because Yahweh is unfolding a plan in what we do, and death is not the end. The life of obedience outlined by Moses is worth living now and promises a rich future. Pie in the sky when you die? Absolutely. But, contrary to what the world would say, that future pie is worth living for.

Job. Another Israelite was fed up with people who took the teachings of wisdom as iron-clad promises from a legalistic God. Solomon had written "The righteous man is rescued from trouble, and it comes on the wicked instead" (Proverbs 11:8), along with many more proverbs in the same vein. Such sayings were meant to be pithy statements of how the world works in general and in the long run, not universal laws. But many people, who wanted to nail God down and get the rules straight so they would feel secure, took the proverbs as absolutes. The righteous prosper and the wicked suffer— that's God's justice. So if you're suffering, you must be wicked. Right?

Wrong. There is a Snake in the grass. Disgusted with small-minded people who made a mockery of Yahweh, this unknown Israelite told the story of Job, a completely righteous man—so good you could hardly believe it. And as the proverbs promised, he was rich, healthy, and loved. But Satan made the accusation that the legalists hadn't thought of: Job isn't righteous because he loves Yahweh; he's good out of pure self-interest. Virtue pays, the Serpent charged. Yahweh buys loyalty with goodies. If Yahweh were to take away the benefits, Job would spit in His face.

This was a severe allegation. The whole human experiment was designed to demonstrate to the cosmos that Yahweh was a Lover who longed to be freely loved by an uncoerced bride, that He deserved to be trusted even in the dark. So Yahweh took Satan up on his dare.

However, when Job lost his wealth, his family, and his health, he had no idea that he was a living test case that those who love Yahweh do so just because they love Him, not because He buys it. Nor did his friends. They quoted at him all the proverbs about how if he was suffering he must have done something wrong. When Job protested that he hadn't done anything to deserve this treatment, his friends furiously denounced him for calling God unjust. To them, if God is in control, life must always be fair. Everything that happens to you must be a direct result of whether you've been good or not.

In the end, Job silenced his accusers by calling upon God to appear and judge his case. He didn't even really care whether his health recovered, so long as he could have an honest, face-to-face relationship with the real God.

Job's friends expected lightning from Heaven to swallow Job up for such a challenge. And when Yahweh appeared in a mighty storm, His response did flatten Job, but not as his friends expected. In an avalanche of questions, Yahweh demonstrated that He indeed had both the wisdom to know how to run the world justly and the power to accomplish what He decided. It is not for a divine lack of understanding or ability that life is unfair, Mr. Job. Life is unfair because the Enemy has corrupted it. There is no way to get rid of evil in the world by force without annihilating everybody, and that Yahweh is unwilling to do. He has another plan, and in the meantime, the good guys will suffer right along with the bad guys. Sometimes even more because the Enemy wants to make the good guys bitter against Yahweh, or at least miserable in their faithfulness. But when the wise are confused in their distress, they won't make petty rules about God to rationalize what is happening. They will, like Job in the end, bow in awe and trust at the One whose wisdom, power, and goodness far surpass their wildest imaginations. Job summed up what he had learned as follows:

> Then Job replied to [Yahweh]:
> "I know that you can do all things;
>   no plan of yours can be thwarted. . . .
> My ears had heard of you
>   but now my eyes have seen you." (Job 42:1-2,5)

Job no longer needed answers to his questions. To glimpse Yahweh once was more than enough for a lifetime of faith in the dark.

Several centuries after Solomon, his proverbs and those of other wise men were collected into the book of Proverbs. That book remains an invaluable guide to practical living; wisdom stands alongside revelation as a priceless gift from God. But Ecclesiastes and Job remind us that wisdom must be understood in light of who Yahweh is: the God whose thoughts and ways are so far beyond our minds that they cannot be reduced to legalistic absolutes to make us feel safe; and the God who is right there with us, infusing our every day with purpose. Life is not fair, but it matters deeply because of who its Author is.

NOTE
1. Some scholars think one of Solomon's court poets composed the Song of Songs for one of Solomon's weddings. Our general practice in this book is to follow traditional beliefs about the authors of books in order not to become mired in scholarly debate. There is wide room for disagreement about authorship when a book doesn't say who wrote it. The Song says it belongs to Solomon, but that could equally mean a dedication. Likewise, Ecclesiastes alludes to Solomon, but never claims him as author.

13

Power Encounters

◆

1 Kings 15–2 Kings 12, 2 Chronicles 13–24

Stalemate

Israel and Judah split because petty despots fancied themselves grand monarchs and refused to submit to a Lord who had the whole people's interests at heart. The result was pathetic. For two centuries, Israel and Judah played a triangle game with Syria. Two of the nations would ally against the third until it was defeated. Then the two would turn on each other. When one feared conquest, it would send money to the third to make a treaty, and the cycle would repeat. This went on until Egypt and Assyria grew strong enough to play, too, and between them gobbled the three others up. (See map, page 360.)

In the meantime the game bled the resources—human and financial—of all three players. Judah fared best because its rugged topography made it less accessible, because it had a stable ruling dynasty, and because Yahweh was faithful to His promise to David. Israel was battered by coups and assassinations; in two hundred years it went through twenty kings from nine families, while Judah went through twelve (including one usurping queen) from one family during the same period. At that point, Assyria destroyed Israel but Judah survived.

The prophetic author of 1 and 2 Kings assessed each ruler according to the covenant standard. Using David as the standard for an A, he evaluated the Judan kings' faithfulness to Yahweh (from Rehoboam to the Babylonian Captivity) and came up with ten Fs, two Ds, one C, three Bs, three A minuses, and only one fairly solid A, Josiah. And the bright spots in Judah were unparalleled in Israel; all her kings failed. Yahweh did not grade on a curve.

Only one royal family in Israel really succeeded in becoming a dynasty, and it proved to be the most dangerous of all to Yahweh's plan. Through that family, the Snake nearly succeeded, not only in corrupting Israel to the point of no return, but also in exterminating the house of David in Judah. The tactics were military force and politics, but also witchcraft and deception on an unprecedented scale. Yahweh fought back as He had not since the days of Moses and Joshua. Open demonic activity invited open divine response, and (as the Serpent well knew by now) Yahweh's plan depended upon the lineage of David.

Omri

For fifty years after the split, things degenerated. Judah endured two worthless kings, then began struggling back under the long reign of Asa. Israel went through five kings, spent six in civil war, then finally settled down to eleven stable years under the victor, Omri.

He was as shrewd as Jeroboam and realized that to compete with Judah he needed a capital of equal splendor. So he bought a hill near Shechem, named it Samaria after its former owner, and built on it a citadel to rival the fortress of Zion. Omri began, and his son completed, work on grand palaces, administrative quarters, and homes like those Solomon had erected in Jerusalem. In Samaria the houses of the rich priests, nobles, and bureaucrats who served the thriving kingdom were divided from the poor neighborhood by a wall. (Jerusalem definitely had uptown and downtown; the best real estate was upwind from cooking and sewage odors. But nobody had thought of a wall.)

Omri put Israel on the map; his dynasty lasted only forty-four years, but a century and a half later the Assyrians were still calling Israel "the house of Omri." Omri did his best to copy Solomon's Egyptian-style administration.

He also imitated Solomon in making foreign alliances; he married his son Ahab to the Phoenician princess Jezebel. When Ahab became king, he topped Jeroboam by building a temple for Jezebel's god Baal in Samaria itself and dropping all pretense of worshiping Yahweh. Baal became the official state god—a mockery of Yahweh's kingship in Jerusalem.

Ahab, Jezebel, and Elijah

In response, Yahweh brought in the big guns. Ahab's predecessors had tolerated Yahweh's prophets and hadn't even executed them when they graphically prophesied the kings' deaths. They took Yahweh seriously enough not to mess with His envoys. At this time the prophets were grouped in companies—communities in which one who felt called to serve Yahweh could reside and learn with other likeminded people. They lived in austerity on the fringes of the increasingly depraved Israelite society to protest the nation's materialism, and generally didn't bother the king unless Yahweh had a message for him (which wasn't often). Probably they spent most of their time imploring Yahweh not to let their country go to the dogs.

However, Jezebel was a practicing witch, an all-out Viper's daughter and enemy of Yahweh. But He had been grooming a prophet of the stature of Moses and Samuel: Elijah (the name meant "Yahweh is God"). This tough desert dweller in camel-hair shorts arrived in Samaria one day with an official notice:

Israel belonged to Yahweh. If her kings and priests did not recognize Him as their Sovereign, they were in treason. If they thought Baal the storm god was better than the gods of Egypt and Canaan whom Yahweh had dealt with in the past, they were mistaken. And to prove that Baal, Jezebel, and every pagan priest from Hamath to Jericho shouting together couldn't squeeze one drop out of the sky, there would be neither dew nor rain in Israel until Elijah said so.

That was it. Elijah walked out. He went out east alone and Yahweh provided food until the brooks all dried up. Then he went to Sidon (Jezebel's home territory!) and Yahweh directed him to a starving widow. He stayed with her, while Yahweh miraculously replenished her supply of oil and grain. When her son fell ill and died, Yahweh enabled Elijah to raise him from the dead. Yahweh's point: *Unlike Baal, I can take care of My own. And if My people want to spit in My face, I can find faithful people to bless in the seedbed of paganism itself. Remember, My covenant with Israel is for the sake of the nations.*

Single Combat

Nearly three years passed, and Ahab didn't get the message. Jezebel began massacring Yahweh's prophets until Ahab's chief of staff resorted to hiding a hundred of them in two caves and bringing supplies secretly. Yahweh could have let the nation starve, but He had compassion even on traitors. So He sent Elijah back to face Jezebel's prophets.

The challenge was simple. Jezebel's 850 prophets would set up one bull for a burnt offering, and Elijah would set up another. The god who sent fire to consume his sacrifice was the real God; the other was a fake. The people gathered at the site on Mount Carmel agreed to take this single combat as proof.

Baal's prophets exhausted themselves in ecstatic dances, shouting, and slashing themselves to arouse him to act. Elijah poked fun ("Shout louder! Maybe he's asleep! Maybe he's relieving himself!") to underscore the absurdity of carrying on like this for a nonexistent god. Finally, as evening was coming,

Elijah arranged his sacrifice and told the bystanders to pour water on it until even a trench around it was filled. Nothing up my sleeve.

Then Elijah prayed briefly, and lightning struck his sacrifice and consumed the bull, the wood, and even the water in the trench. The people fell prostrate and cried, "Yahweh is God!" At Elijah's order they slaughtered the priests of Baal.

Elijah sent them off to eat while he prayed for rain. When at last a cloud appeared on the horizon, he told Ahab to get down the mountain before the storm stopped him. And full of the Spirit of God, Elijah ran before Ahab's chariot some twenty miles to Jezreel.

Ahab could not have had a more solid incentive to abandon his wife's god and lead the nation back to Yahweh. But although he was stubborn, he lacked real backbone. He could put on a good macho show to cover up his essentially weak masculinity, but Jezebel controlled him. Ahab informed her of the events on Carmel; she sent a death threat to Elijah; and then Ahab did nothing.

Elijah was crushed. As he saw it, Yahweh had played His trump card and it had made no ultimate difference. Like many people, he apparently assumed that if Yahweh would demonstrate His majesty publicly, everyone would turn to love and faithfulness. But with the witch still in charge, there would be no national repentance. He had failed. The Snake had won.

But Yahweh had known since Eden that power would not win love. He had made a real offer and had stripped Israel of the excuse that He was absent and silent, but the results did not surprise Him. And while He loved this crusty prophet, He couldn't have him sulking in a cave in the Sinai desert. (Ironically, Elijah had fled to Horeb, where so many years ago Yahweh had twisted a discouraged Moses' arm into leading Israel out of Egypt.) This time, Yahweh showed His envoy a little object lesson.

Fireworks isn't My trump card. I can come in storm and wind when I want to. But you know that mostly those aren't My style.

Mostly I come in a whisper to people like you who are willing to listen. And there are seven thousand more in Israel who are listening. So don't give up—I haven't. We're not going to beat this Snake with pyrotechnics. You'll see: It's only going to take a whisper.

Elisha

But it was going to be a loud whisper for a while with opponents like Jezebel still at large. Yahweh gave Ahab every chance, miraculously intervening in battles against Syria, and sending prophet after prophet to encourage him or get in his face with tough reality checks. He did humble himself before Yahweh enough to die in battle instead of murder. But he kept letting his wife cajole him into acting like a Phoenician tyrant, and he had no respect for Yahweh's messengers.

Ahab's eldest son carried on his tradition; he died without heir, having consulted a Philistine god for healing and having tried to murder Elijah. His brother Joram succeeded him. Early in Joram's reign, Elijah was taken into Heaven in a flaming chariot, and his office as Israel's head prophet passed to his protégé, Elisha.

Now Elisha had the nerve to ask for a double dose of Elijah's spirit (a.k.a. Yahweh's Spirit) in his life. And Yahweh (who likes that kind of spunk if it accompanies humility and love) granted the request. The national cleansing for which Elijah had prayed and sweated, Elisha led into being. Elisha did twice as many spectacular miracles as his mentor.

The miracles were eye-catching exhibits of Yahweh's character. Some (such as a famine) trumpeted judgment against Israel's depravity. Many more displayed His compassion upon the innocent (helpless widows and hungry prophets) who suffered for that depravity along with the guilty. Some were to protect Israel and Judah from destruction by Syria. And one was yet another reminder that Yahweh's plan concerned more than twelve tribes.

Syria's commander-in-chief received healing from leprosy because he humbled himself enough to obey a seemingly childish instruction from Elisha; this adversary of Israel went away with such respect for the God of Israel that he took back some dirt in order to worship Him on His native soil. It was a disgrace: the glory of Yahweh was under the noses of Israel's leaders every day, and they failed to perceive it, while a foreigner was overcome by it on his first encounter. Who were the real chosen people?

Yahweh gave Joram twelve years of Elisha's miracles to catch on to what Israel was supposed to be about—being a light to people like this Syrian officer. Joram did take down the phallic symbol in honor of Baal that had adorned the capital in Ahab's day. But it was a weak gesture, and finally Yahweh told Elisha to put an end to Omri's dynasty.

Jehu

The selected instrument was Jehu, an Israelite army commander and opportunist. After being anointed by one of Elisha's prophetic students, Jehu led his men out to meet Joram and his nephew Ahaziah, the king of Judah, as they were returning from battle against Syria. He dispatched them, then rode to make short work of the witch-queen mother, Jezebel. Then followed a bloodbath of the remaining seventy male heirs of Ahab, all of their supporters, and every Baal-worshiper Jehu could find.

Yahweh rewarded this thoroughness with a promise to give Jehu a four-generation dynasty. But Jehu was no more faithful to Yahweh than Jeroboam had been, so Yahweh allowed Syria to slowly whittle Israel away. There would be blood and more blood until the nation recognized on whom its life depended.

Athaliah and the Attempted Takeover of Judah

All the same, Yahweh-worship was legal again in Israel and the poison of Jezebel was neutralized. But not before it had infected Judah. This was the Serpent's real goal.

Let's catch up a little on events to the south. Early in the reign of Ahab, when Jezebel was just getting rolling, Jehoshaphat inherited the throne of Judah. Like his father Asa, Jehoshaphat was basically a good king, appointing honest judges and doing his best to quell the Baal-worship Rehoboam had encouraged. Under Asa and Jehoshaphat there were basically good relations among the priests who taught the law of Yahweh, the king who administered the law, and the prophets who assessed how well the nation and its leaders were keeping the law.

But Asa and Jehoshaphat had one weakness: when threatened with war, they tended to make foreign alliances rather than trusting Yahweh. Prophet after prophet rebuked both father and son for doing this. Yahweh enabled miraculous victories when the kings took the risk to ally with Him only. But they didn't get the message.

This no-alliance rule wasn't a petty whim of Yahweh's. It was given to prevent the near disaster that occurred because Jehoshaphat allied with Ahab. Jehoshaphat married his son Jehoram to Ahab's daughter Athaliah. Now unity among the twelve tribes was a great idea, but this was neither the time nor the method with Israel such a cesspool of witchcraft.

The result was that Athaliah (who was a spiritual daughter of Jezebel in every way, if not her physical daughter also) corrupted Jehoram. Her Jezebel style was evident when early in his reign Jehoram murdered all of his brothers so as to have no rivals for the throne. Things got so bad that Elijah himself wrote a warning to Jehoram, but the king ignored the letter and contracted the illness Yahweh sent to punish his wickedness. Jehoram was such an appalling king that his people refused even to give him a royal funeral or bury him in the royal crypt.

All of Jehoram's sons but one—Ahaziah—had died in a Philistine attack. His mother, Athaliah, controlled Ahaziah's every move, and he would have been as poisonous a king as his father if Jehu had not killed him along with Joram when seizing the kingship of Israel.

When Athaliah saw that the Yahwists had killed both her nephew Joram and her son Ahaziah, she was ripe to fulfill her Viper Lord's scheme. She set about slaughtering every surviving person descended from David, including her own grandsons. When apparently all were dead, she proclaimed herself queen of Judah.

If Athaliah had succeeded, the Davidic lamp would have been extinguished and the kings of Israel would have claimed Judah when she died, since she was a daughter of an Israelite king. There would have been no son of David to fulfill the prophecies, and Israel would have been a united pagan nation.

But Athaliah's sister-in-law hid an infant son of Ahaziah. For six years a priest named Jehoiada nurtured the child, while Athaliah ruled. At last Jehoiada staged a quick coup and crowned Joash.

Joash ruled well until Jehoiada's death. And even though later he turned rotten and murdered Jehoiada's prophet-son for denouncing him, and even though his own officials eventually assassinated him in return, the house of David survived in his sons.

C·H·A·P·T·E·R

14

Enforcing the Covenant

◆

2 Kings 13–17, Amos, Hosea, Jonah

Prophetic Portfolios

Yahweh gears His tactics to fit the situation. His use of prophets is a case in point.

David needed counselors who would guide and support him in his commitment to serve Yahweh. His Lord sent Gad and Nathan. Solomon wanted no prophets, and got none. When the nation split, the southern prophets continued to follow the pattern of Nathan to the degree that the kings imitated David. Prophets, priests, and kings worked together in the good times. In the bad times, the prophets were often silent, as under Solomon.

Things were different in the northern kingdom. The trouble there was not just a diluting of Yahweh-worship, but a total sellout to Baal or Jeroboam's state-run pseudo-Yahwism. The lines between good and evil were sharp. The Enemy's tactics included open witchcraft. Open supernatural assault demanded overt confrontation: the power encounters and miracles of Elijah/Elisha.

In the background, of course, there were always "the sons of the prophets," members of the prophetic communities who supported the plan through hidden intercession and who recorded key events for posterity. Indeed, even Elijah and Elisha spent most of their ministries in this hiddenness.

But interestingly, Yahweh did not instruct the prophetic communities to collect the sermons of their leaders. We have few or no recorded public messages of the prophets from 1400 to 800 BC.

This pattern shifted around 800 BC. The biblical books from Joshua through 2 Kings (minus Ruth, which is a short story) are the Former Prophets—the history of Israel and Judah from a prophetic viewpoint. But the books from Isaiah to the end of the Old Testament (minus Daniel, something of a special case) are the Latter Prophets—collections of public prophecies delivered between about 760 and 460 BC.

Why the change? Why do we have the collected messages of Isaiah, Jeremiah, and Amos, but not those of great prophets like Samuel and Elijah? And why did the miracles fade out— the nature miracles like the preventing and bringing of rain, and the divine guidance for battle? (Isaiah did give one miraculous sign that was immediately fulfilled—Isaiah 38:7. But he was no Elisha.)

Public Notices
To understand what Yahweh was doing, we need to remember that the prophets were His ambassadors for covenant enforcement. They pointed out violations of the terms to which Israel had agreed under both Moses and Joshua. The prophets also notified the people about the consequences of their choices. Those consequences—blessings for obedience and curses for disobedience—had all been spelled out through Moses and accepted by the people. So there was nothing cruel about Yahweh letting them take effect.

Up until 760 BC, Yahweh was patient with generation after generation of treacherous, callous children. The prophets proclaimed only limited consequences for evildoing. There was no need to record their messages in detail; the gist sufficed to let later generations learn from what had happened.

But from 760 until 460 BC, Yahweh wanted a permanent record of His memoranda. This was not a time for power encounters through prophets (although angels were occasionally deployed), but for a legal record of repeated warnings of covenant violation.

The reason was that Yahweh intended to unleash the full consequences for rebellion. He was going to obliterate the nation. As a just ruler, He wanted a permanent log that He had done everything possible to turn His people from their disastrous course. He wanted to leave later generations in no doubt of the lengths to which He had gone to restore His people.

The prophets' messages during these three centuries fell into two patterns:

MEMO

To: Israel/Judah

From: Yahweh

Subject: Covenant violations

You have violated our agreement at Sinai in the following ways:_____. As you recall, the consequences we agreed upon for such breach of contract were:_____. This note is to inform you that the consequences will be imposed if you do not change your attitude.

Yahweh sent this message repeatedly for fifty years before destroying Israel, then for another hundred before demolishing Judah. In the meantime, and even more after the destructions, He also addressed this to the destitute survivors:

MEMO

To: Israel/Judah

From: Yahweh

Subject: Pardon for covenant violations

Because I am a compassionate Father and I love you, I am going to forgive your crimes and restore you to a glory you can hardly imagine, as follows: _____.

Just two basic messages repeated over and over. Sounds simple—and boring. Yahweh knew His people wouldn't respond to dry memos, to some code-enforcer citing paragraph 9.5.1 of a law book. And He had too much personality for that anyway. So instead, He sent His emissaries with ironic, scathing, lyric, funny, grieving poems to recite. Near Easterners were accustomed to hearing poetry—they found it more gripping and memorable than lectures. Like good songs, the prophecies would stick in the people's minds.

So each book of the Latter Prophets is a collection of poetic messages spoken by a prophet. In some cases, the oracles may have been collected, or even recorded, by the prophet's followers. Rarely do we know the exact circumstances in which the prophet delivered a given poem. Nor are we usually sure even where one prophecy ends and the next begins. Most modern translations guess at the divisions between oracles, but in the original Hebrew they are all run together. We have no way of knowing whether two adjacent messages were delivered days or years apart, or to the same or different audiences. It is clear from the few recorded dates that the collectors weren't concerned with putting the prophecies in chronological order.

Add these uncertainties to the fact that we aren't used to reading poetry much any more, and you can see why the prophets are hard to interpret. They use colorful, figurative language, jump from subject to subject, and don't even say whether they are talking about the present, the near future, or the far future. They can be talking about a situation in their own time, then shift without warning as they glimpse something in a distant century, for a prophet sees from Yahweh's perspective of eternity. It's like taking an aerial view of a highway rather than driving along it. Maybe we'd rather have memos.

But since we don't, we'll try to see what Yahweh was trying to get across to His people through each of the latter prophets. We'll begin with those in the northern kingdom because it lasted only until 721 BC.

A Bull Market in Israel

The prophets were quiet in Israel from the time Jehu became king in 841 BC until about 797 BC. During that time, the kings tolerated Jeroboam's fake religion, but Baal worship wasn't totally taking over as under Ahab. Yahweh let Syria gnaw at Israel until Syria virtually took over. Not even this slow hemorrhage got the people's attention.

So Yahweh tried another tack. Assyria, far to the northeast of Syria, had been a looming threat since Ahab's day. (See map, page 360.) Jehu had had to pay Assyria tribute to keep his throne. But afterward Assyria fell on hard times internally. It barely managed to defeat Syria in 805 BC, but was exhausted in the effort. Assyria's weakness and Syria's defeat were crucial, for they left a power vacuum for Israel to fill. Around 795 BC, a prophet named Jonah foretold that Israel would soon retake all the territory that had been lost since the time of Solomon—quite a bit of real estate.

Jeroboam II inherited the crown of Israel in 793 and set about fulfilling Jonah's words. With both Syria and Assyria weak, and with Israel controlling the major north-south trade routes, the nation exploded into financial and military prosperity. But only the powerful profited. They became fabulously rich as merchants, then began to employ sharp lawyers to acquire the land of small farmers. They built huge houses, furnished them extravagantly, and held endless dinner and drinking parties. Those who lacked either the money, intellect, or connections to play legal hardball found themselves land-less, destitute day laborers.

Worst of all, the wealthy attributed their success to Yahweh's favor. They reveled in being the chosen people, and business at the shrines of Bethel and Dan boomed. Worship services were packed. The prime topic of sermons was "when Yahweh has His day"—when He would come and perma-nently defeat Israel's enemies.

Business was also good at pagan shrines. As the nation grew increasingly secular and materialistic, it was easy for people to celebrate the festivals of both Yahweh and the other gods. Yahweh worship had never been too pure in Israel any-way. People liked to hear the old stories about Abraham and Jacob—the ones that made them feel important—but they also enjoyed the earthier pleasures of fertility rites.

Amos

It made Yahweh grind His teeth to be marketed. Israel had not learned to take Him seriously in the fireworks on Mount Carmel, nor in oppression by Syria. He gave the nation about thirty-five years of prosperity under Jeroboam II to muster some gratitude, and when it was clear that nothing but smug-ness was forthcoming, He sent Amos.

Amos was in the livestock business a few miles south of Jerusalem. He was informed on the Law of Moses, as well as on international affairs. He had never been part of a prophetic community, but when Yahweh told him to take time off to carry a message to the northern kingdom, he consented.

Biting irony was the tone of the speeches Yahweh gave Amos. Amos would stand outside the shrine at Bethel, or in the thoroughfare of Samaria, and announce, "This is what Yah-weh says: . . ." He caught the crowd's ear by declaring how Yahweh would judge the pagan nations for atrocities against

Israel, then won applause by denouncing Judah, and finally zeroed in on his real target:

> "For three sins of Israel,
>   even for four, I will not turn back my wrath.
> They sell the righteous for silver,
>   and the needy for a pair of sandals.
> They trample on the heads of the poor
>   as upon the dust of the ground
>   and deny justice to the oppressed. . . .
> Now then, I will crush you
>   as a cart crushes when loaded with grain."
>   (Amos 2:6-7,13)

Was Israel Yahweh's chosen people? Undoubtedly. But election has a price:

> "You only have I chosen of all the families of the earth;
>   therefore I will punish you for all your sins."
>   (Amos 3:2)

Amos got into big trouble with the authorities by comparing rich women lounging with chilled wine to Israel's top breed of cattle and for predicting that Assyria would soon chew Israel to bits. But when threatened, Amos coolly informed his accuser of the fate he and his family would soon face for their vileness.

The prophet did not enjoy these hard words. Yahweh deliberately selected messengers who would grieve and pray for the wicked rather than revel in their destruction. But He who at Bethel had transformed deceitful Jacob into humble Israel could not tolerate Jacob's descendants celebrating at Bethel by transforming "justice into bitterness" (5:7). Pride and self-congratulating religion disgusted Him.

For nine chapters, Amos graphically detailed the obliteration Israel could expect. But in a final prophecy, Yahweh granted him a glimpse of hope:

"In that day I will restore David's fallen tent.
I will repair its broken places, restore its ruins,
and build it as it used to be." (9:11)

With Yahweh, even the end is not final because a promise
is never broken.

Hosea

Israel's elite ignored Amos the doomsayer, so eventually Yahweh sent the prophet home to take care of his livelihood and collect his messages for posterity. Meanwhile, Yahweh was preparing a different stripe of man to present His plea in a startlingly different way.

Toward the end of Jeroboam's reign, Yahweh asked an ordinary Joe named Hosea to marry a woman he knew would be unfaithful. She bore him three children, and Yahweh gave each of them symbolic names: "God-Scatters," "Not-Loved," and "Not-My-People." (Imagine growing up with the name Not-Loved!) Then Hosea's wife ran off, became a hooker, and ended up a slave. And Yahweh told him to buy her back and love her as He loved the Israelites, even though they were prostituting themselves with fertility gods.

The whole wild scenario was an object lesson for Hosea's neighbors and a chance for him to truly share Yahweh's anguish at being jilted by the people to whom He had poured Himself out. Like an enraptured husband, Yahweh had showered this nation in affluence. But she had seen it all as payment from her paramours, the gods of prosperity and power. Now, through the prophecies of a man who had been there, Yahweh could weep at how as a lover He had wooed Israel, how as a spurned husband He had let her chase her suitors and end up trapped in prostitution, and how incredibly He would allure her again when the consequences of her betrayal hit home. Not-Loved would become Loved, and Not-My-People would again become My People.

Hosea pulled no punches in cataloging Israel's whoredom:

"I will not punish your daughters
    when they turn to prostitution,
nor your daughters-in-law
    when they commit adultery,
because the men themselves consort with harlots
    and sacrifice with shrine prostitutes—
a people without understanding will come to ruin!"
    (Hosea 4:14)

He talked of marred ecology, drunkenness, debauchery, and unjust lawsuits. But he also affirmed Yahweh's mad passion even for such degenerates:

"How can I give you up, Ephraim?
    How can I hand you over, Israel? . . .
My heart is changed within me;
    all my compassion is aroused." (Hosea 11:8)

If His bride would only abandon her strategies for living without Him, Yahweh promised to forgive everything.

Hosea was from Israel, but his book is dated according to the reigns of Judah's kings. The dates show us that he suffered his marital troubles toward the end of Jeroboam II's reign, but that he addressed his adulterous country all the way to the end.

Jeroboam II ended a glorious forty-one-year rule in 753 BC. His son Zechariah succeeded him with all due pomp—it was still a bull market in Israel. Six months later, Zechariah lay dead in a bloody public assassination. His killer held the throne for one month before another army officer, Menahem, murdered him in another coup. Menahem managed to hold the crown for ten years by paying off the king of Assyria with money from a tax that crippled Israel's upper class. A shrewd young king had led Assyria out of hibernation and into a series of well-executed military campaigns that led to Menahem's doorstep. Israel really had no choice but to buy Assyria off. (Other than casting itself on Yahweh's mercy—a plan which occurred to nobody but Hosea. He predicted that bribing Assyria would fail in the long run.)

There were those in Israel, however, who thought there ought to be a third alternative: tough it out against Assyria while ignoring Yahweh. An officer named Pekah set up a countergovernment in the part of Israel that lay east of the Jordan River. He led a civil war first against Menahem and then against his son Pekahiah, who kept up his father's pro-Assyrian policy for two years. At last Pekah managed to assassinate Pekahiah. Pekah promptly rebelled against Assyria, and (one didn't need to be a prophet to foresee it at this point) Assyria promptly overran Israel and conquered everything except the capital city and its environs. Captives were deported to other corners of the empire. To avert total disaster, an officer named Hoshea murdered Pekah, declared himself king, and surrendered to Assyria.

Hoshea lasted for nine years. But when Assyria discovered that he was secretly conspiring with Egypt to throw off the Assyrian yoke, the siege engines rolled again for the last time. After a hideous three-year siege, Assyria took Samaria and deported 27,290 people—virtually all who had failed to flee to Judah. Six kings, but only thirty-one years, had passed since Jeroboam II's death.

The prophet Hosea must have escaped, for his book was apparently compiled in Judah. He lived to see his mission fail utterly as Yahweh dealt with His adulterous bride.

Jonah

Possibly there was one man who would have been more devastated by these events than Hosea. Back around 795 BC, young Jonah had predicted Jeroboam II's victories and the abundance that would follow. Toward 750 BC, things were crumbling and Assyria was on the rise. And Yahweh gave this patriotic prophet an incredible assignment: "Go to the great city of Nineveh and preach against it, because its wickedness has come up before me" (Jonah 1:20). Now Nineveh was a major city of Assyria (soon to be its capital). If Jonah had believed that Yahweh was properly nationalistic and vindictive, he would have set off whistling. But Jonah knew that Yahweh could not be trusted. Nineveh was bound to repent, Yahweh would forgive, and that would be disgusting.

In Jonah's defense it should be noted that the Assyrians were not nice people. When they conquered an area, they demolished buildings, burned trees, slaughtered animals, skinned captives alive, impaled corpses on stakes, stacked heads in heaps, tortured and mutilated captured leaders, deported whole populations to other parts of their empire to discourage nationalist uprisings, and generally practiced rule by terror.

So in order to avoid giving the message that might cause Nineveh's repentance and deliverance, Jonah caught the first boat to the other end of the Mediterranean world. However, Yahweh sent a storm, Jonah let the sailors throw him overboard to save themselves, and Jonah spent three days in the belly of a large fish thinking things over. In the end he cried out to Yahweh, who had the fish vomit him onto land.

While inside the fish, Jonah wrote a poem of thanksgiving and resignation ending, "What I have vowed I will make good. Salvation comes from [Yahweh]" (Jonah 2:9). Then he went to Nineveh, and sure enough, the Ninevites responded to his warning by instantly repenting. Jonah was furious. He accused Yahweh, "O [Yahweh], is this not what I said when I was still at home? That is why I was so quick to flee to Tarshish. I knew that you are a gracious and compassionate God, slow to anger and abounding in love, a God who relents from sending calamity" (Jonah 4:2)!

So Yahweh gave him a little lesson in which He provided a vine to shade Jonah and then shriveled it with heat. When Jonah protested His harshness, Yahweh replied: "You have been concerned about this vine, though you did not tend it or make it grow. . . . But Nineveh has more than a hundred and twenty thousand people who cannot tell their right hand from their left, and many cattle as well. Should I not be concerned about that great city?" (Jonah 4:10-11).

How it galled Jonah and grieved Yahweh that Assyria responded to a single message from a prophet, while Israel ignored the records of Moses, the miracles of Elijah, and the warnings of Amos and Hosea. It was unspeakable that repentant Nineveh became Yahweh's agent to destroy stubborn Israel. But while Yahweh had chosen Israel as His bride, He was not her national pet. He loved all nations—even wicked Assyria—and He wanted no one to forget the purpose of His covenant: "All peoples on earth will be blessed through you."

15

Meanwhile Down South

◆

2 Kings 15–16, 2 Chronicles 26–28,
Isaiah 1–11, Joel, Micah

House of Cards

Judah was not much better than Israel during the eighth century BC. One year after Jeroboam II took over in the north, Uzziah became king in the south. He benefited from the weakness of Assyria and Syria, and from his new control of trade routes through his territory, in just the same ways as Jeroboam did. During his fifty-two-year reign, Uzziah fortified Jerusalem, built towers and cisterns for his livestock holdings, expanded his army, strengthened his defenses to the southeast and southwest, and developed inland and maritime trade. Agriculture also boomed. But as in the north, legal maneuvering increasingly concentrated wealth and power in the hands of the upper class, while the poor grew poorer and poorer.

Uzziah started out devoted to Yahweh, but like Solomon, he let success go to his head. One day he decided to emulate the old Jebusite priest-kings like Melchizedek. When he entered the Holy Place of the temple to burn incense, Yahweh struck him with leprosy. Yahweh had separated the roles of prophet, priest, and king on purpose, and He was not about to let Uzziah upset the balance of power.

Having reached beyond his right, Uzziah lost even what he had. Lepers were quarantined as contagious, so Uzziah spent the last decade of his life as king in name only. His son Jotham dictated policy and ran the daily business of state.

Jotham took over in 750 BC, about the time Amos started making trouble up north. Jotham was not a bad king: he respected Yahweh religion, continued renovating Jerusalem, and fought some successful battles. While Israel convulsed in one coup after another, Jotham kept his house stable. But he was not concerned enough to discourage either the fertility cults with their magic and debauchery, or the ruthless legal tactics of his upper-class supporters. Greatness scored higher with Jotham than ethics. So as strong as the nation was, it was like a kingdom built on a net and suspended over a crevasse. With business booming, nobody wanted to notice that the net's moral fiber was being slowly chewed away by the moths of pleasure and self-interest.

Joel

Nobody, of course, but the prophets. The book of Joel has no date—it could have been written any time in Judah's history because it addresses the situation Judah's prophets were up against for centuries. The gist of Joel's message is that Yahweh was going to send a plague of locusts to prod complacent Judah into repentance. It was the same basic message Jonah took to Nineveh: turn or pay.

Locusts don't seem too threatening to modern city dwellers, but farmers of Joel's day had reason to dread a scourge that could strip a tree in minutes, a field of grain in hours. Yahweh's people were fond of talking about "the day of Yahweh" when He would destroy their enemies, but like Amos, Joel warned that the day would strike at home first. This locust plague was a small-*d* day of Yahweh, and it would be bad enough that the nation had better do some serious soul-searching.

But the locusts were only a foretaste. In one of those prophetic time shifts, Joel saw through the immediate situation to the big-*d* Day of Yahweh at the end of the age, when He would pour out His Spirit on anyone who was open to it, offer salvation from disaster to the nations, and judge both them and His people according to the integrity of their hearts.

Yahweh showed Joel awesome special effects, including, "blood and fire and billows of smoke. The sun will be turned to darkness and the moon to blood" (2:30-31). But "everyone who calls on the name of [Yahweh] will be saved" (2:32).

Isaiah's Commission

Did Judah pay attention, as Nineveh had? Maybe—they were not destroyed when the Assyrians flattened Samaria. But the change didn't stick. In 740 BC, the year Uzziah finally died, Yahweh appeared in a vision to a young courtier named Isaiah. He was not much older than eighteen, but wellborn, well educated, and well connected. He was on his way to the top until Yahweh burst in. Here is Isaiah's account:

> I saw the Lord seated on a throne, high and exalted, and the train of his robe filled the temple. Above him were seraphs, each with six wings: With two wings they covered their faces, with two they covered their feet, and with two they were flying. And they were calling to one another:
>
> "Holy, holy, holy is [Yahweh] Almighty;
> the whole earth is full of his glory."
>
> At the sound of their voices the doorposts and thresholds shook and the temple was filled with smoke.
> "Woe to me!" I cried. "I am ruined!" (Isaiah 6:1-5)

Isaiah knew himself to be a man with a dirty mouth—full of malice and deceit like his countrymen. But one of the seraphs seared his mouth with an altar coal, and in that instant of agony Isaiah was prepared for a mission. "Whom shall I send?" asked a voice. Isaiah answered, "Send me!"

His mission was to tell his people what they didn't want to hear until—just like Pharaoh—they thoroughly calloused their hearts against the God to whom they didn't want to listen. Isaiah's task was to expose their willful blindness and deafness by doing everything he could to sway them, and failing. His job was to fail.

Fun. And what he would have to hang onto for the next six decades was that memory of the thrice-holy Lord, the thundering voices of the angels, and the scalding coal against his lips. That, and an ongoing jumble of hints about events from tomorrow to eternity. Isaiah came away from this experience with a favorite title for his God, not a very popular one among his lighthearted kinsmen: the Holy One of Israel.

The Bubble Bursts

While Jotham was toiling to prolong the prosperity, a rejuvenated Assyrian army under King Tiglath-Pileser was beginning to swallow up kingdoms north of Israel. (See map, page 360.) It didn't take a prophet to see what was coming. But no matter how Isaiah tried to get through to him—lyrical parables with heavy punch lines (Isaiah 5:1-7), mournful laments (1:4-9, 5:8-30), or sharp rebukes (3:13-26)—Jotham and his administration were not interested. Isaiah carefully recorded his reproofs of haughty women, ruthless moguls, and "champions at mixing drinks," even though nobody cared.

But their bubble was bursting. In 735 BC Jotham made his son Ahaz co-regent, possibly because Jotham was ill. Israel and Syria had allied against the Assyrian peril, and they threatened that unless Judah joined them, they would invade and put their own man on Judah's throne. Jotham refused to play ball, but he was also too smart to ally with Assyria. For three years Judah's well-financed army kept Israel-Syria at bay, while Jerusalem's complacence oozed away.

Ahaz

Then Jotham died in 732, leaving Ahaz in control. Weak, amoral, and vain, he was not the man for a crisis. Yahweh bored him; he preferred the pleasures of Baal. And he was terrified that Syrian siege engines might roll up to his window any day. Cornered and thinking himself so clever, he decided to put an end to this anxiety by hiring Tiglath-Pileser to get his neighbors off his back. He would become an Assyrian vassal, of course, but so what? It was inevitable anyway. Better to spend some cash than be overrun.

By now, Isaiah was well known as a prophet in the capital. No doubt Ahaz would have gotten rid of him if he had not been an aristocrat and backed by Yahweh. But he was swimming upstream in this administration.

Yahweh told Isaiah to tell Ahaz his scheme was madness. Don't worry about Israel and Syria, He said—they were small potatoes. The real menace was Assyria. "Be careful, keep calm, and don't be afraid. . . . If you do not stand firm in your faith, you will not stand at all" (Isaiah 7:4,9). You're on thin ice, and your only hope is a real God.

Ahaz was not impressed. So, Isaiah said, you don't believe Yahweh can handle it? Okay, ask for a miraculous sign—anything. Ahaz wouldn't do it; if it came true, he'd be obliged to believe in this inconvenient God and His unmanageable prophet. So Isaiah gave him a sign anyway: a certain virgin would have a son and would name him Immanuel, "God Is With Us." Before this child reached his teens Assyria would wipe out Syria and Israel, and when the boy reached teenage he would have nothing but curds and honey to eat because war would have ravaged Judah and made agriculture impossible.

The virgin may have been a new wife whom Isaiah or another courtier was about to marry. If so, and if Immanuel was born about a year later, Isaiah's prophecy came true right on schedule: thirteen years later Syria and Israel no longer existed and Judah's agriculture was in shambles. (Did even

Isaiah know that his sign would have a fulfillment seven centuries later that would dwarf this one by comparison?)

Ahaz went ahead with his plan. He sent Tiglath-Pileser a fortune in treasures, and Assyria obliged him by sacking and deporting Syria and most of Israel. Then Ahaz traveled to Damascus to meet his Assyrian lord. He was genuinely impressed by what he saw, and even sent his priest sketches of the Assyrian royal altar to copy and install in Jerusalem.

This was the beginning of full-dress paganism in Judah. Ahaz ordered Yahweh's temple closed; hereafter, official state sacrifices would be offered on the new altar. The old bronze altar of Yahweh he would keep, however, for divination (as though Yahweh would have anything to do with him). Other altars began to proliferate around town, and soon Ahaz was sponsoring child sacrifice, sexual rites, and spirit channeling.

Isaiah was shaken. He could see what Israel was reaping for her crimes; refugees were pouring into Judah every day with new tales of atrocities. And Judah was plunging headlong into the same insanity. The palace buzzed with intrigue (a coup? a treaty with Egypt?). The people were drowning their panic in alcohol, sex, and politics. But Yahweh told Isaiah:

> "Do not call conspiracy
>   everything that these people call conspiracy;
> do not fear what they fear,
>   and do not dread it.
> [Yahweh] Almighty is the one you are to regard as holy,
>   he is the one you are to fear,
>   he is the one you are to dread,
> and he will be a sanctuary;
>   but for both houses of Israel he will be
> a stone that causes men to stumble
>   and a rock that makes them fall." (Isaiah 8:12-14)

Yahweh gave Isaiah an awful glimpse of the dark times ahead. But He also let him see a light that would pierce the shadows from Galilee in the northern kingdom.

For to us a child is born,
    to us a son is given,
    and the government will be on his shoulders.
And he will be called
    Wonderful Counselor, Mighty God,
    Everlasting Father, Prince of Peace.
Of the increase of his government and peace
    there will be no end. (Isaiah 9:6-7)

Snapshots barraged Isaiah: Israel's destruction, Assyria's ultimate defeat, the emergence of a faithful remnant from the nation's ashes, and that larger-than-life future King:

A shoot will come up from the stump of Jesse;
    from his roots a Branch will bear fruit.
The Spirit of [Yahweh] will rest on him—
    the Spirit of wisdom and of understanding,
    the Spirit of counsel and of power,
    the Spirit of knowledge and of the fear
        of [Yahweh]—
and he will delight in the fear of [Yahweh]. (Isaiah 11:1-3)

Offspring of Eve, Lion of Judah, Son of David—Isaiah doubtless knew the prophecies. But Mighty God? Everlasting Father? Isaiah faithfully recorded the promises and spent his time rearing his family and a circle of followers who would stay faithful to Yahweh even in the dark.

Micah
One of Isaiah's allies in these grim days was a small-town prophet named Micah. His little book tells the same tale as Isaiah's early messages (there are even some word-for-word overlaps), except from the viewpoint not of a courtier steeped in political intrigue, but of a villager who daily watched wealthy landholders extort the family farms out from under their owners. As Hosea had shared Yahweh's grief at Israel's

adultery, Micah wept with Yahweh that the same poison was infecting Judah. Prophets-for-hire harassed Micah for predicting disaster, but he could only say what he saw. He may have been a country bumpkin, but Yahweh showed him not only the fall of Samaria before it occurred, but also Babylon taking Judah into exile, Yahweh freeing a remnant, and the reign of the Davidic king in the last days. Micah added another piece to the puzzle about this King: he would be born in David's hometown of Bethlehem.

C·H·A·P·T·E·R

16

Judah Seals Her Fate

◆

2 Kings 18:1–21:18, 2 Chronicles 29:1–33:20, Isaiah 13–66

Hezekiah's Good Times

Who knows how, but Isaiah was appointed chaplain for crown prince Hezekiah. He weathered the Ahaz administration for eight years, then another twelve in which father and son reigned together. His one goal as a statesman was to groom Hezekiah to be a real Davidic king.

Faithful waiting paid off. In 715 BC when Ahaz died, Isaiah found himself in midlife as a trusted royal counselor at last. Hezekiah was utterly devoted to Yahweh; his first act as king was to reopen the temple, which his father had closed. It took the Levites weeks to clean out the years of accumulated grime, dispose of the occult objects Ahaz had collected, and get things running again. Then Hezekiah held a lavish rededication ceremony modeled on Solomon's, and after that a two-week Passover festival. He even invited Israelites who had managed to survive the Assyrian deportations six years previous. It was a glorious expression of the chosen people reunited in obedience to Yahweh.

Hezekiah looked and acted like Solomon reborn—the young Solomon in his temple-building days. Everyone hoped that this renewed devotion would lead to another golden age. They resented it when Isaiah continued to point out that the renovation was only skin deep: overt occultism might be dwindling, but materialism, greed, treachery—all the old vices—were still going strong.

So Isaiah's life was still far from easy. The other counselors disdained him for exposing their hypocrisy; they were pro-Yahweh for political expedience only. And Hezekiah, although honestly devout, was also a rash and idealistic patriot. It galled him that Judah was still vassal to pagan Assyria; each time he paid his annual tribute he was reminded of his father's mistakes.

Some of his advisors proposed that Judah ally with Egypt to throw off the Assyrian yoke. Isaiah unleashed his complete verbal arsenal against this counsel, which amounted to relying on what people could manipulate—intrigue and military hardware—rather than on Yahweh. He cried,

> Woe to those who go to great depths
>   to hide their plans from [Yahweh],
> who do their work in darkness and think,
>   "Who sees us? Who will know?" (Isaiah 29:15)

> "In repentance and rest is your salvation,
>   in quietness and trust is your strength,
>   but you would have none of it.
> You said, 'No, we will flee on horses.'
>   Therefore you will flee!
> You said, 'We will ride off on swift horses.'
>   Therefore your pursuers will be swift! . . ."
> Yet [Yahweh] longs to be gracious to you;
>   he rises to show you compassion. (30:15-16,18)

Again and again Isaiah faced off against Hezekiah's ministers, countering their ridicule with steel-eyed messages.

But his efforts came to nothing. When a new Assyrian king was engaged in securing his position in 705 BC, Egypt, Judah, and several other vassals seized the chance to revolt. The first year all was quiet when Jerusalem sent no tribute; King Sennacherib was busy stabilizing his throne in his new capital, Nineveh. The second year was fine.

In 703 Hezekiah fell seriously ill and survived only because Yahweh answered his desperate prayers. Then envoys arrived from Babylon (see map, page 360), another Assyrian vassal, ostensibly to congratulate Hezekiah on his recovery but actually to urge him to join a military campaign against their overlord. Strongly tempted to agree, Hezekiah entertained the diplomats regally. He even gave them a tour of his entire royal treasury to show that he was as much to be reckoned with as his ancestor Solomon. Isaiah was aghast when he heard about the incident. In a flash he saw it all: troops marching, overrunning Jerusalem, sacking the palace, carrying everything back to Babylon. It would not happen yet, but sometime after Hezekiah's death.

Hezekiah was used to these premonitions from his old teacher. He was still basking in his restored health and the admiring murmurs of the Babylonian entourage. "The word of Yahweh you have spoken is good," he told Isaiah. But he was thinking something else: "There will be peace and security in my lifetime."

Rude Awakening

Selfish fool! For all his patriotism and loyalty to Yahweh, Hezekiah's real goal was a successful, pain-free life. He wanted to make the history books as a great king without having to endure hard times. So far, faithfulness to Yahweh had paid off handsomely, but his faith was about to receive its first real test.

By 701 BC, Sennacherib had gotten things together at home and was ready to deal with rebels. His army swept through Syria and Samaria to Judah and began to gobble up city after city. Soon he reached Lachish, thirty miles southwest of Jerusalem and the last stop before the capital itself. Panicking, Hezekiah sent a message of capitulation and an offer to pay as much tribute as Sennacherib asked. The king's price was eleven tons of silver and a ton of gold; Hezekiah had the gold plating stripped from the temple doors to fulfill it.

But Sennacherib had no intention of going home without beating the nationalism out of Hezekiah. He continued his siege of Lachish and dispatched officials to demand complete surrender. They urged the guards on Jerusalem's walls to turn against Hezekiah, detailing the pathetic state of Judah's army, the failure of every other nation's gods to resist Assyria, and the horrors of famine that would come with a long siege. They even pointed out that Yahweh's own prophets (such as Isaiah) had predicted this Assyrian invasion.

The Jerusalemites steeled themselves against this psychological warfare, and Hezekiah sent a message to Isaiah: ask Yahweh to hear how the Assyrians have mocked Him and to rebuke them.

Sennacherib had made this a test case of his power versus Yahweh's. Yahweh accepted the challenge. While Hezekiah kept praying desperately each time Sennacherib sent another threatening message, Yahweh told Isaiah what He thought of the Assyrian king. One night Yahweh sent an angel with bubonic plague to decimate the Assyrian army, and followed that with some news from Nineveh that obliged Sennacherib to call off his siege and hurry home. As Yahweh had promised, he never returned; twenty years later his sons assassinated him in his temple.

Yahweh and the Nations

The dispute between Sennacherib and Yahweh hinged on whether Yahweh had the power—which the other gods lacked—to defeat this human king. Yahweh accepted this duel in order to demonstrate (for anyone paying attention) that He was not just another national deity but the Ruler of the

Nations, and not just in the abstract but in the details of each nation and life.

Yahweh made a strong point of this fact to Isaiah, a statesman embroiled in international politics. He gave Isaiah prophecies of judgment on every one of the nations around Judah at one time or another; they are collected in chapters 13 through 23 of Isaiah's book. Then chapter 24 culminates in a vision of the whole earth laid waste—ecological holocaust because humans, the earth's stewards, have defiled it in their self-absorption.

But always Yahweh comforted Isaiah with glimpses beyond desolation: a banquet Yahweh would spread for His own among all peoples when He would wipe away every tear and swallow up death forever.

Manasseh
Judgment and joy seesaw in Isaiah 24–35; the prophet must have grown dizzy in those late days of Hezekiah between the tense statecraft and wild insights from Yahweh. Only a pitiful remnant of Judah survived the onslaught of 701 BC, and the king, in his late fifties by now, was not the confident patriot he once was. After five years he appointed his twelve-year-old son, Manasseh, as co-regent and began planning to pass the crown. He lived another decade, but we hear nothing of more reforms.

Manasseh became sole king upon his father's death in 687. He reigned fifty-five years, longer than any other king of Israel or Judah. He was Yahweh's curse on a persistently rebellious people: they had played church for twenty-eight years under Hezekiah without pausing in their unethical business practices. So Yahweh gave them the kind of king they deserved. Manasseh reinstituted the ways of Ahaz, and then some; he put pagan altars and a fertility pole in Yahweh's temple, sacrificed his own infant son, consulted mediums, and practiced sorcery. Those who opposed him he executed.

Among the executed were probably some of the prophets

who announced that Yahweh was going to wipe out Judah as He had Israel because Manasseh was worse than the Canaanites had been. It was the rampant bloodshed, more than anything else, that Yahweh refused to forgive.

Isaiah's Last Assignment

Isaiah was getting on toward seventy years old, fifty of which he had spent toe to toe with three kings and their charlatan counselors. Now, as Manasseh showed his colors, Yahweh pulled his chief prophet back from the front lines to record some tidings for future generations.

His first glimpse had come that day when Hezekiah crowed about the Babylonian envoys. All the destruction that was still a century away had flooded in on him. But it was not primarily his job to foretell those days. Instead, he scribbled oracle after oracle—twenty-six chapters' worth—about the times after the destruction. Chapter 40 opens with "Comfort, comfort" for a Jerusalem demolished for her crimes and for the people carried off from her to Babylon. Isaiah saw a highway built through the desert on which Yahweh would come to lead His people back to their land.

Why did Yahweh announce this return 160 years before it happened? Yahweh was trying another tactic in His appeal to the nations, including the returning remnant. His displays of power had not convinced them to abandon worthless idols; perhaps His foreknowledge would. Repeatedly Isaiah saw a law court in which Yahweh sat now as judge and prosecutor, now as defendant. He summoned the nations to face Him with their charges that He was weak or unworthy of worship. In His own defense, Yahweh points to a warrior from the east named Cyrus, whom Yahweh would raise up to deliver His people even though he knew nothing of the Holy One. Who but the King of the Earth could predict what He would do 160 years before it occurred, a century before it even appeared necessary? Who else could foretell the fall of an empire before it had risen, and name both the empire and its conqueror?

Isaiah's perceptions were so accurate that modern scholars maintain they must have been written after the fact. But the style of these chapters is too masterful an imitation of the earlier ones, and the whole point of this section is that Yahweh knows ahead of time what He is going to do.

The Servant

Besides His preannounced deeds, Yahweh called one other witness into court: Israel. He viewed them not as Israel and Judah, two political entities, but as Israel, His people. "My servant," He called them, a term He had previously used only of men like Moses, Joshua, and David, for in the Near East a king's "servant" was a trusted royal envoy. And to drive home the intimacy, He added, "whom I have chosen, you descendants of Abraham My friend." And He repeated the covenant commitment: "I am with you." I am Immanuel. I am Yahweh.

"You are my witnesses," He told His people as the nations gathered to hear their testimony, to the fact that "I am he. Before me no god was formed, nor will there be another after me. I, even I, am [Yahweh], and apart from me there is no savior. I have revealed and saved and proclaimed I, and not some foreign god among you. You are my witnesses . . . that I am God."

The scene shifts. The witnesses are in court to give account for their failure to keep the covenant and be real witnesses to the nations. Yahweh's servants have failed in their mission.

Now there is another Servant: Israel-but-not-Israel, with a strange mix of qualities: a ruler filled with Yahweh's Spirit like the judges of old, but gentle to the weak and bringing justice not only to Israel, but to the nations. Yahweh tells this Servant,

"It is too small a thing for you to be my servant
    to restore the tribes of Jacob
    and bring back those of Israel I have kept.
I will also make you a light for the Gentiles,
    that you may bring my salvation to the ends of the
    earth." (Isaiah 49:6)

Yet the Servant is not quite the liberator one might have expected after David. He is one who "know[s] the word that sustains the weary" (50:4), who endures abuse and continues to serve:

> I offered my back to those who beat me,
>   my cheeks to those who pulled out my beard;
> I did not hide my face
>   from mocking and spitting.
> Because the Sovereign [Yahweh] helps me,
>   I will not be disgraced. (50:6-7)

Servanthood is less and less attractive, even for those who follow the Servant. It is a confusing picture, made worse in the final song (52:13–53:12). On the one hand,

> See, my servant will act wisely;
>   he will be raised and lifted up and highly exalted.
>   (52:13)

But on the other hand, consider this:

> His appearance was so disfigured beyond that
>   of any man
>   and his form marred beyond human likeness. . . .
> He was despised and rejected by men,
>   a man of sorrows, and familiar with suffering. . . .
> Surely he took up our infirmities
>   and carried our sorrows,
> yet we considered him stricken by God,
>   smitten by him, and afflicted.
> But he was pierced for our transgressions,
>   he was crushed for our iniquities;
> the punishment that brought us peace was upon him,
>   and by his wounds we are healed. . . .
> [Yahweh] has laid on him the iniquity of us all.
>   (52:14, 53:3-6)

How could it be that "he was cut off from the land of the living" and "assigned a grave with the wicked, and with the rich in his death," yet "he will see his offspring and prolong his days, and the will of Yahweh will prosper in his hand"? Somehow, this Servant would be the ultimate guilt offering, the perfection of all the bulls and rams offered in the temple, bearing in His own body the crimes of humanity. Yet, "After the suffering of his soul, he will see the light of life and be satisfied."

One wonders what Isaiah made of these prophecies. Did he think the Servant was a renewed Israel, suffering for the crimes of the nations? Did he envision some great prophet like Moses? Did he connect the Servant Songs to his visions of the Davidic king decades earlier? How could he reconcile the affliction and triumph, the death and the life after death?

The Kingdom

The third thing Yahweh talked to Isaiah about at length was the restoration of His Kingdom. Alongside the highway, Isaiah kept seeing the desert blossom as Yahweh irrigated it with springs and pools for His thirsty ones. Once Yahweh explained that this water represented His Spirit that would restore life to a dead people and knit them to Him in faithfulness.

Another image Yahweh used was the barren woman (Zion) whom He had rejected for her adultery but whom He would take back to Himself and bless with many children. Isaiah saw Zion's sons and daughters streaming home from exile, followed by the mighty of the nations bearing lavish gifts. Peace and abundance would reign among a righteous people devoted to their deliverer. They would not even need the sun anymore because Yahweh would be the source of light in their midst.

Yahweh painted the restoration in glowing colors: a new sky and a new earth in which a century would be a short life-span, farmers would cultivate their lands in safety, wolves and lambs would live at peace together, and above all, the intimacy of Eden would return.

The Invitation

Yahweh did not show all of this to Isaiah to sate his curiosity. He was laying up a storehouse of promises for the remnant who would return to Judah after exile in Babylon. Theirs would be hard times, and they would be tempted to slip back into the callousness that was getting Judah into trouble now. So, interwoven among the threads of glory were invitation and warning. Isaiah quotes Yahweh:

> "Come, all you who are thirsty,
>   come to the waters;
> and you who have no money,
>   come, buy and eat! . . .
> Why spend money on what is not bread,
>   and your labor on what does not satisfy?
> Listen, listen to me, and eat what is good,
>   and your soul will delight in the richest of fare."
>   (55:1-2)

> "Surely you will summon nations you know not,
>   and nations that do not know you will hasten
>   to you,
>   because of [Yahweh] your God." (55:5)

For just as the Servant's job is to be a light to the nations, so those who return to Yahweh will also receive that task, which was always Israel's purpose. "For my house will be called a house of prayer for all nations" (56:7).

Yahweh knew already what the returnees would fall into; He described it at length to Isaiah: bloodshed, deceit, plots, avarice, corrupt courts—the same old song. He would raise up prophets like watchmen on the walls of Jerusalem to intercede for the city as Moses had done, but many of them would be lazy. So Isaiah's messages swing from hope to judgment and back again. But even though his last word details the agony of those who spurn Yahweh in the last days, the closing chapters as a whole ring with joy because vindication does not all depend on human faithfulness:

> He saw that there was no one,
>   he was appalled that there was no one to intervene;
> so his own arm worked salvation for him,
>   and his own righteousness sustained him. . . .
> The Redeemer will come to Zion. (59:16,20)

Whoever the Servant is, and whatever his followers do, one thing is certain. The Redeemer—the Kinsman who buys His people out of slavery (Yahweh Himself)—will come to Zion.

17

Strolling Toward Disaster

◆

*2 Kings 21:19–23:27; 2 Chronicles 33:21–36:8;
Jeremiah 7–20, 26; Nahum; Habakkuk; Zephaniah*

Amon

Yahweh managed to catch Manasseh's attention toward the end of his life. Manasseh apparently got involved in a Babylonian rebellion against Assyria and was dragged off temporarily to Babylon. His time in prison led to some change of heart regarding Yahweh, and he prayed to the God of Israel for deliverance. After he was pardoned and sent home, he tried to take Yahweh more seriously and reduced his own pagan practices, but he did virtually nothing to reform his people.

He died at the ripe age of sixty-seven, and his twenty-one-year-old son, Amon, took over. Amon, who had not had the pleasure of walking to Babylon with a hook in his nose, had not seen the light about Yahweh. He was such a vile king that after two years his officials assassinated him and tried to take over, but the coup was put down and Amon's son, Josiah, was crowned.

Zephaniah

About the time eight-year-old Josiah became king, one of his older cousins began receiving some public prophecies. Zephaniah was a great-great-grandson of Hezekiah and familiar with the court and current politics. Observing the wreckage left by Manasseh and Amon, he blasted Jerusalem with several brief oracles. His visions focused now on the atrocities committed by the leaders of his nation, now on the destruction they would reap, now on the Day of Yahweh at the end of the age. His poetry is stark:

> "Their blood will be poured out like dust
> and their entrails like filth.
> Neither their silver nor their gold
> will be able to save them
> on the day of [Yahweh's] wrath."
> (Zephaniah 1:17-18)

Zephaniah saw the fate of Judah's enemies—even Assyria—as well as that of Judah herself, since Yahweh played no favorites. He heard Yahweh's astonishment that even the city where He had put His Name did not respond to His correction. Yet like most of his prophetic brothers, he closed with a song of triumph about the day when Yahweh would forgive and restore.

Josiah

Temporary relief was in sight, for like Joash two centuries earlier, Josiah had the benefit of virtuous tutors. At the age of sixteen he committed himself to seek Yahweh, and at twenty he launched a campaign to morally disinfect Judah and Israel. First he had his father's and grandfather's paraphernalia, such as phallic symbols and astrological gear, thrown on the garbage heap. He tore down the altars of child sacrifice and expelled the homosexual prostitutes from Yahweh's temple. Then he traveled across his land and even to Samaria and

Bethel desecrating shrines and slaughtering pagan priests. (He rebuked priests of Yahweh who were officiating outside Jerusalem, but he didn't kill them.) At last he went home (to the relief of large sections of his people) and set to work repairing the temple, which had had no upkeep for a century.

Jeremiah

Twenty-year-old Josiah launched his religious purge in 627 BC. The following year when it was well underway, Yahweh called a young priest (or priest-in-training) only slightly older than Josiah to be a prophet with an international portfolio. Jeremiah gave the stock response to a calling (Who, me? I'm no public speaker. I'm nobody!), and Yahweh gave His standard retort: Don't be scared. I am with you.

Jeremiah had the distinction of receiving possibly the very worst assignment of any prophet. Many had to prophesy Judah's destruction; Jeremiah got to do it for forty years, during most of which he endured death threats and imprisonment, and at the end of which he got to savor every bitter moment of famine and slaughter.

His first seventeen years were tolerable because Josiah was alive and working for the same ends. He made the job of restoring Judah's integrity seem possible, and he protected Jeremiah from active persecution. Jeremiah could stand in Jerusalem's marketplace and express Yahweh's grief over His wanton bride, His sorrow that His people preferred to dig their own wells to slake their thirst for security and importance rather than drink from Yahweh's fountain. Yahweh's envoy was free to accuse Judah's finest of murder and graft. Those were the years when Yahweh begged shamelessly, "return, return." But few listened.

The Book of the Covenant

One day during the temple renovations, the priest in charge was fetching money to pay the workmen. In a back storeroom he discovered a scroll, which he passed on to Josiah's secretary.

Josiah was appalled when he heard the scroll read, for it turned out to be some or all of Moses' writings—the Book of the Covenant with its commands, blessings for obedience, and curses for treachery. It was obvious to Josiah that Samaria lay in ruins and his own nation was barely hanging on against crop failures and the ever-present threat of Assyria all because they had thumbed their noses at their King.

The book of Moses made it quite clear that crimes on the level of Manasseh's and Amon's would lead to destruction. (It's a hint of how low things had fallen that Moses' writings were utterly unknown in Josiah's day.) Josiah dispatched four of his officials to a prophetess to inquire what Yahweh was going to do about these crimes and curses.

She reported that, yes, Yahweh was indeed going to obliterate Judah for its villainy, but because Josiah had humbled himself before Yahweh, He would take the king's life before the destruction took place so that he would not have to suffer through it.

Wonderful news. Josiah called a mass meeting of the elders of Judah and the entire population of Jerusalem to renew the covenant. He had the book of Moses read and made the people pledge to obey it. Then he threw the greatest Passover celebration in history: 41,400 animals were cooked or burnt.

No doubt Yahweh appreciated Josiah's attempt, but He knew His fickle people were simply following their leader to avoid his wrath and would revert to their old ways as soon as they had a more compliant king. So Yahweh continued to move nations into position like chess pieces for His checkmate of Judah. For Jeremiah, the visions and sounds of an army swarming toward Jerusalem were like nightmares. He obediently reported what he saw; but he also wept:

> Oh, my anguish, my anguish!
> I writhe in pain.
> Oh, the agony of my heart!

My heart pounds within me,
I cannot keep silent. (Jeremiah 4:19)

Yahweh told him He would save Jerusalem if Jeremiah could find one honest man in the city. But as hard as he looked, he failed. Yet daily, it seemed, other prophets were coming out with grandiose pronouncements of Yahweh's favor and protection, and the priests spoke pious platitudes.

Nahum and the Rise of Babylon

Nahum was one of the few true prophets of this period who had something popular to say. He had the job Jonah wanted: he received a technicolor preview of Nineveh's fall. The city had abandoned its earlier repentance and reached new heights of brutality in the 640s and 630s. Nahum's staccato style throbs as Nineveh, soaked in blood and sorcery in its lust for gold and power, is crushed, then blown away like locusts in the wind.

Josiah's magnificent Passover was in 622 BC. In 612 Nineveh fell to an alliance of Media and Babylonia. (See map, page 360.) The surviving Assyrian forces regrouped, but after three years of fighting they were pushed west across the Euphrates. The Egyptians (who wanted to be rid of Assyria for good) allied with Babylonia and began to march north to squeeze the Assyrians from the other side. Josiah feared Egypt would swallow Judah up if Assyria were defeated, so he led his army out to cut Egypt off. But as He had promised, Yahweh let the thirty-nine-year-old monarch die in battle. Egypt and Babylonia, under the brilliant general, Prince Nebuchadnezzar, cut down the remains of the Assyrian army. The neo-Babylonian Empire was dawning.

Josiah's First Two Sons

When a bleeding Josiah arrived in Jerusalem and later expired, the whole nation mourned bitterly. Jeremiah composed laments for the lost king that were national treasures for centuries. But times were tense; Jehoahaz, Josiah's second-oldest son, was quickly chosen as his successor.

However, the Egyptian pharaoh paused on his way home from smashing Assyria to arrest Jehoahaz, imprison him in his military headquarters in Syria, appoint his elder brother king, impose a stiff vassal tribute upon Judah, and carry Jehoahaz back to Egypt to die.

Jehoiakim, Josiah's eldest, reigned eleven cruel years. Dishonesty, oppression, ambition, and injustice were the order of the day, along with renewed idolatry and debauchery. For the first four years Jehoiakim was a vassal of Egypt.

Habakkuk
The prophet Habakkuk was disgusted with the way Judah behaved during the late years of Josiah and the early ones of Jehoiakim. It looked to him as though Yahweh was going to let the rich nobility squeeze the life out of the poor forever. Habakkuk finally got fed up with praying for justice and complained to Yahweh: "Why do You tolerate wrong?"

Yahweh coolly responded that He was about to punish Judah's wickedness by overrunning the land with an even more ruthless people: the Babylonians.

That's worse! Habakkuk protested. You're the Rock, the Holy One. "Your eyes are too pure to look on evil, You cannot tolerate wrong." How can You let such vicious people who worship themselves be Your instruments of justice? How can You let the wicked triumph?

This question was burning in the minds of more than one prophet who had heard the predictions about Babylonia. So Habakkuk stationed himself like a watchman to hear what Yahweh wanted him to tell the rest about this complaint.

Yahweh was not the least offended that His servants were challenging His methods. He told Habakkuk to take a memo and save it for later generations who would also wonder about His justice. Yahweh's reply was to detail both the Babylonians' offenses and the judgment He would impose. Habakkuk would have to be patient, but in due time the wicked would get theirs.

Like Job, Habakkuk stood in awe when Yahweh actually showed up to answer his complaint. He composed a song exalting Yahweh's power as a deliverer. He concluded, looking around at the way aristocrats were raping the land and looking forward to even worse devastation when the Babylonians arrived:

I heard and my heart pounded,
    my lips quivered at the sound;
decay crept into my bones,
    and my legs trembled.
Yet I will wait patiently for the day of calamity
    to come on the nation invading us.
Though the fig tree does not bud
    and there are no grapes on the vines,
though the olive crop fails
    and the fields produce no food,
though there are no sheep in the pen
    and no cattle in the stalls,
yet I will rejoice in [Yahweh],
    I will be joyful in God my Savior.
        (Habakkuk 3:16-18)

Jeremiah's Complaints

We don't know whether Jeremiah got to hear this interchange between Habakkuk and Yahweh, but we do know that he was asking rather the same questions early in Jehoiakim's reign.

Here's why: Yahweh told him to stand in the doorway of the temple and rebuke the worshipers for coming there after making shady business deals all week. He added that both temple and city would be ravaged because of this behavior. The priests and others whose livelihoods depended upon the temple demanded that Jeremiah be executed. The crowd agreed vehemently at first, until some elders argued that Hezekiah hadn't executed Micah for saying essentially the same things. Jeremiah was released—a close call since Jehoiakim had another prophet hunted down and executed at about this time. And shortly thereafter, Jeremiah heard of a plot among his fellow priests—his relatives—to murder him.

Jeremiah was devastated. Yahweh had ordered him not to pray for this worthless nation, but Jeremiah just couldn't bring himself to stop. He wept and wrote heartrending laments about the sufferings he saw coming to Judah. He couldn't understand why he was being treated like a traitor. So he said, You know, Yahweh, I'd like to have a word with You about Your justice: "Why does the way of the wicked prosper? Why do all the faithless live at ease?" (Jeremiah 12:1). And Yahweh's incredible response was, You think it's bad for you now? Just wait! Later, when Jeremiah complained again, Yahweh promised that the day would come when Jeremiah's enemies would come crawling to him for counsel. But He also added that Jeremiah had better give up the pity parties. The only real comfort Yahweh had to offer was the honor of a noble mission and His old promise: *I am with you.*

Incredibly, as Jeremiah continued to pour out his pain, he also continued to draw enough strength from Yahweh's presence to see his galling job to the end. He both yelled and trusted when a priest had him beaten and restrained overnight in the temple.

His offense that time was gathering a crowd at the Potsherd Gate, smashing a clay pot, and declaring that Yahweh would smash the nation just like that. Yahweh was continually giving him these bits of theater, like the time when he had to bury a linen belt until it rotted to symbolize how pure-white Judah, which had been the belt around Yahweh's waist, would be ruined.

18

Babylon's Triumph

◆

2 Kings 24:1–25:30; 2 Chronicles 36:9–23;
Jeremiah 21–25, 27–52; Lamentations; Obadiah

Babylon's First Attack

Jehoiakim was a smug vassal of Egypt from 609 until 605 BC. In that year, Jeremiah announced that for twenty-three years he had been warning Judah, and now the warning period was over. Judah was about to begin seventy years of captivity in Babylon.

At about the same time, Jeremiah got a series of words predicting the same judgment on Judah's neighbors: Egypt, Philistia, Edom, Moab, Ammon. And he got a long, spectacular preview of Babylon's end after the seventy years were up. None of this comforted him much.

That year, 605 BC, Prince Nebuchadnezzar defeated Egypt soundly (at the same place where the two nations had fought as allies against Assyria four years earlier). Just as he was sweeping south to absorb Samaria and Judah (see map, page 360), news arrived that his father had died and he was now king of the Babylonian Empire. To assert himself as the new overlord, Nebuchadnezzar confiscated some of the holy objects from the temple and some of the young men from royal and noble families. The latter would be trained to serve in the growing Babylonian bureaucracy that administered the empire. (Among these noble captives were Daniel and three of his friends, about whom we'll hear more later.)

It was possible that this shock might soften the people's hearts, so Yahweh made another appeal; He told Jeremiah to record all of the messages he'd been given about both Judah and the nations, then read them aloud in public. So Jeremiah dictated, and his secretary, Baruch, recorded everything. Then, because Jeremiah was under house arrest, they agreed that Baruch would take the scroll to the temple to read it on an opportune day when the people would be gathered there.

Their opportunity didn't come until the following winter (December 604 BC). One December day found Baruch at a temple gate reading Jeremiah's scroll. The son of Jehoiakim's secretary of state heard him and ran to tell his dad what was going on. Jehoiakim's cabinet ministers were aghast when they heard Baruch's oration, and told him, "You and Jeremiah, go and hide. Don't let anyone know where you are." Then they told the king about the scroll. Jehoiakim had it read aloud, and every few minutes he sliced off the section he had heard and threw it in his fireplace. His officials begged him to take Jeremiah's words seriously, but he just sat in grim silence until the scroll had been entirely read and burned, then he sent some of his men to arrest Jeremiah and Baruch.

But the two were successfully hidden. After they had heard Jehoiakim's response, Yahweh told them to rewrite the scroll and add a word for the king: because of his contempt for Yahweh, his lineage would be cut off and his body unburied.

Babylon's Second Attack
So Jehoiakim and his people were unmoved. They played the role of an obedient vassal to Babylonia from 604 to 602. However, in 601 Nebuchadnezzar took on Egypt again but failed to

break her. That encouraged Jehoiakim to rebel, even though Jeremiah warned against it. Babylonian troops and their allies arrived swiftly to quell the Judahite uprising with a series of raids.

When the raids failed to subdue Judah, Nebuchadnezzar himself arrived with his army to besiege Jerusalem. In 598 Jehoiakim died (cause unknown) just before the Babylonians completed their siege. The city fell on March 16, 597. It was looted, and ten thousand people were deported this time. King Jehoiachin, Jehoiakim's son, was among the captives. Nebuchadnezzar put Jehoiakim's uncle (Zedekiah, a third son of Josiah) on the throne as his puppet king.

Jeremiah Versus the False Prophets

Zedekiah was as weak as Jehoiakim was spiteful. Jerusalem overflowed with "prophets" claiming that within two years Babylon would be defeated, the temple articles and captives taken by Nebuchadnezzar would be returned, and Judah would be restored. In 593, Yahweh told Jeremiah to wear an ox yoke around to drive home the point that the yoke of Babylon was there to stay. Eventually one "prophet" splintered the yoke in a public quarrel with Jeremiah, claiming that Yahweh was going to break the yoke of Nebuchadnezzar within two years. Jeremiah accused that man of being a false prophet and announced he would die that year for preaching rebellion against Yahweh. Two months later the man was dead. For the time being, Zedekiah heeded Jeremiah and stayed loyal to Babylon.

That same year (593) he sent envoys to Babylon and even visited there for reasons unknown. Jeremiah sent a letter with the envoys to the Jews in exile, telling them to settle down and pray for the prosperity of their pagan towns, for they would be there seventy years. He warned them to ignore the prophets with the two-more-years prediction, but encouraged them, with words from Yahweh, that seventy years of exile was not forever.

"For I know the plans I have for you . . . plans to prosper you and not to harm you, plans to give you hope and a future. Then you will call upon me and come and pray to me, and I will listen to you. You will seek me and find me when you seek me with all your heart. I will be found by you . . . and will bring you back from captivity." (Jeremiah 29:11-14)

A letter came back from a prophet in Babylonia to the chief priest in Jerusalem, demanding that he imprison Jeremiah for telling the exiles that they would be gone seventy years. (The Babylonian contingent had its share of false prophets.) But Jeremiah was temporarily in favor as long as Zedekiah was inclined to loyalty, so the priest gave the letter to Jeremiah. And a second time Yahweh announced a false prophet's death.

Babylon's Third Attack
It didn't take long, though, for an ambitious new pharaoh to stir up a pro-Egyptian faction in Jerusalem. Zedekiah succumbed to it (despite Jeremiah's reproof) and revolted. So for a third and last time Nebuchadnezzar set out for Jerusalem, determined to swat this pesky city for good. He arrived on January 15, 588.

Zedekiah panicked and sent several of his officials to beg Jeremiah to seek information from Yahweh or ask Him to do what He did back in Hezekiah's time, a century earlier.

But Jeremiah retorted that Yahweh was now doing what he had been predicting for thirty-eight years. He added that anyone who resisted Nebuchadnezzar would die, but anyone who surrendered would survive. Yahweh would protect those who had been taken into exile, but those who stayed with Zedekiah He would reject. And if the king and his men really wanted help from Yahweh, let them show it by reforming the corrupt courts, ceasing to rub out their enemies, paying workmen fair wages, cutting back on their luxurious lifestyle, and giving justice to the many oppressed poor in the city. Jeremiah also denounced Jerusalem's prophets for simply telling her leaders what they wanted to hear. They were the worst of all, putting their own words into the mouth of the living God.

But as the siege wore on and things looked blacker and blacker, Yahweh began to give Jeremiah some hopeful messages. Yahweh was going to discipline but not destroy His people. Eventually He would punish their captors. Once again they would be in covenant relationship to their Bridegroom, their Father, their God. Yahweh spoke as He did to Isaiah in his latter years:

"I have loved you with an everlasting love;
    I have drawn you with loving-kindness.
I will build you up again
    and you will be rebuilt, O Virgin Israel. . . .
The time is coming . . .
    when I will make a new covenant
with the house of Israel
    and with the house of Judah." (Jeremiah 31:3-4,31)

But these messages of hope were for future generations. To Zedekiah's face, Jeremiah's message was that Nebuchadnezzar would burn Jerusalem to the ground, but first Zedekiah had a chance to die and be buried honorably.

A Pause in the Fighting

A moment of respite came when Egypt marched out to aid Judah, and Nebuchadnezzar had to suspend his siege until he could beat off the Egyptians. Zedekiah begged Jeremiah to pray that the Babylonians wouldn't come back, but the seer said it was useless. In hopes of pleasing Yahweh and gaining some willing soldiers, Zedekiah declared that all Hebrew slaves in Jerusalem were free. At first his officials and the other slave-owners agreed to this, but afterward they changed their minds. (After all, Nebuchadnezzar was withdrawing. Maybe they could have their lives and their servants, too.) Jeremiah said this was just more proof that this people had no intention of obeying Yahweh (whose law required that Hebrew slaves be freed after seven years), and repeated his word of destruction.

Then Jeremiah took the opportunity provided by the lull in fighting to try to get to his hometown to settle some family matters. However, the captain of the guard arrested him at the gate, accusing him of trying to desert to the enemy.

Zedekiah's officials imprisoned him as a traitor, despite his protests. Zedekiah secretly released him for a private audience; the king wanted to know what Yahweh had to say, but he feared his officials, who hated Jeremiah. But all Yahweh had to say was, "You will be handed over to the king of Babylon." Zedekiah didn't dare release Jeremiah, but he did grant him a less miserable prison and a reasonable food ration until supplies in Jerusalem ran out.

However, Zedekiah's officials were still fuming that Jeremiah was telling the people they would survive if they surrendered but would die if they resisted. The bureaucrats told the king that this was sheer treason and undermined morale, and finally convinced him to let them throw the prophet into a cistern (they wanted to kill him without overtly having his blood on their hands). The sixty-year-old prophet spent days up to his hips in mud in an abandoned well. But Zedekiah couldn't stick to anything when pressured, so another official persuaded him to have Jeremiah returned to his previous prison.

Promises
Nebuchadnezzar had soon dealt with the Egyptians and was back at Jerusalem's gate, as grim as ever. The defenders were tearing down their luxurious houses in order to hurl the stones at the builders of siege ramps; the grain ran out and people started eating anything they could find. Jeremiah sat in jail, once again receiving words from Yahweh that contradicted everything his senses told him.

For decades Jeremiah had heard messages of doom while

Judah lounged at ease. Now when catastrophe was imminent, Yahweh instructed him to buy his cousin's field back home in order to keep it in the family. Jeremiah did what he was told, but asked what on earth Yahweh was thinking. "Ah, Lord Yahweh," he said, "You can do anything. You know everything that goes on in people's hearts. You've done miracles to keep Your covenant with us through thick and thin. You've been totally right to send these Babylonians to obliterate us. I know You can do anything, but—if You're going to destroy and exile us, why am I buying this field?"

Yahweh responded, "I am [Yahweh], the God of all mankind. Is anything too hard for me?" (32:27). Yes, in justice He was going to smash Judah, but because of His unearthly love He was going to forgive and restore His people, even transform their hearts so that they would be able to be faithful. Jeremiah might never get the use of that field, but his descendants would.

I am Yahweh who made the earth, He said. "Call to me and I will answer you and tell you great and unsearchable things you do not know" (33:3). Great and unsearchable things: how He would heal His people, restore them to peace and security, and raise up an unending heritage of the royal and priestly lines. Above all, "a righteous Branch" would "sprout from David's line." Zedekiah's name meant "Yahweh is my righteousness," but he failed to live up to that name. But the Branch and his city would be called "Yahweh Our Righteousness" in truth (23:5-6, 33:15-16). The goal of all of this was the original plan: Yahweh would have the seed of a people passionate for Him, and "this city will bring me renown, joy, praise, and honor before all nations on earth that hear of all the good things I do for it" (33:9). A faithful Jerusalem would be His bait to draw the nations.

The End

By July of 586 the famine was so bad in Jerusalem that mothers were cooking their babies. Jeremiah urged the king to save himself by surrendering, but Zedekiah was paralyzed with fear of both his officials and those Jews who had already deserted.

On August 14, 586, the attackers finally broke through the wall. Zedekiah tried a desperate escape, but Nebuchadnezzar caught and blinded him, executed his sons, and hauled him off to Babylon. The invaders burned the temple and every prominent building to the ground, took everything of value, smashed the walls, and took captive all but the poorest, who would keep the land productive so that it could be taxed.

Rage and Weeping

Two poems express the breadth of prophetic response to the calamity of 586 BC. Obadiah denounced the Edomites for gloating at Jerusalem's destruction and aiding her enemies. His rebuke stands as a permanent warning to those who watch others suffering Yahweh's discipline: "You should not look down on your brother in the day of his misfortune" (Obadiah 12), for your own discipline may not be far behind.

Jeremiah (or possibly another eyewitness) responded by painstakingly shaping his grief into five poems; in the first four, each verse begins with a successive letter of the Hebrew alphabet. The book of Lamentations begins with a look at Jerusalem weeping like a destitute queen, now a hideous wretch.

> See, O [Yahweh], how distressed I am!
> I am in torment within,
> and in my heart I am disturbed,
> for I have been most rebellious.
> Outside, the sword bereaves;
> inside, there is only death. (Lamentations 1:20)

The prophet wails his grief in tightly crafted verses, but finds the "Yet" of David. Surveying smoking rubble, starving infants, corpses everywhere, he writes:

I remember my affliction and my wandering,
the bitterness and the gall.
I well remember them,
and my soul is downcast within me.
Yet this I call to mind
and therefore I have hope:
Because of [Yahweh's] great love we are not consumed,
for his compassions never fail.
They are new every morning;
great is your faithfulness. (3:19-23)

His closing is a mix of confidence, questioning, and humility, knowing that only Yahweh could bring such a people to real repentance:

Restore us to yourself, O [Yahweh], that we may return;
renew our days as of old. (5:21)

To Egypt

The commander of the Babylonian imperial guard, who was in charge of cleanup operations, had heard of Jeremiah. Both he and Nebuchadnezzar knew the prophet had been counseling submission for years, and they suspected that here was a man of great character, if not even of divine appointment. So when the commander found Jeremiah in prison awaiting deportation, he freed him. He offered the old man hospitality in his own home in Babylon, but Jeremiah, loyal to the end, insisted on staying with the survivors in Jerusalem.

Nebuchadnezzar had appointed as governor a Judan named Gedaliah who, like Jeremiah, had long advocated nonresistance to the Babylonians because their conquest was a judgment from Yahweh. The commander committed Jeremiah to Gedaliah's protection. Gedaliah set up an office in Mizpah, a few miles north of Jerusalem, and urged the farmers to gather the harvest that was just coming ripe—in short, to resume business as usual.

But a surviving relative of Zedekiah assassinated Gedaliah and more than a hundred of his supporters, took captive the rest of Gedaliah's group (including Jeremiah), and tried to flee to Ammon. Another group of Jewish army officers intercepted the assassin and freed the prisoners. Then, terrified of Babylonian reprisal, they begged Jeremiah to ask Yahweh what they should do next.

Yahweh promised to protect them if they stayed in Judah and took care of His land. He also promised that if they fled to Egypt because they didn't trust Him, the death they feared would come upon them there. Sure enough, the officers had no intention of trusting Yahweh and staying in Judah; they had already made up their minds and were only hoping for someone to justify their decision. They had the gall to accuse Baruch of inciting Jeremiah to say the wrong thing. Then they forced Baruch, Jeremiah, and the rest of the remnant to go with them to Egypt.

Poor Jeremiah. It wasn't long before the new arrivals in Egypt met earlier Jewish fugitives and all were practicing a mix of Jewish, Egyptian, and Babylonian religion. In particular, they were making cakes in the shape of Ishtar, the Babylonian Queen of Heaven, and burning incense to her. Hadn't they learned anything from the cataclysm they had just been through, Jeremiah wanted to know. Yes, they said, we've learned that things started falling apart back home when we stopped worshiping Ishtar, and we're not going to make that mistake again. Jeremiah threw up his hands and prophesied the murder of the current pharaoh as a sign of the eventual annihilation of the Jewish community in Egypt.

Postscripts

In 561 BC, some twenty years after Jeremiah's death, a new king of Babylon declared an amnesty for the Judan captives there. He released Jehoiachin from prison and assigned daily rations from the royal household to support Jehoichin and his five sons. The lineage of David was hanging on by a hair.

19

A Prophet in Exile

Ezekiel

The Exile was Yahweh's judgment on His people, but as in the time of Moses, He was able to use such tragedy productively. These few generations did more to transform Judaism (the faith of the people of Judah) than all the centuries since Joshua. A few key people spearheaded the transformation; the prophet Ezekiel was one of them.

Ezekiel's Call

A handful of Jews were taken to Babylon in 605 BC, but thousands went in 597. (See map, page 360.) For the decade until Jerusalem was crushed, these clung to the hope that any day now, Yahweh would work a miracle and bring them home. They huddled in holding patterns and eked out livings in their makeshift settlements along the canals of the Euphrates River. They were also largely unwilling to face any responsibility they may have had for their sufferings.

Among these exiles of 597 was a priest-in-training named Ezekiel. Four years later, on his thirtieth birthday, he was eligible to be anointed as a full-fledged priest. But in Nippur, a Babylonian city a thousand miles from Jerusalem, there was not much for a priest of Yahweh to do. No temple, no sacrifices. About the only work was teaching the writings of Moses.

But Yahweh had another assignment for this priest. That year, 593 BC, was when King Zedekiah sent envoys to Babylon and later went there himself. It was the year Jeremiah wrote to the exiles, advising them to settle in for seventy years and ignore those among them who were prophesying a speedy return. (For that, one of those exiled prophets urged that Jeremiah be executed.) The ice under Jerusalem was daily growing thinner, and the expatriate leaders were incompetent.

In that year, Yahweh blasted His new priest with a vision: a blazing windstorm, in the midst of which were four living creatures, glowing with fire. Each had four faces and four wings, and they stood as the four corners of a square, outstretched wings touching. Resting on their spread wings was a crystalline expanse, upon which stood a sapphire throne. On the throne Ezekiel could make out a manlike figure gleaming like white-hot metal and fire. This was a physical representation of the glory of Yahweh; the Presence that had led Israel through the desert, indwelt the tabernacle, and inhabited Solomon's temple was now appearing to the exiles in Babylon.

Ezekiel had the usual response to such a sight: he hit the dirt. Yahweh breathed His Spirit into the prone form so that Ezekiel could stand up, then began issuing instructions to His new prophet, whom He addressed as "son of man." "Son of" in Hebrew parlance signified someone's essence: a "son of iniquity" was a thoroughly wicked person; a "son of Abraham" was a person with a character like Abraham's; and "son of man" (or "son of Adam") referred to an utterly human, Adam-like person, in contrast to the Holy God.

Yahweh appeared to Ezekiel in this terrifying way to strengthen him for a harsh task. The Jewish exiles were *rebellious*. Yahweh had a woeful message for them, just like the one Jeremiah was giving the Jews back home. Ezekiel would need the same tough hide Jeremiah had to withstand abuse from people who didn't want to hear what he had to say.

The Spirit of Yahweh literally picked Ezekiel up and dropped him in a nearby village of exiles. For a week he sat dazed by his encounter, feeling Yahweh's anger against His people's stubbornness churning in his own gut.

Free to Choose

Yahweh compared the prophetic task to that of a watchman, stationed on the heights of a city to inform its people about the progress of a battle or approaching couriers. Jeremiah was posted in Jerusalem to warn about the coming holocaust. Ezekiel's job was to notify the exiles that each of them was as individually accountable for his own actions as Jerusalem was as a whole for hers.

The exiles were saying they were suffering for their parents' crimes, or for the nobility's corruption—it was always someone else's fault. Yahweh wanted them to face the fact that in His sight, each of them lived or died by his own virtue or vice. It's true that Yahweh allows parents' sin to taint their children's lives, for no man is an island. But the children always have enough freedom to choose darkness or light. Even a person who has been wicked since birth retains the freedom to choose to change—not enough power to break ingrained habits on his own, but enough to reject them in principle and wholeheartedly seek Yahweh's help to reject them in practice.

In their heart of hearts, the exiles suspected that Yahweh enjoyed saddling people with inherited sin and then zapping them for it. To this Yahweh retorted, "Do I take any pleasure in the death of the wicked? . . . Rather, am I not pleased when they turn from their ways and live?" (Ezekiel 18:23).

Living Message

Like Hosea, Isaiah, and Jeremiah, Ezekiel often had to live his message. First, Yahweh made it impossible for him to speak except when giving a direct message from his Boss. This silence went on for seven years until Jerusalem's destruction, and symbolized the nation's refusal to listen.

Then Yahweh told him to build a clay model of Jerusalem under siege (the real siege was as yet five years off), and to lie on his side in front of it one day for each year of the treason of Israel and Judah. For 430 days Ezekiel had to lie there eating nothing but vegetarian patties baked on cow dung (a taste of famine food) embodying what Yahweh had suffered for 430 years. For it was really He who had borne the nation's evil all those years, and He who would suffer with His people every anguish of siege, starvation, and slaughter. Ezekiel, the son of man, was a living picture of what Yahweh was willing to bear for love of treacherous children. And like Hosea, the prophet was able to enter into the intimacy of Yahweh's grief and share it with Him as a friend.

The Glory Departs
The next year Ezekiel saw a dreadful thing: in a vision of Jerusalem he watched the glory rise from the temple and depart. Out the front gate of the city it went, and stopped over a nearby hill called the Mount of Olives. Jerusalem had abandoned Yahweh; now He was abandoning her. Ezekiel cried out in horror, but Yahweh was unmoved.

Covenant Sentence
Ezekiel saw in detail what was coming on Jerusalem: the famine; Zedekiah fleeing the city through a hole in the wall; the bloodshed. He directed some scathing tongue-lashings toward both Judah and the exiles. Jerusalem was a woman Yahweh had found as an abandoned baby, raised tenderly, and finally married and adorned as a queen. But she had used her fame and wealth to become a whore and attract gigolos, so Yahweh was handing her over to be torn apart by her lovers. Ezekiel described both idolatry and international intrigue in graphic lewd imagery.

He had choice words for Judah's leaders, both in Jerusalem

and Babylon. They were like shepherds who cared nothing for their sheep, only for themselves.

And from a thousand miles away, Ezekiel fought the same battle Jeremiah was fighting against the false prophets who predicted that everything was going to be okay. Real prophets, said Ezekiel, would be repairing the gaps in the moral and spiritual wall of the city, so that it could stand against all upheavals in the Day of Yahweh. But instead, when the leaders of Judah built a flimsy wall, these prophets simply whitewashed it to look like a solid piece of justice and commitment.

Every bleak picture, though, held its ray of hope. One day, when Yahweh's adulterous bride was humbled, He would take her back as wife. He would take His sheep from the false shepherds and give them a true shepherd: a son of David. Ezekiel saw the same restored remnant glimpsed by every other prophet since Hosea first announced doom: fabulous harvests in a land without war; true love between Yahweh and His people; a new covenant written on the heart. Over and over He explained the purpose of both destruction and restoration: "Then they will know that I am Yahweh."

News of the End

In August of 586 BC, Yahweh told Ezekiel that the next day he would lose the delight of his eyes: his wife. He was not to show any sign of mourning, for on that same day the exiles would lose the delight of their eyes and their hopes would crumble: Jerusalem would fall. In his silence, Ezekiel had only Yahweh with whom to share his grief. For if lying on his side before a model of Jerusalem had let Ezekiel taste Yahweh's suffering, here was the ultimate empathy; both God and man saw their beloved brides die that day, and wept together alone.

Five months later the first captives arrived with news of the final desolation of the Holy City. For seven and a half years, Ezekiel had been unable to speak except when delivering a message from Yahweh. Now his tongue was loosed to greet the refugees. All this time his job had been to urge the exiles to turn from the self-centeredness to which, insanely, they still clung, despite the ordeals they had suffered. His tactic had been to predict destruction as a sign of Yahweh's rage.

But now that the worst had happened, Yahweh gave him a new assignment: to sketch out yet more of the glorious future He planned, so that hope might accomplish what warning had not. Again He gave Ezekiel a series of visions: Israel was like a valley of dry bones, but Yahweh would breathe into them until they were again a great army. He would bind Israel and Judah together again into one nation under one Davidic king.

> "I will give you a new heart and put a new spirit in you; I will remove from you your heart of stone and give you a heart of flesh. And I will put my Spirit in you and move you to follow my decrees and be careful to keep my laws. You will live in the land I gave your forefathers; you will be my people, and I will be your God." (Ezekiel 36:26-28)

World powers would amass to destroy the new kingdom, but Yahweh would reduce their armies to carrion. Yet Yahweh was quick to reiterate the purpose:

> "It is not for your sake, O house of Israel, that I am going to do these things, but for the sake of my holy name, which you have profaned among the nations where you have gone. . . . Then the nations will know that I am [Yahweh] . . . when I show myself holy through you before their eyes." (36:22-23)

Yahweh's eye was ever on the nations.

Enigma

The final section of Ezekiel's book is puzzling—its symbolic meaning seems clear enough, but its literal fulfillment confounds the imagination. The prophet saw the temple rebuilt in

Jerusalem according to a plan of mammoth proportions—the entire complex covered a square mile with wide buffer zones between it and the rest of the city.[1] The plan drove home the point that Yahweh's holy place was utterly separate from the commonplace city of getting and spending around it. No longer would Yahweh's house sit cheek-by-jowl next door to a palace like Solomon's. In fact, the priests and Levites would have about twenty-one square miles each around the temple precincts to form a further buffer between the holy and the common. The city itself would be only a quarter the size of the holy area.

Yahweh gave Ezekiel detailed regulations for the priests who would serve Him in His house. The overall picture is of the tabernacle system of Leviticus radically revamped and expanded, but still largely intact. And the overall message is HOLINESS, including the absolute need for blood sacrifice to cleanse the people enough to live even at arm's length from a Holy God.

Ezekiel saw the glory move back into Yahweh's dwelling place just as he'd seen it abandon Solomon's temple before Jerusalem was burned. He also saw a river flowing out of the temple, giving life to everything it touched. He saw how Yahweh would redistribute the Promised Land in equal portions to the twelve tribes—no more of this amassing of wealth in the hands of a few. And finally, Yahweh renamed the city. It would no longer be called *Yerushalayim* (Jerusalem), but *Yahweh-Shammah*: Yahweh Is There.

NOTE
1. The lengths of the Hebrew measurements are somewhat debated, but this is a ballpark figure.

20

Ambassador
to a Pagan Court

♦

1 and 2 Kings, Daniel

Four Ambassadors

While Ezekiel was berating his countrymen in their impoverished villages, Yahweh was doing something quite different
with four Jews taken to Babylon back in 605 BC. It seemed that
a rapidly expanding empire prompted Nebuchadnezzar to
recruit administrative staff from among the conquered nations.
It wasn't easy to find people with the intellect and basic education to master the classical literature of Babylon (written in
an ancient and complex language), the official language in
which state business was done (Aramaic), and the intricacies
of Babylonian magic, divination, and dream interpretation. A
royal administrator had to know all of these, and in addition,
had to be physically perfect and handsome in order to fittingly
represent his master.

So in each captured country, Nebuchadnezzar's officers
selected a few young noblemen who showed potential for
such studies. In Judah they found four. These teenagers agreed
to have their names changed as a sign of submission to

Nebuchadnezzar, even to receive names derived from the names of Babylonian gods. They agreed to study the literature of sorcery and nature worship even though Yahweh had forbidden such practices. They were apparently secure enough in their commitment to and understanding of Yahweh that they could immerse themselves in their neighbors' thought-world without having their own convictions undermined. (These four, at least, had benefited from the labors of Zephaniah, Habakkuk, and Jeremiah.) Their firm foundation enabled them to serve as Yahweh's ambassadors to a pagan court, ambassadors who understood the people they were reaching well enough to speak their language and touch them where they lived.

The Limits of Conformity
The four captives were willing to do all this in order to identify with the culture to which Yahweh had sent them, but thereafter they repeatedly drew lines they would not cross. Over and over they had to discern between the conformity that won them an audience in the culture, and the conformity that would have meant selling out and losing their message.

The first line they drew was refusing to eat the king's food. Young administrators-in-training were housed separate from the palace, but they were fed from the royal kitchens to signify that they were the king's men. But the king's meat and wine were routinely offered to pagan gods before being served, and in the Near East, regularly eating someone's food was powerfully symbolic of swearing allegiance to him. The four young Jews just could not in good conscience eat food that linked them to Babylon's gods so firmly.

So their leader, Daniel, maneuvered their steward into feeding them vegetarian diets and no wine. Yahweh confirmed this stratagem by giving them better health than their colleagues who ate the king's food. He also demonstrated the old proverb "The fear of Yahweh is the beginning of wisdom" by enabling His ambassadors to excel in all aspects of their training in wisdom by the end of their two-year course.

This limit to conformity was private, but later the four Jews had to risk their lives to maintain their principles. At one point, Nebuchadnezzar experimented with uniting his multiracial empire under one state religion, and commanded officials from all of his provinces to bow down before a statue he erected. Daniel (who by then was one of the king's chief officials) managed to evade the directive, but his three friends were seen by envious colleagues (who reported them to the king) and thrown into a furnace for refusing to worship the state idol. These three told Nebuchadnezzar flatly that their God was able to rescue them from the flames, but even if He chose not to, He deserved their loyalty. When miraculously the flames did not consume the men, Nebuchadnezzar was so awed that he praised this powerful God and on the spot declared Judaism legal in his empire.

Decades later, Daniel found himself in a similar position. Jealous fellow courtiers, out to get Daniel, convinced a new king to decree that for a month no one could worship anyone but him, knowing that Daniel would ignore such an order. That time, God demonstrated His power to protect His own by preventing a den full of lions from devouring Daniel.

Messages from the God of Heaven

Most of the time, however, Daniel and his friends were able to go about their duties in a corrupt, pagan government, serving Yahweh and His justice in quiet ways. But in a few key instances, Yahweh employed Daniel as His spokesman to these people who knew nothing about Him.

Daniel's book reflects his (and Yahweh's) sensitivity to speak in ways his hearers could grasp. When addressing non-Jews, Daniel avoided Yahweh's personal name and instead used titles that would say something to his hearers: God, the God of Heaven, the God of My Fathers, the Great God, God Most High. The whole middle section of his book is written in

Aramaic, rather than Hebrew, to demonstrate God speaking to all nations in the international language. And when God wanted to get messages across to the kings Daniel served, He used dreams and omens because Babylonians were prepared to hear from the gods in this way.

God really wanted to give Nebuchadnezzar a chance. The king was insecure about having risen so fast to become lord over a huge empire, so God gave him a dream showing the kingdoms of men as a huge statue of a man. Nebuchadnezzar's kingdom was the head of gold (the first and greatest). But after him would follow a silver, a bronze, and an iron kingdom of ever-decreasing glory. The feet of the statue were iron mixed with clay: strength and fragility mixed. And finally would come an eternal kingdom founded by God, not humankind, that would smash and replace all human kingdoms.

The message: Your human empire is secure for a time, O Nebuchadnezzar, but the God of Heaven is lord over all nations and the whole scope of history. For a time He will allow human kingdoms to rise and fall, but at the end of time He will sweep them all away and establish a kingdom that will last.

God enabled Daniel to interpret this dream for Nebuchadnezzar at the very beginning of his career; the young Jew could hardly have been more than twenty, but he proclaimed the truth about God's supremacy to a man who held Daniel's life in his hands. Daniel was quick to credit God, rather than his own skill, for the interpretation, since it was only God's answer to desperate prayer that gave Daniel the insight to explain the dream and save his own life.

Sadly, the king responded only by recognizing Daniel's God as one more powerful deity in a pantheon of gods. So some forty years later, God sent him another dream, which Daniel again had to interpret: unless Nebuchadnezzar acknowledged that he was subordinate to the God of Heaven, and showed it by ceasing to oppress his own subjects, God would reduce him to insanity until he yielded. This is just what happened. But although Nebuchadnezzar did eventually admit that God was the real one in charge of the world, he seems to have died before he truly understood what that fact implied.

The Changing of Kingdoms

Just as Nebuchadnezzar had dreamed, the Babylonian Empire was a flash in the pan that God raised up briefly to discipline His people. He had promised Babylon's fall to Habakkuk, Jeremiah, and Ezekiel; He had told Jeremiah it would happen seventy years after the Captivity began; He had even told Isaiah the name of the man who would do the job.

Sure enough, in 549 BC, a Persian king named Cyrus defeated his overlord and became king of the vast Median Empire north and east of Babylon. Two years later he absorbed Asia Minor, west of Babylon, and cast his eye on Babylon itself. Nebuchadnezzar had been dead for fifteen years, and the current king of Babylon was Nabonidus. Now Nabonidus had allied with Cyrus years earlier and was not concerned to build up defenses against him. Instead, Nabonidus dabbled in ancient literature. The priests of Babylon resented his attempts to replace their gods with another, so he fled to Arabia, leaving his son Belshazzar in charge.

Belshazzar ruled the Babylonian Empire the whole time Cyrus was jaunting around building his own empire. By 540 BC Belshazzar could see he'd made a fatal mistake in letting his army go to seed, but it was too late. In the autumn of 539, with the Medo-Persian army on his doorstep, Belshazzar was losing his grip. To drown his terror he threw a wild banquet, even calling for the sacred vessels of Jerusalem for his drinking cups.

Toward the end of this drunken feast, the horrified ruler saw writing appearing on the wall opposite him: words about weights of money. His mother told him to summon an old magician named Daniel to interpret the message. Daniel explained that God had weighed Belshazzar's worth and found him wanting; that very night Babylon fell to Cyrus.

Wider Visions

With experiences like these, there was no doubt in Daniel's mind who was in charge of the volatile world he lived in. But what about the other Jews scattered around the Near East? Some were settling in to make good livings in commerce and manufacturing; others were barely making it.

Jeremiah and Ezekiel were dead, and Yahweh sent no emissary to replace them. But one prophetically minded Jew sorted through the annals written by the prophetic communities since Solomon's time and wrote a sweeping history to answer the question in everyone's mind: *Why did Yahweh let this happen?* In this book, which we call 1 and 2 Kings, the author traced how Israel's and Judah's kings failed to lead their people to keep the covenant, and showed that the Exile was the natural result of rejecting their Lord.

Some priests began to understand that keeping the covenant was essential, and they started codifying the books of Moses and the prophets into a system of religious practice that could hold its own against pressures to assimilate into local culture. If Yahweh kept His promise to restore them, they were determined never to break the covenant again.

But all of these activities were focused on the Jewish community, which was carefully insulating itself from the alien world around it. Daniel could not afford such a narrow perspective, and God's focus had always been wider. Also, now that Judah would never again be an independent state, but would be continually subject to the pagan kingdoms of Nebuchadnezzar's dream, God had to prepare His people to survive under regimes that would make it difficult for them to live His way. In the furnace and the lions' den, Daniel and his friends had received foretastes of what would happen when the interests of a secular state clashed with loyalty to the true God; the four forerunners escaped miraculously, but it would not always be so. Living in the corrupt world without being absorbed by it would demand the toughest kind of faith.

So Yahweh gave Daniel four visions to encourage the generations that would follow him. They echoed the glimpses Isaiah and Ezekiel had had of the far-distant future, but they also represented to a new kind of prophecy, which we call apocalyptic (from the Greek word *apokalypsis*, "revelation" or "unveiling"). In weird, symbolic pictures, Yahweh sketched highlights of what He had in store.

The Son of Man
The visions built on Nebuchadnezzar's dream of the statue. Daniel received the first two while Belshazzar was still reigning. In the first he saw four wild animals that represented the four kingdoms. The ruler of the fourth kingdom spoke boastfully of his power, but God appeared as the judge of men and kingdoms, and the fourth animal was slain. Then appeared "one like a son of man," who received from the judge authority to rule and even be worshiped by all nations in an everlasting kingdom.

Who was this "son of man" with whom Yahweh would share His worship? Yahweh had used the term for Ezekiel to emphasize the prophet's mere humanness. But this Son of Man was the ultimate human, the true Son of Adam promised at the beginning, the One who alone of all His brothers bore the image of God untainted. He was not just the son of David, a king for a tiny nation, but King of all.

Wonderfully encouraging, but there was an ominous note. The fourth kingdom would be crushed, but not until after its king had blasphemed God and oppressed His servants cruelly. Those who remained faithful even to death, however, would reign with the Son of Man.

Babylon, Persia, Greece
The second vision, which Daniel received in 551 BC just as Cyrus was beginning to put Persia on the map, zeroed in on the second and third of the four kingdoms. The first was Babylon; its days were already numbered. Persia was number two, and Greece (which was just starting to be noticed as a power)

was number three. An angel described to Daniel one of the kings of the Greek empire: a conniving despot who would war against God and His people. This vision so appalled Daniel that he spent days in bed, sick and exhausted.

Suffering and Perseverance

Daniel's third vision came just after Cyrus conquered Babylon in 539 BC. Daniel had been reading Jeremiah and figured that the seventy years were about over, so he went to Yahweh with mourning and fasting, begging Him to forgive and free His people. As faithful as he had always been, Daniel saw in himself the same corruption that stained his people; he confessed passionately and threw himself on Yahweh's mercy. In response, an angel came to say Yahweh was granting his request. Jerusalem and the temple would be rebuilt, but beyond that, sixty-nine weeks of years remained until an anointed king would come. He would then be killed and there would be war, the destruction of the temple, treachery, and abominations before justice would be inflicted on a false ruler.

Two years later, Daniel was fasting to understand what he had seen, and a fourth vision came: an angel so terrifying that Daniel was overwhelmed and had to be strengthened repeatedly just to stand up and talk. This warrior angel was battling the spirit princes who stood behind the earthly kingdoms arrayed against God's people. He gave Daniel more details of Persia and Greece (astonishingly accurate as to what would happen in the 200s and 100s BC) in which proud kings would rise and be dashed to dust, and one particular king would exalt himself to divine status, ravage Israel, and finally be crushed. In those terrible times the people of God would suffer horribly, but "the people who know their God will firmly resist" and "those who are wise will instruct many" (Daniel 11:32-33). Then the angel spoke of the end of the age, when after cataclysmic distress the dead would be raised to either eternal life or eternal shame.

Kings and Kingdoms

The details of all this were opaque to Daniel. From our hindsight we can see the rise and fall of Babylon, Persia, Greece, and a fourth kingdom: Rome. We know of a wicked Greek king, Antiochus IV, who did set himself up as divine and persecute the Jews in Israel, but we also find elements of Daniel's visions that look past that king. It appears that Antiochus was going to be a foretaste of many rulers who would tyrannize God's people for refusing to worship what is human, and of a final ruler who would be the epitome of this type. In the face of such oppressors, the message of the visions is clear: "The people who know their God will firmly resist."

21

Return to Jerusalem

◆

Ezra 1–6, Haggai, Zechariah

First Return: 537 BC

"This is what Yahweh says to his anointed,
    to Cyrus, whose right hand I take hold of
to subdue nations before him
    and to strip kings of their armor. . . .
I will go before you
    and will level the mountains;
I will break down gates of bronze
    and cut through bars of iron. . . .
For the sake of Jacob my servant,
    of Israel my chosen,
I summon you by name
    and bestow on you a title of honor,
    though you do not acknowledge me.
I am [Yahweh], and there is no other;
    apart from me there is no God." (Isaiah 45:1-5)

197

A century and a half after Isaiah recorded these words, King Cyrus of Persia rode victorious through the gates of Babylon, having absorbed most of the Near East into his empire. He had never even heard of the God of Israel, but Yahweh had selected him carefully nonetheless. Cyrus viewed politics and religion in a way utterly unlike his Babylonian predecessors. Convinced that sheer force could not make a large empire stable, he sought to win his diverse subjects' good will by tolerating their cultural distinctives. Instead of forcing everyone to worship Persian gods, he encouraged each nation to seek its own gods' favor for him. He sent people back to their homelands, returned confiscated religious objects, and financed the rebuilding of temples. This policy was so successful that his successors continued it.

So it was only months after Yahweh told Daniel his prayers were granted that Cyrus issued an edict that Jews in his empire could return to Jerusalem and rebuild their temple. A bare fifty years had passed since the city's destruction and not quite seventy since Daniel's capture; in response to prayer, Yahweh had mercifully trimmed the time of suffering.

Only about fifty thousand of the exiles decided to make the trek back to Judah. The rest—the majority—preferred to stay where they had settled, bought houses, and built businesses. After all, many had been born in Babylon and knew Judah only as a story.

But those who stayed behind were glad to help finance the resettlement. And Cyrus's treasurer counted out every last gold dish and silver bowl that Nebuchadnezzar had carried off from the ruined temple. And the returnees were on the whole a prosperous bunch with slaves and considerable personal funds. It was a promising start.

Even after several generations, most of the company could trace their lineage and even their village of origin; roots mattered when the covenant was so tied to family. A few priests who could not prove their ancestry were even barred from officiating because the leaders remembered what had happened in Moses' day when unauthorized priests tried to claim the office. For fifty years and more, the priests and Levites had been poring over Moses and the prophets, analyzing what had gone wrong. This time they were determined to take Yahweh seriously and do everything by the Book.

Temple Foundations

The returnees took about three months to settle into villages around Judah. Then in the autumn of 537 BC they gathered in ruined Jerusalem to celebrate the Feast of Tabernacles. The temple site was a heap of rubble, but they rebuilt the altar and began offering the sacrifices precisely as laid down in Leviticus, the priestly handbook. If their primary reason for existing as a people was to be "a kingdom of priests and a holy nation" (Exodus 19:6) as a model to the other nations, then worshiping Yahweh took top priority.

Hence, on top of planting their first crops in a land quite different from Babylon, the community's chief task that first wet winter was to line up craftsmen and material to begin rebuilding the temple in the spring. There was a bittersweet celebration when the foundation was laid in May of 536: the young shouted for joy, while the old who had seen Solomon's temple wept.

Everything was going great until a delegation arrived from Samaria (the region that used to be called Israel but was now named after its former capital). They were pleased as punch to welcome their new neighbors and help them build a Yahweh temple. Why, they'd been worshiping Yahweh ever since they came to Samaria! But the Jews knew that these Samaritans were equal opportunity religionists imported from all over the Near East by the Assyrians. They would be glad to support a Yahweh cult along with their other gods and thereby slowly assimilate the well-heeled newcomers into their system.

So the Jews turned the delegation down flat. They welcomed with open arms anyone who wanted to join them to serve Yahweh exclusively, but "open-mindedness" and "many paths to the divine" had gotten the covenant nation in hot water the last time, and they had no intention of repeating that mistake.

Rebuffed, the Samaritans showed their true colors. They launched a campaign of intimidation, ridicule, and threats to discourage the rebuilders. They even hired professional help in cutting supply lines and causing trouble with the legal authorities. They had no intention of letting a distinctly Jewish state become a power in the region.

The campaign succeeded, but only because the Jews were not really prepared for the realities of recolonization. They had marched out full of idealism, their ears ringing with the words of Isaiah and Ezekiel about restoration. They probably expected the land to sprout abundance of its own accord, and certainly to support them in the comfortable lifestyle they had been carving out in Babylon. A few poor crop years and a little scorn from their neighbors, and they were no longer in the mood to build a temple. Priorities shifted to self; when the people had nicely paneled houses and full stomachs, then it would be time again to think about building a house for Yahweh.

The Temple Restarted: 520 BC

So things sat for sixteen years. In the meantime, Cyrus died in 530 BC, and his son Cambyses secured the throne by murdering his brother and hiding the body. Cambyses had soon swallowed Egypt into his empire, but then he died suddenly in 522. In the ensuing struggle for power, one of Cambyses' officers and distant relatives, Darius, gained the upper hand. But he had all kinds of trouble stabilizing his reign; for two years he contended with rebel factions, two of which claimed to be led by Cambyses' vanished brother. It was a credit to Darius's talent and toughness that he finally managed to impose order by the middle of 520.

In August of that year Yahweh knew the time was ripe to

prod His people back into action. A series of disastrous harvests because of drought and hail had gotten their attention; the despondent community was a pale shadow of the cocky crew who first set out from Babylon seventeen years earlier.

A prophet named Haggai announced that the crops would keep failing until the people started building Yahweh's house instead of pouring everything into their own. A temple was a national focal point—an essential if Judah was to remain distinct as Yahweh's nation against intense pressures to merge into the surrounding culture.

Haggai's calm reasoning stung into action the community's two leaders: Governor Zerubbabel (a grandson of King Jehoiachin, and therefore a potential Davidic king) and Joshua (or Jeshua) the high priest. They promoted the building project in earnest, while Haggai cheered them on: "Be strong!" "I am with you, declares Yahweh."

To those who didn't think much of the stark brick-and-beam structure after the splendor of Solomon's temple and those in Babylon, Haggai painted a grand picture of how Yahweh would shake the heavens and the earth and overturn kingdoms. "The desired of all nations" would come, the prophet said, and the glory of this house would be greater than that of Solomon's. From the day the rebuilding began, the harvests would start turning around. And most importantly, Yahweh had chosen Zerubbabel as His "signet ring," His pledge of full payment on the promises about the Son of David.

Zechariah

Haggai delivered just four messages in four months; once construction was well underway, his job was over. But that same autumn a young priest named Zechariah took up the task of encouraging the builders. The following February he received a series of strange visions—angelic horsemen, horns and craftsmen, a woman in a basket—symbolic messages to spur the Jews on. Yahweh was going to overturn the oppressing nations, cleanse Judah, and fill Jerusalem to overflowing. Zechariah saw Joshua in his high priestly robes bloodstained with the crimes of his people; the robes were stripped off of him and replaced with clean ones, and Yahweh repeated His promise to send the Son of David: "I will remove the sin of this land in a single day" (Zechariah 3:9). Did anyone wonder what would have to take place on that single day to remove the land's sin?

Zechariah saw two olive trees providing oil for a lamp: king and priest, anointed with Yahweh's Spirit, fueling the holy service of His people. He saw Joshua crowned as king: the royal and priestly offices intermingled in a way impossible under Moses' law, since kings had to come from Judah and priests from Levi.

The meaning of all this was not too clear, especially statements like, "I [Yahweh] will live among you and you will know that [Yahweh] Almighty has sent me to you" (2:11). God sending God?

But on the whole, it sounded as though any day now Persia would be overthrown, Jerusalem would be again the resplendent capital of an independent nation, and a son of David would reign. Some of the prophecies gave the distinct impression that Zerubbabel himself might be that king (although what to make of a king with a priestly role of cleansing sin?).

In any case, it was all upbeat enough to keep the builders going when the next round of threats to their project surfaced. Another delegation arrived, this time from the Persian provincial governor. The empire had been in disarray for two years, and any sign of a local uprising—such as building fortifications with large blocks of stone—demanded investigation. The Jews quaked when the governor made out a full report, including names of those involved, and sent it to the Persian capital.

But Yahweh had everything under control. First He moved the governor to let the Jews continue building until a verdict came from King Darius. Then He moved Darius to the same attitude as his grandfather. Cyrus's original decree authorizing state aid in the building of the Jewish temple was found in the archive of a remote Persian city. So Darius ordered the governor not only to permit the construction, but even to finance it out of local taxes. Darius even decided to pay for the daily offerings so that both these citizens and their God would support his regime. Palestine was a key region, what with Egypt so volatile, and it was in Darius's best interest to please his subjects so easily.

With ample funds, the Jews finished the temple in less than three and a half years. Zechariah kept up morale in Yahweh's double-edged fashion. On the one hand, he predicted extravagant blessings: Jerusalem full; all the exiles restored; abundant crops; nonJews streaming to Jerusalem to seek Yahweh. But there was a catch. Zechariah relayed Yahweh's instructions to the people:

> "These are the things you are to do: Speak the truth to each other, and render true and sound judgment in your courts; do not plot evil against your neighbor, and do not love to swear falsely. I hate all this." (8:16-17)

Sharing in this glorious future depended on the people's response.

Hope Deferred

Nonetheless, it was a bright day in 516 BC when Joshua and Zerubbabel dedicated the new temple, just seventy years since the destruction of the first one. Those who remembered the opulence of Solomon's temple found the bare-bones replacement disappointing; there was no gold, one lampstand instead of ten, and even the ark of the covenant had been lost and had to be replaced by a slab of stone. The dedication ceremony squeezed the impoverished community to the limit, but even so it was stark compared to Solomon's lavish affair (700 animals versus 22,000). Yet although the kingless nation under Persian domination was a pale shadow of its former glory, the people were full of hope.

But year passed into year; Jerusalem remained in ruins and Darius showed no signs of falling off his throne. To keep the people going, Yahweh gave Zechariah an even wilder series of prophecies, basically encouraging but bewildering in their contradictions. He told of an army (the Greeks?) sweeping through Palestine and routing Judah's enemies, then the Jews battling victoriously against the Greeks, and more glimpses of national greatness. The people would abandon their corruption; Yahweh would come Himself to battle against their enemies and reign as King in their midst; and the nation would be so pure that even the horses' gear would bear the insignia of the high priest's turban: "Holy to Yahweh." Yet the Davidic king would come on a donkey, a symbol of peace, rather than on a war horse when he triumphed over the oppressors. How could a man of peace defeat Israel's enemies? And Zechariah also saw the king as a shepherd rejecting his rebellious flock and its greedy shepherds, and tossing away his wages: thirty pieces of silver, the price of a slave.

With hindsight we know Zechariah was seeing jumbled-together events that would happen over the course of one century, five centuries, even twenty-five. Why didn't Yahweh spell things out more clearly? The Jews got the understandable impression that "soon" meant "in our lifetime," or certainly not centuries and millennia away. When Zerubbabel died and nothing earth shattering seemed to be happening, the Jews not surprisingly cooled in their spiritual fervor. They kept up the temple sacrifices, of course, but it all became more and more a matter of religious duty than of passionate devotion.

Yahweh couched His messages as He did, knowing that His people would grow fickle through disappointment. What if He had told them back in 520 BC, "Build this temple now, even though you're going to live in poverty and oppression for five and a half centuries until the King comes, and even then he won't be the military general you wanted, you'll sell him for a slave-price, and you'll have another couple thousand years to struggle through"? Surely the Jews would have thrown up their hands right then and said, "This is too much. What's in it for us?" So instead, Yahweh told them just enough to encourage them, just enough to give them a chance to respond *if* they trusted Him. He could have burst in right then, ousted Persia, and dropped the Jews into the lap of luxury. But that would have been just what Satan had said about Job: Yahweh buys love. He didn't want the kind of love that had to be bought; He wanted the Abrahams who would hang on in the dark.

This generation of Jews were not Abrahams. After Zechariah's final prophecies the Bible falls silent on that generation, and we hear nothing more of the restored community for sixty years. By that time, rot and complacency had settled in, and while Yahweh was not finished with the nation, there was no more hinting that glory was just around the corner.

What would have happened if that generation had held faith through the years of hard work and waiting under foreign oppression?

C·H·A·P·T·E·R

22

Looking Toward the Future

◆

Ezra 4:6-23, 7:1–10:44;
Nehemiah; Esther; Malachi

Esther

Meanwhile, the scene shifts back to the Persian capital, where Yahweh was beginning to deal with a quiet threat to His people's existence.

Darius was a superb leader. He solidified the Persian Empire from India to northern Sudan, improved the bureaucracy, instituted the use of coins, standardized weights and measures, introduced a new law code, and took a strong interest in his subjects' welfare. But he also imposed burdensome taxes to support his administration and building projects, such as his lavish palace at Susa, his new capital.

Darius's son Xerxes[1] (pronounced "Zerk-seez") succeeded him on his death in 486 BC. The new king was bold, ambitious, handsome, stately, and thoroughly self-indulgent. The empire was crumbling under Darius's taxes, but Xerxes did not have his father's diplomatic skill. He burned Athens, took sacred treasures from Egypt, destroyed temples in Babylon after a revolt, and denied a Jewish request to rebuild the walls of

Jerusalem. He seduced his niece, abandoned his sister-in-law to death for rebuffing his advances, and wiped out his brother's whole family. When a bridge he commissioned collapsed in a tempest, he ordered the sea flogged and had the builders beheaded.

It took Xerxes a couple of years to quell revolts in Egypt and Babylon after his father's death. Then he spent a while finishing his fabulous citadel at Susa. But by 483 he was ready to tackle empire building. He invited all the prominent men of his domain to spend six months in Susa, to admire his wealth and power and to help him plan a campaign against Greece. The culmination of that session was a seven-day debauch before the launch of the war.

On the seventh day Xerxes summoned his loveliest possession, his queen, to display herself for his guests. She refused to come, possibly because she objected to the manner in which she was to be displayed. At any rate, the Persian nobles agreed that such conduct would undermine wifely submission, so Xerxes deposed his wife and declared that he would choose a new queen upon his return from Greece.

The Greek venture was catastrophic; Xerxes gave the Greeks two of their most glorious historic victories. When his army limped home in 479 BC, Xerxes was ready for the distraction of a new batch of girls for his harem. So his attendants planned a beauty contest in which the prettiest girls from across the empire would be commandeered, given beauty treatments, and allowed to spend one night with the king. When Xerxes found one that suited him, she would be queen. The rest would spend the remainder of their days locked in the hot, cramped harem, living like nuns.

One of the unlucky ladies was Esther, a Jew from the tribe of Benjamin. She quickly found favor with the eunuch in charge of the harem, who coached her on how to win the king's notice. Sure enough, she became queen in January of 478 BC.

An orphan, Esther had been raised by her uncle Mordecai.

Upon becoming queen she had him appointed as a judge, and while sitting among the other officials one day, Mordecai overheard a plot to assassinate Xerxes. He told Esther, and she told Xerxes, who duly executed the plotters and recorded Mordecai's service in his record book.

Sometime later, Mordecai irritated one of Xerxes' officials by refusing to bow to him. This Haman was a descendant of the king of Amalek whom Mordecai's ancestor Saul was supposed to have executed six centuries earlier (1 Samuel 15). Haman was also an insufferable boor, and Mordecai saw their rivalry as a symbol of the war between the sons of the Snake and the sons of God.

Haman saw it that way, too. He wheedled Xerxes into issuing an irrevocable edict authorizing pogroms against a certain unnamed race. The Jews mourned when they heard of the edict issued on April 17, 474. Mordecai urged his niece to intercede with the king. But Esther knew her husband's volatile moods. Initiating contact with him could mean instant death, and she hadn't seen him in a month.

Mordecai's response was curt:

If you remain silent at this time, relief and deliverance for the Jews will arise from another place, but you and your father's family will perish. And who knows but that you have come to royal position for such a time as this? (Esther 4:14)

A Mind with a plan lay behind the destiny of every Jew; Esther's choice was simply whether to accept the risks of her assignment or fail in the purpose for her existence. She accepted.

As it turned out, her shrewd tactics and some "coincidences" won the execution of Haman and a second edict that the Jews could protect themselves against anyone who tried to carry out the previous irrevocable edict. March 7, 473, was a bloodbath, but the Jewish people survived.

The book of Esther was probably written sometime between Xerxes' death in 464 BC and the end of the Persian Empire in 331, most likely by a Jew living in one of the Persian cities. The hairbreadth deliverance is celebrated annually as the Feast of Purim, when the book is read. But the most notable feature of the book is that not once is Yahweh named or even alluded to. Fasting is mentioned, but not the prayer that certainly accompanied it. The coincidences—that it was Esther whom the harem officer and the king favored, that Mordecai happened to overhear a conversation, and on and on—are simply left to dangle as "well, that's what happened." Nothing is attributed to Yahweh's intervention. It's as if the writer is saying, "That's how life looks from down here. We see only what happens; we can only guess where Yahweh's hand is touching." The God who dealt with Pharaoh through technicolor plagues could deal with an even worse tyrant like Xerxes by placing a gutsy woman in the right place at the right time.

Ezra
Xerxes' successor, Artaxerxes, again had to deal with revolts in Egypt. To maintain order and loyalty in Palestine, he authorized a priest named Ezra to lead a second party of Jews back to Judah in 458 BC, and then to enforce the Jewish law on all Jews there. Artaxerxes also made a grant to pay for sacrifices in return for the goodwill of the Jewish God and people.

Ezra was an impassioned student, practitioner, and teacher of Moses' Law. He soon whipped temple worship into shipshape condition and began teaching Moses' instructions. The people were shocked to find out how many things they were doing that directly contradicted Yahweh's laws. Some of the leaders admitted to Ezra that many Jewish men had married nonJewish women, who were now leading their husbands and children to practice the mixed local religions. It may have been (as happened a generation later) that the men were even divorcing their Jewish wives in order to marry into the families of influential local landowners. But at the very least they were endangering the existence of a nation devoted to Yahweh.

In response Ezra did not rebuke the men; he was consumed with the horror of how this disregard must make Yahweh feel. He tore his clothes and hair as signs of mourning and sat in silence for hours, appalled. Then he went to the temple in his torn robes, fell to his knees, and sobbed a prayer of confession. He knew Yahweh had every right to wash His hands of this mob and bring in another batch of exiles through whom He could fulfill His plan. His grief cut the people's hearts deeper than any accusation; they came to him weeping and promising to divorce their foreign wives.

A committee of the leading Jews sat for three months reviewing each family's case and found 110 men guilty of marrying wives who had not converted to worship Yahweh exclusively. The committee decided these persistent idolaters had to be divorced; it was a human tragedy of mammoth proportions, but spiritual purity (not ethnic purity) was the reason for this community's existence.

Nehemiah

For twelve years Ezra strove to keep the unruly Jews in line. By 446 he had made enough progress that they were ready to try rebuilding Jerusalem as a proper national capital. But three local nonJews informed Artaxerxes that if this city were restored, the Jews would almost certainly revolt and try to set up an independent state. Since he had had to quell a Palestinian rebellion in 454 BC, Artaxerxes took the warning seriously and ordered the work halted until further notice. The Jews' enemies went a step further and demolished and burned what had already been done.

The Jews were mortified, but Yahweh had an ace up His sleeve. Back in Persia, one of Artaxerxes' trusted officials happened to be a Jew of faith and nerve called Nehemiah. When Nehemiah heard that the reconstruction had been wrecked, he spent four months fasting and praying for Yahweh to do something. By April of 445, he knew *he* was that "something." Through prayer and natural shrewdness he worked his whole strategy out before approaching Artaxerxes with it. Miraculously, the king agreed to send Nehemiah as the new governor of Judah with a royal escort, letters to the local Persian officials, and even a requisition for timber from the royal forests.

Upon his arrival in Jerusalem, he inspected the demolished walls and again had a plan entirely mapped out before presenting it to the Jewish leaders. Their new governor's take-charge confidence impressed them, and they summoned their people from around Judah to help build the city wall.

The governors of Samaria and Ammon, however, were not pleased. They were used to running the region, and this new Jewish governor would be a pest once he had a defensible city. But Nehemiah dismissed both their ridicule and their threats: "The God of Heaven will give us success."

The Jews flocked from their villages and set to work. When scorn failed to daunt the builders, their enemies tried raids. Nehemiah countered with his typical spiritual-practical approach: "We prayed to our God and posted a guard." The work halted temporarily for a total call to arms, but thereafter the builders were able to make progress as long as their weapons were at hand. It was a grueling two months in which not even Nehemiah got much sleep or even changed his clothes.

The next problem was internal. Nehemiah had diverted the people from farming to building, and many of them were already in economic trouble. They'd had to mortgage their land to feed their families during a bad crop year, and if their harvests failed this year, their creditors would take everything. Some farmers had even sold daughters to support the rest of their children, and the Jewish buyers were selling the girls to pagans. These peasants were dedicated to Nehemiah's cause, but "you can't eat walls."[2]

Nehemiah was shocked that Jews were willing to buy the lands and even the children out from under their countrymen with the attitude that business is business. The governor had himself been lending money, but he was now convinced that even fair lending was improper when a brother's life was at stake. He made his fellow rich men swear that everything foreclosed or bought from a debtor would be returned, that interest would no longer be charged on loans, and that anything a fellow Jew could not pay back would be treated as a gift. To set an example, Nehemiah went so far as to refuse to take a salary from taxes on his people; for the next twelve years he lived off what he had earned in Persia. (That included supporting a household of 150 people plus guests.) To him, sacrificial concern for his people was a leader's sign of love for God.

Nehemiah endured plot after plot from his enemies — murder attempts, false rumors that he was conspiring to become king, efforts to disgrace him before the people. His blunt prayers for justice and protection punctuate his memoirs (which form most of the book of Nehemiah).

Once the city had a wall with gates and guards, Nehemiah addressed himself to populating it so that it would not just be a shell, easily cracked when his back was turned. He was also concerned to help Ezra in his ongoing campaign to keep the people focused on Yahweh. So the two of them summoned the whole community to Jerusalem for the autumn festivals. For a solid six hours on the first day, Ezra read from the books of Moses while the Levites interpreted the teaching so that the people could grasp it clearly. The people wept as they saw how far short they fell of this standard, but Nehemiah told them to go home and celebrate: the strength to move toward this holiness would come not from self-punishment, but from joy in Yahweh.

For a week they lived in tents on city roofs, celebrated their ancestors' desert wandering, feasted, and listened to Moses' teaching. Toward the end of the month they gathered again for a day of hearing the teaching, confessing their offenses, and worshiping. Then they cast lots for the one family out of ten who would move into the new city. Nehemiah's book carefully records the name of each of those families as a sign that this was an ordered people, a network of men and women with a past and a future. Finally, the community held an elaborate festival to dedicate the wall—and hence the whole city—to Yahweh as His holy place. It was not the vast complex envisioned by Ezekiel, but it was the city of God for now.

Nehemiah governed Judah until 433 BC, at which time he returned to Artaxerxes' court. Sometime thereafter he got himself commissioned to another term as governor and showed up back in Jerusalem to find that things had gone to seed. One of his archenemies had secured family connections with the high priest and had made an apartment out of one of the temple storehouses! One of Nehemiah's first official acts was to throw Tobiah's belongings out of the room. Then he ordered it purified and refilled with the incense and grain that belonged there.

Next he found that the people had broken their pledge to finance the temple services; the Levites had had to go back to farming to make ends meet. He dealt with that in short order. After that he disciplined the Jewish leaders for permitting commerce on the Sabbath in the Holy City—he locked the gates and posted guards until the merchants got the message that this day belonged to Yahweh. Finally, when he found that once again Jewish men were preferring pagan wives, and that many of their children couldn't even speak the Jewish language, he handled the men in Nehemiah fashion: he exploded and even slapped some of them around. Haven't you idiots gotten the message yet? Yahweh wiped us out once for degenerating into just another idolatrous nation, and He won't hesitate to do it again. We exist to be a light to the nations, not to imitate their madness.

Malachi
The last prophet of the Old Testament may have been at work during the days of Ezra and Nehemiah, or just after. He addressed the same issues they faced: the Jews, disappointed

that none of the great things Haggai and Zechariah promised had happened, were settling into lukewarmness. They doubted Yahweh's love for them, since He had not come to His temple in power, nor liberated His people from their overlords. They doubted His justice, since the wicked were still prospering more than the good. So they continued to go through the motions of worship, but they cut corners, offering to Yahweh only what they didn't want. The priests set scandalous examples, and the people followed them in divorcing their first wives in order to make more socially advantageous marriages with pagans.

To this community who said it didn't matter what they did because Yahweh had gone on vacation, Malachi declared that Yahweh was going to send a messenger in the spirit of Elijah to prepare for His own coming to His people. Then they would find out that God showing up was not as pleasant as they thought. For He would come like a blazing sun—purifying and healing to those who were willing to bear the heat of holiness, but a consuming fire to those who were only casually interested in religion.

The Silent Years

Most of the Jews completely ignored Malachi. So after his death, the prophetic voice fell silent in Judah, and the land held its breath, awaiting the Elijah-messenger. Yet a handful of people here and there retained the fire in their hearts and continued to seek Yahweh's presence, not just His gifts. They fulfilled one of Yahweh's promises through the prophet Isaiah:

I have posted watchmen on your walls, O Jerusalem;
    they will never be silent day or night.
You who call on [Yahweh],
    give yourselves no rest,
and give him no rest till he establishes Jerusalem
    and makes her the praise of the earth. (Isaiah 62:6-7)

For four hundred years the hidden watchmen prayed.

NOTES
1. Many Bible versions translate this name as "Ahasuerus." Xerxes and Ahasuerus are the Greek and Hebrew versions of this king's Persian name.
2. Derek Kidner, *Ezra and Nehemiah* (Downers Grove, IL: InterVarsityPress, 1979), page 95.

23

The Silent Years

◆

Greece and Rome

Persia fell to Alexander the Great in 331 BC. When Alexander died in 323, his generals dismembered his empire, and the next century and a half saw the Middle East shredded as two Greek empires sparred for control. Judah (now called Judea) played pawn and trophy in this game, but was largely able to govern herself as one of the many sacred temple-states in the Greek domain.

But around 190 BC, Daniel's fourth beast—Rome—began to prowl eastward. Two Jewish priests took advantage of their Greek overlord's terror by taking turns offering bribes for the high priesthood. (The high priest was effectively the ruler of Judea.) Patriotic and godly Jews banded together in 168 BC behind the more legitimate of the two bribers, and their stance landed them in rebellion against their king. Guerrilla war and religious martyrdom followed for several years while the king, Antiochus IV, handed the Jewish temple over to the local cult of Zeus. A statue of Zeus (or rather his Syrian equivalent, Baal

Shamem) was erected in the temple. To the distraught Jews this was a clear fulfillment of Daniel's prophecy that an "abomination of desolation" (*siqqus meshomem* in Hebrew, which sounds like a pun on Baal Shamem) would desecrate the temple.

Eventually, though, Antiochus could no longer afford to bog his armies down in a pointless war with Judea. The ban on Judaism was lifted, and the temple was cleansed in a ceremony celebrated thereafter as the Feast of Dedication, Hanukkah. As Daniel had predicted, Yahweh came through for His people.

However, the guerrillas had no intention of settling for religious freedom. They fought for twenty years until they won control of a free Jewish state. Politically free, at any rate. For in the meantime, the legitimate line of high priests had all fled to Egypt, and the new Jewish governor was popularly acclaimed the first of a new dynasty of high priests. His sons took the title "king" as well as high priest and mimicked Greek kings in their despotism without mimicking any of the redeeming features of their culture. At length two sons of this dynasty fell into civil war and left the door open to a nonJewish politician named Antipater. Antipater cut a deal with the Roman general Pompey, and almost overnight in 63 BC, Judea became a Roman subprovince.

Roman rule may have been no worse than the graft-ridden Judeans deserved, but it was very bad indeed. Arrogant toward "inferior races" and gluttonous for plunder, the Romans did not endear themselves to their subjects. Antipater was assassinated in 43 BC for being Rome's toady, but his sons carried on his pro-Roman policy. They effectively ran Judea, the high priest having been reduced to a figurehead. After the elder son was killed in an invasion from Rome's enemies, the younger son, Herod, was named "king of the Jews" once he restored order. Herod was as good a friend to Rome as he was a stench in Jewish nostrils, so he retained his throne right through the transition from the Roman Republic to the Roman Empire under Augustus Caesar in 27 BC.

Hasids and Pharisees

Back in the time of Malachi, bands of faithful Jews started meeting together to support each other in resisting the general spiritual snooze. They called themselves Hasidim because they maintained *hesed*—covenant faithfulness to Yahweh. Psalm 119 reflects their twin passions for Yahweh and His laws:

> I have sought your face with all my heart;
> > be gracious to me according to your promise.
> > (verse 58)

> Oh, how I love your law!
> > I meditate on it all day long. (verse 97)

The Hasids strove in vain to keep their Jewish brothers from adopting Greek customs. They supported the guerrilla war against Antiochus but broke with the new Jewish kings when they proved to be no better than debauched Greeks. Those who broke away (around 145 BC) came to be called Pharisees, meaning "separatists." Their hallmark was ritual purity—strict adherence to the food laws, the Sabbath, and other practices that made it difficult to have normal social contact with nonJews. They invested incredible energy in studying the Law of Moses, and in the process developed a body of tradition about how to interpret and apply it. That tradition eventually came to rank as sacred as the Law itself.

In some ways, the tradition made it easier for the average person to feel confident about obeying Yahweh. For instance, Exodus 16:29 said, "no one is to go out" on the Sabbath. The Pharisees decided that Yahweh couldn't have meant to confine everyone to his or her house, so in light of Numbers 35:5 they concluded that one could go 2,000 cubits (about three-fourths of a mile) from wherever one designated as "home" for the day. If one wasn't sure what counted as "work" on the Sabbath, one could refer to the thirty-nine classes of work outlined by the Pharisees' rabbis.

But sometimes the interpretation pushed so far as to

virtually nullify the original intent of a law. And more often than not, the tradition became so complicated that only an expert could remember it, let alone follow it. And the more one focused on getting all of the complex rules right, the less attention one tended to give to the other Hasid distinctive: "I have sought your face with all my heart."

One tradition that may date back well before the Pharisees emerged as a party had to do with Yahweh's name. Exodus 20:7 declared, "You shall not misuse the name of [Yahweh] your God." His name deserved honor because it expressed the essence of His character. It was not to be used flippantly, and certainly not in false oaths, magic, or fake prophecy. But the Jews came to feel that it was really too holy to be used at all. So when reading the Law and the Prophets, they would substitute the title "Lord" for the name "Yahweh." They referred to Him as "Lord" or "our Father in Heaven" or even as "Heaven." When the Scriptures were rendered into Greek, the translators used the Greek word for Lord, *Kyrios*. In keeping with that practice, we will from now on call Him "the Lord" or "God."

Sadducees and Common People

Over against the Pharisees stood the Sadducees, whose name probably comes from their having been members of the *syndike*, or ruling council. They were the favored party of the Jewish kings, so although they comprised only a few of the richest priestly families, they held great political power. They controlled the high priesthood and the temple with its lucrative treasury. On the religious side, they rejected the Pharisees' tradition and claimed to hold the old, pure doctrine. They accused the Pharisees of getting many beliefs—such as bodily resurrection, rewards and punishments after death, predestination, and angels and demons—from Persian religion. They had a much more tolerant, expedient attitude toward pagan overlords than the Pharisees.

While the Sadducees dominated the temple and the ruling council, the people endorsed the Pharisees. This gave the Pharisees enormous influence beyond their numbers (there were only about six thousand of them even in the first century AD). The quarrel could get hot; around 90 BC one high priest-king was pelted with citrons (similar to lemons) on the Feast of Tabernacles because he poured the holy water on the ground next to the altar like a Sadducee instead of on the altar as the Pharisees taught. He later dealt with the opposition by having eight hundred of the rebellious rabbis crucified.

However, the Pharisees and Sadducees were forced to tolerate each other when both sat on the Sanhedrin, the national ruling council. This was easier once Herod and Rome had reduced both to carving out turf under foreign rule. And Pharisees and Sadducees could agree on one thing: the common mob of artisans and peasants were barely Jews, either because they were disgustingly lax about keeping the laws and traditions, or just because they were rabble. This rabble, who formed the largest segment of the population, had neither time nor education for doctrinal debates. They were just trying to survive under a crushing load of taxes levied by Rome and priestly Jerusalem.

Essenes, Qumran, and the Zealots
Three other groups filled out the Jewish landscape at the turn of the first century AD. The Essenes were basically monks—they lived in monastic communities, avoided sex and other forms of physical indulgence, and maintained their devotion to the Lord through strict separation from the world. Their brotherhoods grew because families would give them sons to raise. Even Herod held them in high esteem because they had the only prophets whose words came true.

A similar community, or network of communities, is best known by its main settlement at Qumran. This group was dedicated to the study of and adherence to prophetic writings, especially the book of Daniel. They went to the desert to prepare to be the Lord's instrument when He would come to judge the earth. Their mandate was Isaiah 40:3—

In the desert prepare the way for the LORD;
make straight in the wilderness a highway for our God.

Purity, common property, menial labor, self-denial, and ritual cleansing were key features. The Qumranites criticized the Pharisees for supporting the sacrificial worship at the Jerusalem temple, even though the high priest there was no longer of the branch of Aaron's family to whom King David had assigned the high priesthood. In fact, they considered the Pharisees generally lax about the Law. These were serious spiritual Green Berets.

The Zealots turned up as a formal party around 6 BC just after Herod's death. They held that it was against God's law to submit to a Gentile ruler. They adhered to most of the Pharisees' doctrines, but while the Pharisees were content to let the Lord break the foreign yoke in His own time, the Zealots felt called to be the instruments by which He would accomplish that purpose. Depending upon your point of view, they were freedom fighters, guerrillas, or bandits.

24

The Silence Breaks

◆

Matthew 1:1–4:11, Mark 1:1-13,
Luke 1:1–4:13, John 1:1-51

Shadow Hopes

On the evening of earth's great disaster in Eden, the Lord promised that a Son of Eve would someday crush the Snake who had led humankind into misery. As time went on, the Son of Eve was revealed to be a Son of Abraham, Son of Judah, Son of David. Isaiah saw him as a Warrior King, full of the Spirit of God. But he also gave him titles no man could claim for himself: Mighty God, Everlasting Father, Prince of Peace.

Isaiah also glimpsed someone whom he dubbed "the Servant of the Lord." Like the Son of David, He would establish a regime of justice. It would be not just a Jewish nation, for He would also bring the Gentiles the same deliverance from darkness. Yet somehow, before He attained His glory He would suffer unspeakably, bearing in His body the full cost of His people's crimes. He would die and yet reign—a paradox.

Daniel saw another kingly figure: "one like a son of man" who would receive dominion over the whole earth forever. One *like* a man? He glimpsed the coming of the King who would suffer and reign, and even heard a timetable that might pinpoint the King's arrival within a decade or so. Micah learned the King would be born in Bethlehem. Zechariah implied that the Deliverer would be Priest as well as King, staining His holiness with the people's corruption in order to cleanse it away.

And yet God had told several prophets that He would not share His glory with someone else. He Himself would come to deliver His people: "Then suddenly the Lord you are seeking will come to his temple" (Malachi 3:1). There was also that odd bit in Zechariah about God apparently sending God.

But the fine points of these prophecies were largely lost on a nation shuddering under the weight of Rome. The people had long pinned their hopes on the Anointed One (*mashiach*, or Messiah), the anointed king of David's line who would come to liberate them. The sufferings, the promises to the Gentiles, the inscrutable titles—these perplexities blurred amid the shining vision of Someone Who Will Get Us Out of This Mess!

God Becomes Man

Perhaps the wildest fantasy a Jewish woman could have would be mothering the Messiah. She would have to consummate a marriage with a man of David's line, of course. How else did one have babies?

But God had never done anything the way humans expected, and He wasn't changing that pattern in the last years of Herod the Great, king of the Jews. Adolescent, virgin Mary lacked the only requirement for motherhood history had ever known. She had, however, all of the qualities God required: the right lineage, and the same attitude of total trust and devotion that had won Abraham titles like "righteous" and "friend of God."

The stump of David had run into hard times since noble Zerubbabel led his compatriots back from Babylon more than five centuries earlier. But peasant Mary's blood was royal enough, and she was engaged to a man with comparable pedigree. So the Spirit of God came upon her and completed what was lacking in her egg's twenty-three chromosomes for the making of a man. It was that simple.

Simple. All it required was for that Person of divinity who had eternally been joined as a Son to a Father to empty Himself of His infinity and pour Himself into a single human cell. It required nothing but a divine self-humiliation that made Heaven gasp.

It was God's joke on the wisdom of men. Greek philosophers had recently been defining God as an unmoved Mover, utterly detached from the base material world, utterly beyond feelings or any touch from the earth at all. For their part, the Jews had walled their God off behind multiple layers of temple courts and fully expected that if they slit the throats of the right animals every day, God would stay in line. But the Lord who had thundered to Moses, whispered to Elijah, and wept with Hosea was not about to be banished to some hygienic spiritual plane where He wouldn't interfere with human plans. And while some were watching the skies, waiting for Him to ride in on a cloud, He snuck into their midst incognito, in a teenager's womb.

One of the baby's biographers called him "the Word"— God's self-expression, revealing in human form everything the Unpronounceable One had ever been. In a day when His people had grown afraid to utter His name, God chose a new one.

Jesus was the Greek version of that name; the Hebrew equivalent was *Joshua*, "Yahweh saves." The baby's namesakes were the general who led Israel to possess the Promised Land, and Zechariah's high priest. Another name lingered in the background, for the impossible birth recalled one of Isaiah's more obscure predictions: "The virgin will be with child and will give birth to a son, and will call him Immanuel [God with us]" (Isaiah 7:14).

By rights, this Jesus was in every way a king. Son of David and Son of God—who could dispute His claim? But the road to His throne would be the thorny one of a God who had always preferred to woo rather than ravish.

A certain Matthew, another of Jesus' biographers, said it all in the genealogy that opens his book. The women he chose to mention in Jesus' ancestry were Tamar (who seduced her father-in-law because she saw no other hope of gaining her rights), Rahab the prostitute, Ruth (who came from an explicitly blacklisted foreign nation), Uriah's wife (Bathsheba, whom David seduced and whose husband he subsequently murdered), and Mary (whose neighbors were all certain she was a slut). Surely this boy bore in His bloodline all the worst that men and women could do to each other. He was a true son of Adam, and "Son of Man" was the title He chose for Himself.

To drive the point home, God had the baby born in a stable. It was indeed in Bethlehem, but the only people who showed up to mark the occasion were a mob of shepherds (who ranked extremely low on the Pharisees' list of law-abiding servants of God) and some Persian magicians. The prominent priestly families were notified, but declined to attend. Herod responded to the news by decreeing that all unweaned boys in Bethlehem be slaughtered. His only interest in a Davidic king was to stamp out a rival. But of course Herod was a Snake's pawn, and the Snake knew well enough who Jesus was.

It was pathetic. Haggai and Malachi had both extolled the glory of the day when "the desired of all nations" would come to His temple. But when Mary brought her newborn to fulfill the proper rites, only an elderly saint and a closet prophetess noticed. The priests were busy elsewhere. Jesus made hardly a ripple in the human world when He arrived, but behind the scenes heaven and hell were holding their breath.

John the Baptizer

A few months before Jesus' birth, God had given a son to a cousin of Mary's in one of those postmenopausal conceptions He had made famous with Sarah. This child may have been raised in one of the monastic communities scattered around

Judea, for he emerged from the desert twenty-something years later as an ascetic firebrand. But whereas the folks at Qumran were preparing for the Day of the Lord by walling themselves off, John intended to prepare for it by slapping his countrymen into line.

He was in fact the first capital-*P* Prophet the nation had seen for four hundred years, and it was his business to summon every man, woman, and child to prepare. His chosen piece of theater was baptism, a ritual washing that converts from paganism usually underwent as a sign of being cleansed from their idolatrous past. John insisted even "good" Jews needed this bath. He hugely impressed the common people with his wild appearance and hellfire sermons on the banks of the Jordan River. The religious leaders rolled their eyes.

Perhaps the first and last time John was ever stopped in his tracks was when his cousin Jesus arrived to be baptized. He had been warning everybody that Someone was coming who would baptize them with fire rather than mere water, and here was the Coming One looking at him serenely, waiting to be dunked. John tried to refuse. Jesus did not deny that He had no need to be cleansed, but He maintained that He needed to identify fully with the people to whom He was sent. Furthermore, His Father had chosen this occasion to publicly declare that Jesus was the Son of God and was empowered by the Spirit of God. It was the first time in history that God publicly paraded His strange nature: there were Three of Him who related to each other as Father, Son, and Spirit; yet there was only One of Him.

Entrance Exams
Before He had lifted a finger in His Father's service, Jesus emerged from His bath in the Jordan mantled in His Father's approval: "This is my Son, whom I love; with him I am well pleased" (Matthew 3:17). This conviction would be the bedrock of His life; in a whirlpool of popular acclaim and rejection, He would have one relationship to stand on. For it

was His job to relive the trials of Adam and Israel, and prove faithful where they had failed.

First the ancient Snake met Jesus in the desert and coaxed Him to make Adam's choice: Take by force what the Father could give by grace. Be a Messiah of Your own making. Choose physical comfort, pride, or personal glory. And always the refrain: "If you are [*really*] the Son of God. . . ." Doubt Your Sonship. Doubt Your Father's love.

Jesus faced this assault not with His divine strength, but with only the weapons available to all people. He quoted from Moses' sermons about what Israel should have learned during her forty years in the desert. What Israel never did learn, Jesus clung to at the core of His being.

Those long desert days were His last test before His real work began. He was about thirty years old and had never yet done anything that anyone had taken special notice of. But now He headed back to where John was still preaching and baptizing and did more nothing. The Baptizer, however, told his followers that Jesus was "the Lamb of God, who takes away the sin of the world!" (John 1:29). In other words, "Follow that One instead. Somehow He is the fulfillment of all that the temple system represents." John probably didn't even know what he was saying when he pushed his own followers to abandon him. Yet five of them ended up accompanying Jesus on the eighty-mile walk north to the Sea of Galilee, where Jesus had been raised and where He was still based.

C·H·A·P·T·E·R

25

The Kingdom

◆

Matthew 4:12–20:34, Mark 1:14–10:52,
Luke 4:14–18:43, John 2:1–10:42

New Wine

The Son of God yielded His divine power when He confined Himself to humanness. But at His baptism, Jesus received the power of God's Spirit, just as the prophets before Him had done. And His total surrender to the Father made Him more open to the Spirit than any prophet; for the first time ever, a human walked in the full authority of the Holy Spirit. What God had intended for Adam, this second Adam lived.

His first public use of this power was to supply wine for a wedding feast. It was an entirely appropriate debut. God liked parties. He had told Isaiah that His Kingdom was going to be like one immense party with the best food and the finest wine. And weddings were His favorite, since they reminded Him of the union He would one day have with His Bride, the people He loved.

So Jesus selected six huge stone jars, slimy with the scum of ceremonial Jewish washing, and ordered them filled with water. To the wedding guests who drank the water-become-wine, the miracle probably meant little. But to the five men who had followed Jesus from the Jordan, this was a hint. The King who had commanded the Jewish Law for a season and a purpose was about to change the stagnant water it had become into fresh wine for a royal feast. All that washing in dirty water had grown pointless. It was time for men and women to be washed in fire and drink the new wine of the Kingdom.

The Kingdom at Hand

This was Jesus' message as He began to visit synagogues and preach in the streets: "Repent"—turn around, change your thinking, shake the dust out of your heads—"for the Kingdom of God is at hand." The King has arrived. Dump out your jars of scummy water and get ready for fresh wine.

To demonstrate His kingship and His Father's character, Jesus set about fulfilling Isaiah 61:1-2. Luke records Jesus' words:

> "The Spirit of the Lord is on me,
>   because he has anointed me
>   to preach good news to the poor.
> He has sent me to proclaim freedom for the prisoners
>   and recovery of sight for the blind,
> to release the oppressed,
>   to proclaim the year of the Lord's favor."
>   (Luke 4:18-19)

From sunup to sundown He healed the sick, cast demons out of people, and proclaimed that the day of liberation had come.

Of course, He meant the day of liberation from the Snake and from the madness that had gripped Adam's kin since the beginning. Freedom from people's insane efforts to feed their spirits with work or sex or possessions or power. Freedom from old bitterness and senseless grief. But the people persisted in not seeing past their noses. To them "the Kingdom of God has drawn near" could mean only that Daniel's sixty-nine weeks had drawn to a close, and that God was about to smash the last of the great world empires and erect on its ruins a Jewish kingdom that would endure forever. The Son of David would be a general leading a supernaturally equipped Jewish army to victory against Rome and an earthly golden age.

Upside-Down Values

Consequently, Jesus' teaching about the values of Kingdom citizens made virtually no sense to anybody. *You think it's good to be rich and well fed and laughing and popular,* He said. *That's right, we sure do,* was the universal response. *Well, you're wrong. The really fortunate people from now on are the poor, hungry, weeping, and rejected.* What? He made Himself somewhat clearer by explaining that He was referring to those who knew their spiritual poverty, mourned over it, and hungered to have their intimacy with God restored. One should envy those people, for they were ripe to enter God's Kingdom.

Jesus maintained that this was often easier for people who didn't have a lot of physical comforts or even necessities to rely on. He certainly wasn't prejudiced against rich people, especially those who treated their wealth as a tool to serve God. But He had a special fondness for the vulnerable of all sorts, and He was constantly warning against the subtle temptation to worship money. None of this made sense to a nation committed to the iron-clad rule that wealth equals God's favor and poverty equals God's displeasure.

Then there was Jesus' teaching on forgiveness:

> "If someone strikes you on one cheek, turn to him the other also. If someone takes your cloak, do not stop him from taking your tunic. Give to everyone who asks you, and if anyone takes what belongs to you, do not demand it back. . . .
>
> "Love your enemies, do good to them, and lend to them without expecting to get anything back." (Luke 6:29-30,35)

The idea of not retaliating against injuries was so foreign to any sane reasoning that no one knew what to do with it. Why would someone just lie down and let people take advantage of him? Doesn't that just encourage unscrupulous people—most of all the Roman soldiers, who would intimidate the last dime out of a person if he let them? Certainly, the Sadducees preached cooperation with Rome and the Pharisees agreed under protest, but to a Zealot, turning one's cheek to a Roman was mealymouthed blasphemy.

One could spiritualize Jesus' words to mean merely that one should have a generous and forgiving attitude, but the stark statements themselves went much further than that. Total nonretaliation. Absolute freedom from bitterness.

In fact, everything Jesus said went a lot further than most people were prepared to go. The commands from Mount Sinai forbade murder and adultery; Jesus said those included even hatred and lust (the inner attitudes behind the actions):

> "For I tell you that unless your righteousness surpasses
> that of the Pharisees and the teachers of the law, you
> will certainly not enter the kingdom of heaven. . . .
> "Be perfect, therefore, as your heavenly Father is
> perfect." (Matthew 5:20,48)

Here was a standard so laughably high that one could hardly do anything but throw up one's hands in defeat. It was tempting to ignore it, except that it veered dangerously close to the standard of total holiness laid down in the Law.

After all, the purpose for that radical holiness had always been to attract those who did not know the true God. Jesus told His followers they were like a lamp set on a lampstand so that everyone could see the true light of God and be drawn to it. "Let your light shine before men, that they may see your good deeds" (Matthew 5:16).

What good deeds? Certainly not the "acts of rightousness" the Pharisees liked to do in public: prayer, fasting, giving to the poor. Those were personal disciplines to strengthen one's intimacy with God and should be done secretly (Matthew 6:1-8). Pagans would never be impressed by those; lots of pagans prayed and fasted. No, the good deeds that would make a world sit up and take notice would be forgiveness when they expected vengeance, humility when anyone else would be arrogant, and honest dealings when swindling was standard in the Mediterranean world.

But could the hundreds of the Pharisees' intricate rules really be a lazy compromise of God's real requirements? The mind reeled at the thought. And when His hearers were staggering, Jesus thoroughly confused them by accusing the Pharisees of putting intolerable burdens on the people. He said,

> "Come to me, all you who are weary and burdened, and I will give you rest. Take my yoke upon you and learn from me, for I am gentle and humble in heart, and you will find rest for your souls. *For my yoke is easy and my burden is light*." (Matthew 11:28-29, emphasis added)

Somehow, Jesus claimed, committing oneself to those impossible Kingdom values and approaching them yoked to the King would actually be easier than laboring over the Pharisees' rules.

The Inner Circle

But most of the crowd who mobbed Jesus in search of healings and miracles wanted nothing to do with such demands. Fairly soon He resorted to speaking to them only in parables—little stories with subtle or not-so-subtle points. They were easy to ignore but also hard to forget, and the unspoken punch line was always, "So what are you going to do about it?" For example, He said once, "The kingdom of heaven is like treasure hidden in a field. When a man found it, he hid it again, and then in his joy went and sold all he had and bought that field" (Matthew 13:44). In other words, *How much is God's Kingdom worth to you? What would you be willing*

to give up to gain it? How serious are you about seeking God?
Meanwhile, Jesus focused His attention on that smaller group of people who really wanted to understand what He was saying. Every rabbi had disciples; Jesus was no different in that respect. He was unusual in that He persistently weeded them out with statements like, "Foxes have holes and birds of the air have nests, but the Son of Man has no place to lay his head" (Luke 9:58) and "Unless you eat the flesh of the Son of Man and drink his blood, you have no life in you" (John 6:53). Anybody who would hang around for comments like these was seeing more in Jesus than just a miracle-worker or a potential military commander.

There were at least seventy of these fairly serious disciples. From among them, Jesus selected twelve to be His inner circle—His comrades, confidants, and crack trainees. He called them *apostoloi* (Greek) or *shaluchim*, (Aramaic, the language of Jewish Palestine). These words meant "sent ones," but in Jewish legalese they referred to a special representative, a proxy or ambassador. One could send a *shaliach*, or apostle, to collect religious taxes, deliver a certificate of divorce, or even stand in for the bridegroom in a betrothal. Jesus was the official *shaliach* from the Father, and He was grooming twelve men to carry on that task.

His selection gives one pause. He stayed up all night praying to discern which twelve were the right ones, and here is the group He chose: Simon Peter, a well-meaning if hotheaded fisherman; Peter persistently rushed in where angels feared to tread. Simon's brother, Andrew, one of those disciples of John the Baptizer. James and John, fishermen brothers who bore the nickname "Sons of Thunder" because of their tempers. Simon the Zealot, a revolutionary with violent anti-Roman leanings. Matthew, a tax collector for Herod—the kind of person guys like Simon usually spat at when they met them in the street. Philip, Bartholomew, Thomas, another James, Thaddaeus— we know almost nothing about these five; did they ever do anything? Then there was Judas Iscariot, the only man from

Judea (the rest were backcountry types from Galilee). Being the sharpest with finances, Judas was in charge of the money, but he tended to dip into it for his own purposes.

There wasn't an educated man in the bunch, and all were rough diamonds at best. But these were the men Jesus took with Him everywhere He went. He and the Twelve were joined by some women who paid the bills out of gratitude for healings they had received from Jesus.

Acting Like God

In a culture where even chaste women were considered instruments of the Devil sent to corrupt nice Jewish boys, having women in His entourage was a move guaranteed to raise eyebrows. Rabbis were taught to speak to women as little as possible (including their wives), but Jesus freely chatted with women both alone and in public. He even taught them as disciples (no decent rabbi would have dreamed of having female disciples).

In fact, if He had come to endear Himself to His people, He was going about it entirely the wrong way. He kept declaring God's pleasure with the faith of dirty Gentiles. He attended rowdy parties at the homes of the first-century equivalent of loan sharks and shady businessmen. He talked a lot about humility but was constantly coming out with outrageous statements.

First, He professed the right to interpret the Law with a total disregard for the traditions of the elders. He generally leaned toward the Pharisees' viewpoint rather than the Sadducees', but then He would say, "You have heard [from the rabbis] . . . but I say to you. . . ." He called Himself "Lord of the Sabbath" and said that gave Him the right to ignore the rules for that holy day. His followers did not fast, He said, because one should celebrate when He was present. He even claimed the right to forgive sins, which only God could do, and backed up the claim with miracles.

One day He was at a Pharisee's home for dinner, and a

street woman came in (homes were fairly public in that culture). She drenched Jesus' feet with her tears, then started kissing His feet and wiping them with her hair, and finally poured wildly expensive perfume over them. Jesus acted as though this were a perfectly acceptable way for a total stranger to treat Him in public. He had the gall to declare all her sins forgiven because of this shocking display. His host was speechless at a supposed great prophet acting like He thought He was God.

Face-off

And He didn't stop there. The Pharisees were seething at Him for breaking the no-work rule by healing people on the Sabbath, and in general for implying that He was God's equal. They didn't like the familiar way He called God "My Father" instead of "the Father" or "our Father in Heaven." Everything about Him threatened their neat system and their cozy position at the pinnacle of Jewish society. So they started spreading a rumor that He was casting out demons by the power of the Chief Demon himself. Jesus coolly pointed out the absurdity of this idea; why would the Devil cast out the Devil?

The truth was quite the reverse. Time after time Jesus faced off against the Pharisees and other rabbis. He didn't mince words about their hypocrisy, pride, and greed: "Woe to you, because you are like unmarked graves, which men walk over without knowing it" (Luke 11:44). It incensed Him that they had reduced His Father's commands to a set of external rules that one could practice while entirely sidestepping any real passion for God or compassion for people.

Many of Jesus' parables were barbed arrows aimed at the Pharisees. When they complained that He treated the dregs of society like friends, He told a story about a father with two sons. The older son stayed home to serve his father obediently, while the younger left home with his inheritance, squandered it in wild living, lived hand to mouth for a while, and finally crawled home, hoping for a job on his dad's farm. He was now willing to accept the humiliation he had coming, but the father welcomed him home, restored him to the full privileges of a son, and threw a party. The older son was irate:

"Look! [he said.] All these years I've been slaving for you and never disobeyed your orders. Yet you never gave me even a young goat so I could celebrate with my friends. But when *this son of yours* who has squandered your property with prostitutes comes home, you kill the fattened calf for him!"

"My son," the father said, "you are always with me, and everything I have is yours. But we had to celebrate and be glad, because *this brother of yours* was dead and is alive again; he was lost and is found." (Luke 15:29-32, emphasis added)

Jesus had come to welcome despairing younger brothers home to a Father who longed to throw His arms around them. It broke His heart to see the bitter elder brothers who were wasting their lives serving a Father they resented because they could not understand His love.

Jesus grieved that their spite had blinded them beyond repair. Although He was not given to name-calling, He had a title for them: "You brood of vipers!" (Matthew 12:34, 23:33). After long ages the Son of Eve had come, and the sons of the Snake were waiting. The Serpent had spawned not just among the pagan Romans who taxed Judea to support their decadence, nor the thieves and extortioners of the Jewish underclass, but among the religious leaders whose real gods were security, comfort, tradition, and respectability.

Jesus knew exactly who stood behind the malice in these men's eyes. He told His apostles, "The Son of Man must suffer many things and be rejected by the elders, chief priests and teachers of the law, and he must be killed and on the third day be raised to life" (Luke 9:22).

The Twelve were stunned. Jesus was at the height of His popularity; they were riding a crest to Jerusalem with the anointed Son of David. It was only a matter of time before He directed His power against Rome and the Kingdom began in earnest. But Jesus knew better. Luke writes, "When Jesus left there, the Pharisees and the teachers of the law began to oppose him fiercely and to besiege him with questions, waiting to catch him in something he might say" (11:53-54).

C·H·A·P·T·E·R

26

Jerusalem's Last Chance

◆

Matthew 21:1–26:56, Mark 11:1–14:52,
Luke 19:1–22:53, John 11:1–18:11

To Jerusalem

It was a loyal but motley band who followed Jesus on His last trip to Jerusalem. He had spent most of His ministry in backwater Galilee, but He had visited Jerusalem enough to be known and detested by the leading Pharisees there. He still hadn't done anything to raise the hackles of the Sadducees. Yet.

The apostles knew Jesus was the Messiah; they just didn't have a clue what that meant. Knowing they could only make things worse, Jesus strictly forbade them to discuss His title in public. Peter got into an argument with Him about predicting betrayal and death instead of victory. And one of the apostles' favorite pastimes was debating the pecking order that would go into effect among them once they took charge of the nation. All Jesus needed was these guys explaining His kingship to people.

The way they saw it, Jesus was spiritualizing the whole thing. He fed five thousand leaderless insurgents with bread, then instead of accepting their offer to follow Him in a march on Jerusalem, He alienated everybody by calling Himself "the bread of life." He showed up at the temple at the end of the biggest feast of the year, after the priests had spent a week doing rites to seek rain, and announced at the top of His lungs, "If anyone is thirsty, let him come to me and drink" (John 7:37).

"I am the light of the world." "I am the good shepherd." I am . . . I am . . . I am. He drove the Jews nuts by constantly alluding to Exodus 3:14—"God said to Moses, 'I AM WHO I AM.'" But direct questions like, "If you are the Anointed One, tell us plainly," He would always sidestep. *Look at My actions,* He'd say. *What do you think?*

After all, what good would it have done to claim the title? It was the same as in the garden with mad Adam: the Lord wanted His people to see Him clearly and choose Him for who He was.

Yet after three years of nonstop contact with Jesus, the Twelve still didn't get it. They had watched Him heal and teach and drive out demons. They had thrilled to actually do these things themselves. They had been part of the miraculous feeding of the five thousand with five loaves and two fish. They had asked Him endless questions. They knew more than anybody, and they knew almost nothing.

Royal Parade

So if even the Twelve were blinded by their preconceptions of who the Son of David ought to be, it was no surprise that the crowds approaching Jerusalem for the Passover were entirely in the dark. And for maybe the first and last time, Jesus did exactly what they expected.

About two miles from Jerusalem, the summit of the Mount of Olives reaches 2700 feet above sea level, some 300 feet above Jerusalem. (See map, page 363.) The road from Jericho crests that peak, then descends steeply toward Jerusalem. Near the top lay the towns of Bethany and Bethphage. In one of those villages, Jesus told His disciples to fetch an unridden donkey colt. Such a mount was ritually clean, suitable for sacred or royal use. An unridden colt might be kept in a village for an important visitor, and Jesus was held in awe in this region. Just a few weeks or months earlier He had rocked Bethany by raising one of its citizens from the dead after three days in his tomb.

Jesus' disciples knew at once what He was saying by mounting this colt. He was claiming to be the fulfillment of Zechariah 9:9; He was announcing that He was coming to the capital as its king.

The disciples were ecstatic. They could see it all: Jesus would ride in amid popular acclaim, ascend the temple steps, march into the inner court, and grasp the horns at the corners of the altar. That would signify that He was declaring His kingship. All the people would rise against the Romans, and with the power of God behind them they would quickly oust the pagans and institute the Kingdom.

The disciples' job was to get the crowd behind their nominee. So they started shouting royal acclamations from Psalm 118, such as "Blessed is the king who comes in the name of the Lord!" (Luke 19:38). They threw their cloaks on the ground in front of the donkey in the manner of a proper regal welcome.

The local villagers and probably lots of pilgrims from Galilee who had seen Jesus' miracles soon responded to the revelry. They cut branches from the trees to add to the royal carpet, and joined in shouting "Hosanna"—a cry from Psalm 118 for God to save His people through the king. By the time the entourage reached Jerusalem, it had swelled to a rollicking mob ready to follow their king into battle.

Some Pharisees in the crowd rebuked Jesus for encouraging this riot, but He retorted, "If they keep quiet, the stones will cry out" (Luke 19:40).

Last Chance

Then, with the crowd in His grasp, Jesus let them drop. As He gazed down over Jerusalem from the Mount of Olives, He wept. He knew what her choice today was going to cost her.

He knew how she would look forty years hence, surrounded by Roman armies quelling a rebellion. The citizens would be slaughtered and their temple burned because they would not yield their demand for a military deliverance. They wanted liberty on their terms, under their control. They would not humble themselves before a God who wanted their hearts and the tough choices of self-sacrifice and love. And therefore, although they could quote every scripture about the Lord coming to His temple, they did not recognize Him when He came.

For He did ride up the temple steps and enter the outer court, the one called the Court of the Gentiles because it was supposed to be set aside for Gentiles to pray and perhaps encounter the true God. But He did not proceed to the altar to claim His throne. Instead, He stopped and grimaced at what had happened to the Gentiles' place of prayer. It was mobbed with people buying and selling animals for sacrifice (at stiff prices because it was a cartel), or changing common currency for the coinage in which offerings had to be made (another monopoly). Only someone blind and deaf could pray in this bedlam. Jesus assessed the situation, returned to Bethany for the night, and the next morning returned prepared to take action. He pushed over the money changers' tables and single-handedly drove the whole throng out the front door. Then He sat down to teach a stunned audience about God.

Until now, Jesus had clashed mainly with the "lay" leaders of Judaism—the Pharisees and teachers of the Law. But now He had challenged the chief priests, whose families probably owned the businesses Jesus had just shut down. And the money aside, Jesus was dangerously close to bringing the wrath of Rome down on the Jews' heads. Yet the chief priests couldn't do a thing about Him because the people applauded His behavior as a bold prophetic deed. The crowd was probably a little disappointed that Jesus hadn't claimed His crown, but they still doted on Him and were convinced He had something up His sleeve. So the priests decided to lay aside their animosity toward the Pharisees in the face of a common

enemy. Passover was only a few days away; they were determined to find a way to arrest Jesus as a political activist before
He did whatever further intolerable prophetic antics He was
planning.

Farewells

For three days Jesus taught as an ordinary rabbi in the temple
courts, while the Pharisees and Sadducees tried to trap Him
with trick questions. But He was a master at turning their
questions back on them and making them look like fools.
Eventually they left Him alone, grinding their teeth.

When their frustration was at its zenith, their golden
opportunity dropped from Heaven—or rose from hell. Jesus'
finance man, Judas, appeared in the chief-priestly offices with
a proposal. He had followed Jesus for three years, convincing
himself that he had hitched his wagon to a rising star. But now
it was clear that Jesus was throwing it all away in political
blunders and spiritual nonsense, and Judas had had enough.
For a price, he would reveal where they could find Jesus apart
from the adoring crowds and arrest Him. It was a deal.

That same Wednesday afternoon, Jesus announced a
veiled farewell to His gawking audience. He bore no ill will
toward the many who had heard His words and disregarded
them. Their indifference would be its own judge when those
words returned to them on the Day of the Lord.

On Thursday Jesus did not go to the temple. He spent a
quiet day apart, then celebrated a Passover meal with His
apostles in the evening, a day early. This would be their last
night together, and He had an intense session planned to brief
them for His departure.

As usual, the lesson was full of theater. At some point, He
stripped like a slave and washed His followers' feet. His point:
"Now that I, your Lord and Teacher, have washed your feet,
you also should wash one another's feet. I have set you an
example that you should do as I have done for you" (John
13:14-15). They had bickered and competed long enough. As

Jesus' sent ones, they had to represent His character, and He wanted to be known as one who would submit to the lowest self-abasement and sacrifice Himself for the good of those He loved.

His other drama involved the food at the meal. The fare at a Passover supper was already symbolic: the unleavened bread represented the haste with which the Israelites left Egypt; the bitter herbs recalled their bondage; cups of wine punctuated the dinner at intervals. There was supposed to be a roast lamb to signify the sacrifice whose blood protected Jewish homes from the destroyer. But the official lambs would not be sacrificed until Friday afternoon, and only by the temple priests.

Jesus added two more symbols to this paramount meal of the Old Covenant. A Jewish dinner commenced when the host blessed and broke the bread. When Jesus did this, He added, "This is my body given for you; do this in remembrance of me" (Luke 22:19). Then He made each man eat a piece of the bread and remember His bizarre words about eating His flesh. Human sacrifice was unthinkable; this was too close for comfort.

The meal ended with the last Passover cup, over which Jesus declared, "This cup is the new covenant in my blood, which is poured out for you" (Luke 22:20). Here was Jeremiah's new covenant (Jeremiah 31:31-34), not ratified by the blood of bulls, as was the old covenant at Sinai, but by—what?—this rabbi's blood? Surely the meal ended in confusion, as each man sipped the cup and wondered.

Between the bread and cup came a disquieting lecture.[1] Jesus tried to explain that He was leaving and that in His absence the apostles would face fierce opposition from the world around them. But they needn't feel fearful or abandoned, because someone called the *Parakletos*—the Comforter, Counselor, Helper—would come to their aid. This was the Spirit who had inspired the prophets and who had been enabling Jesus to do His works of power. All the disciples had to do was to remain connected to Jesus like branches to a vine, and everything would be fine. Exactly how one could remain connected to a man who was leaving was left unclear, but somehow it involved obeying His commands, especially the one to love each other.

The disciples were in no way encouraged by these promises and pressed for a better explanation. Where was Jesus going, and why couldn't they go, too? Jesus replied with oriental ambiguity, and the Twelve were left vaguely uneasy.

Jesus knew His men were still woefully ill-equipped to face the next twenty-four hours, let alone the rest of their lives, so He closed the feast with a magnificent prayer for them and for those whose lives they would touch. Then He led them back to their camping site in a garden on the Mount of Olives.

Arrest

Judas had left the dinner early to summon the temple guards to that site. Jesus knew His betrayer's errand, so while His disciples fell asleep, still baffled, He kept vigil and steeled Himself for the ordeal ahead. It was time to fulfill Isaiah's words: "He was despised and rejected by men, a man of sorrows, and familiar with suffering." It was time to do for real what Ezekiel did symbolically when he bore the sin of Jerusalem. It was time to give meaning to the death of every bull and goat whose throat had ever been slit on the bronze altar in fifteen hundred years. For none of that blood and burning flesh had ever paid the cost for God's grief at His children's rejection of Him. It had always been God absorbing the price into Himself, paying the terrible cost in His own suffering. Now He was going to do before all the cosmos what He had really been doing all along. And if human sacrifice was unthinkable because of the exquisite value of human life, what of God sacrifice?

Yet Jesus was human, too, and His every nerve cried out against the coming torture. He had faced His entrance exams in the wilderness of Judah; this was His final exam. In utter frankness, He acknowledged that His will was to walk away from this ordeal. But what Adam had been unable to say, Jesus said to His Father: "Yet not my will, but yours be done."

On the Day of Atonement each year, the high priest sprinkled the blood of one goat on the throne of God as the price of the people's crimes for that year. Then he would lay his hands on a live goat and confess those crimes over it, transferring the guilt to this innocent substitute. Then the scapegoat would be driven into the desert. Here in this garden, Jesus began to live out what fifteen hundred years of goats had symbolized. As high priest and victim in one, He took into Himself the crimes of a planet. He had never before experienced evil within Himself; the weight of it alone nearly killed Him.

The soldiers arrived soon thereafter. It was a farce: They, armed to the teeth and quaking; He, defenseless yet in total control. They were expecting a dangerous revolutionary with an armed band and possibly miraculous powers. They were utterly unprepared for a calm, commanding presence who used the divine name "I AM" to identify Himself. Peter tried to satisfy their expectations by launching the war of liberation, but Jesus squelched him and healed the man he attacked. All in all, it was more a matter of Jesus giving Himself to the soldiers than of them actually arresting Him.

NOTE
1. The Gospel accounts don't make it entirely clear in what order the bread, the cup, the footwashing, and the lecture occurred. This is one possible reconstruction. In general, the Gospel writers seem less concerned about including precise chronology than a modern historian might wish.

C·H·A·P·T·E·R

27

The Death of Death

◆

*Matthew 26:57–28:20, Mark 14:53–16:20,
Luke 22:54–24:53, John 18:12–21:25*

Jewish Trials

The trial, too, was a charade. Roman soldiers had shared in Jesus' arrest on the grounds that He was a political revolutionary. Because such revolutionaries were a severe threat to order in the province, the governor's mandate was to maintain order even if it meant ruthless suppression. The Sanhedrin—the Jewish leaders—honestly feared Jesus might spark an uprising, perhaps unintentionally, but they knew perfectly well He was no guerrilla leader.

The trouble was that they needed Rome to believe otherwise. Their real motive for getting rid of Jesus was that, like every prophet before Him, He was a pain in the neck for men like them. He was making them laughingstocks among the people and jeopardizing their lucrative businesses. But they couldn't execute Him for being a prophet. They might possibly convict Him for blasphemy—claiming to be the Son of God. But if they had Him stoned for blasphemy, He might become something even worse than a live prophet: a martyred one. His disciples might launch a whole movement around Him.

No, the only sensible move was to have Rome execute Jesus on political grounds. They had to convince the governor that He was a threat to public peace, an insurrectionist claiming to be the rightful Jewish king.

So around 3:00 a.m. on Friday, Jesus was marched into the home of the godfather of the chief-priestly families: Annas. Annas had been high priest many years earlier, and since then Rome had appointed five of his sons to that office, probably on his advice. The current high priest was Caiaphas, Annas's son-in-law.

Annas intended to conduct a preliminary interrogation to gather evidence for the real trial. But Jewish legal procedure declared the accused innocent and not even on trial until at least two independent witnesses had given testimony that agreed. Accused people could not be asked to incriminate themselves. Knowing that Annas had no right to interrogate Him, Jesus coolly refused to answer his questions. He politely directed Annas to any of the dozens of people who had heard His teaching in the temple. Had anyone heard Him say anything that could prove He was a false prophet?

An official finally lost his temper and slapped Jesus across the face. But the man who had said, "If someone strikes you on one cheek, turn to him the other also," put His own preaching into practice. Neither cringing nor spiteful, Jesus simply pointed out that this was one more illegality that Annas and company really ought to face up to.

Exasperated, Annas summoned the entire Sanhedrin out of bed to give this upstart His trial. Unfortunately, it wasn't legal to hold a capital trial in the middle of the night. Even after coaching the witnesses, the priests couldn't get them to agree except on a vague story that Jesus had said, "I am able to destroy the temple of God and rebuild it in three days." Jesus didn't bother to explain that He'd really said, "Destroy

this temple [my body], and I will raise it again in three days."
The trial was a show anyway.

Finally Caiaphas asked Him point blank if He was the
Messiah. Jesus responded with an orientalism that implied,
"Yes, but you haven't a clue what that means." To really shake
up His audience, He added an allusion to Daniel's prophecy
about the divine Son of Man coming from Heaven.

That was the last straw for the Sanhedrin. It never
occurred to any of them that Jesus' claim might be true, so the
outrageous apparent blasphemy disgusted them. Some began
to hit and spit on Him. As soon as dawn broke they held a
quick official trial in which they got Jesus to repeat His claim
to be the King, and promptly shuffled Him off to the governor.

Roman Trials

Lucky for them, the Roman workday began at dawn. But the
governor, Pontius Pilate, was less than thrilled to have this
case on his morning docket. He knew his Jewish subjects
detested him for his record of extortion, murder, atrocities, and
social blunders. He had recently provoked a riot by parading
his soldiers with a portrait of the emperor on a Jewish holy day
(the Jews regarded the portrait as an idol). Rome had disciplined Pilate for endangering public order, and he knew Rome
would fire him if there were riots about a supposed Messiah.

Pilate's first dodge was to invite the Sanhedrin to execute
Jesus on religious grounds, such as blasphemy. Roman subjects weren't really allowed to inflict the death penalty, but
Pilate promised to look the other way. But this offer wasn't
good enough for the priests, so Pilate agreed to question Jesus
about His kingship. When it became clear that Jesus' claim had
few or no political overtones, however, Pilate wanted to dismiss the whole case.

He almost got out of it when he learned Jesus was a
Galilean. Technically, that put Him under the jurisdiction of
Herod (son of Herod the Great), who ruled Galilee. But Herod,
who was in town for Passover, found Jesus a bore and

returned Him to Pilate. Herod had been thrilled by a chance to question the famed wonder-worker, but Jesus ignored Herod completely. He wasn't interested in performing for an effete, pompous kinglet.

So back came Jesus to Pilate's office, dressed by Herod in a mock imperial robe. The governor's next sidestep was to have Jesus beaten within an inch of His life. Pilate hoped that would satisfy the Sanhedrin without getting him into serious trouble with this god Jesus claimed to serve. Jesus' serenity in the face of His accusers was getting under Pilate's skin. The man was too lucid to be a madman, and there was something decidedly unnerving about His confidence.

It was customary for the governor to demonstrate his benevolence by freeing one Jewish prisoner at the Passover. When Pilate led Jesus out to the crowd, he expected them to beg mercy for this teacher they so adored. But the sight of Him dripping blood in a royal robe and wearing a crown of thorns changed their infatuation to contempt. The Sanhedrin had already coached the people to request another prisoner's release—Barabbas, a *real* guerrilla captain. Ironically, his name meant "son of the father." For Jesus, the Sanhedrin led the cry, "Crucify!" and the people echoed it. This was the Roman execution for slaves and scum—to Romans it was a disgrace, and to Jews it fulfilled Deuteronomy 21:23, "anyone who is hung on a tree is under God's curse." Such a death would silence any notion that Jesus was a prophet of God.

Pilate was beside himself. It terrified him to think of lifting his hand against one who might be divine (Romans were incredibly superstitious). He confronted Jesus:

"Where do you come from?" he asked Jesus, but Jesus gave him no answer. "Do you refuse to speak to me?" Pilate said. "Don't you realize I have power either to free you or to crucify you?"

Jesus answered, "You would have no power over me if it were not given to you from above. Therefore the one who handed me over to you is guilty of a greater sin."

From then on, Pilate tried to set Jesus free, but the Jews kept shouting, "If you let this man go, you are no friend of Caesar. Anyone who claims to be a king opposes Caesar." (John 19:9-12)

This was too much for Pilate. He feared the gods, but he feared Caesar more. He wanted this god to know that the man's blood was on the Jews' heads, though.

"Shall I crucify your king?" Pilate asked.

"We have no king but Caesar," the chief priests answered. (John 19:15)

It was true. The Snake laughed.

Crucifixion

It was a grisly way to kill, even by the standards of the day. The law forbade crucifying a Roman citizen. The victim was nailed (or tied) by hands and feet to wooden crosspieces shaped like a T, a Y, an I, or a †. He straddled a hornlike projection, which took some of the weight and kept the flesh from tearing away from the nails. It usually took hours for the blood loss from beating, exposure to sun, and restricted circulation and breathing to produce heart failure.

Jesus was half-dead from flogging before He reached the site. But He was aware enough to deliver a mournful prophecy to the women who followed His escort. He felt no bitterness, not even toward those who had plotted His death and now mocked Him as He hung nailed to a pole. It had always been so since the first rebellion; these men were only carrying out what humans had ever longed to do: kill God so that they could rule their lives themselves. Jesus felt only compassion. He said, "Father, forgive them, for they do not know what they are doing" (Luke 23:34).

As Isaiah had foreseen, He was executed among criminals. The two thieves crucified with Him provided an object lesson on the choice being offered an entire planet. One cared only for self and let himself be devoured by his hatred of God and man. The other saw past Jesus' humiliation and acknowledged His kingship. Hatred or humility. Bitterness or faith.

Of the Twelve, only John dared attend the execution. Proud Peter had said he was willing to die for Jesus, but something broke inside him when Jesus refused to let him fight. He didn't understand why his Master had just turned Himself in. Despair clutched him, and outside Annas's house he denied three times that he even knew Jesus. Then he remembered that Jesus had actually predicted this betrayal, and Peter could hardly believe he was capable of stooping so low. Too late, he knew himself.

So while John stood watch at the cross, Peter wept in hiding, one inch from despair and suicide. Judas had already killed himself in too-tardy remorse for his treachery. Believing himself beyond forgiveness, he fulfilled his belief. But Jesus had prayed that Peter's faith would not utterly fail, and in the desperate hours a thread held.

On the other hand, the women of Jesus' entourage were not afraid to show their faces at the cross. Perhaps it was safer for them; no one paid attention to women anyway. Perhaps they had more faith, or more guts, than the men who were huddling in shock somewhere else. Certainly Jesus' mother didn't care whether the Sanhedrin boiled her in oil now that they were killing her Son. But Jesus cared, so He asked John to take her into his household.

That was His last piece of business. Ever since the previous night He had been carrying in His body the guilt of a worldful of perverted humans. Now the full cost of that burden closed in on Him. Evil dug an impassible gulf between the Evil Person and God. Yet now the Son of God was full to overflowing with the evil of the ages. For the first time in His existence, that dark gulf yawned between Him and His Father.

From eternity they had always been intimately one; now the Father was nowhere to be felt.

In the agony of abandonment Jesus found the energy to wail the first verse of Psalm 22: "My God, my God, why have you forsaken me?" It was a song of despair under persecution and divine rejection, yet it ended in a victory to which Jesus clung fiercely:

Posterity will serve him;
    future generations will be told about the Lord.
They will proclaim his righteousness
    to a people yet unborn—
for he has done it. (Psalm 22:30-31)

"For he has done it." The hour had come. It was about 3:00 p.m. on Friday afternoon, and the temple priests were getting ready to slaughter the Passover lambs. That night the Jews of Jerusalem would be feasting on roast lamb to celebrate their deliverance from slavery. A thin column of smoke rose from the temple as a signal that the lambs were about to die. Jesus asked for a sip of wine to rinse His parched mouth. He had one last word to say, and He wanted it to ring.

Tetelestai! Greek accountants scrawled this word across invoices every day. It literally meant "It is finished," but the point was "Paid in Full."

It was over. Peaceful at last, Jesus prayed Psalm 31:5, a song Jews often sang before going to bed: "Father, into your hands I commit my spirit."

The earth shook when its King died, and the heavy curtain that divided God's throne room from the rest of the temple tore from top to bottom.

Reversal

Although a member of the council, Joseph of Arimathea was conveniently absent from the Sanhedrin meeting that condemned Jesus. Perhaps he was not notified because he was known to be a follower of Jesus. At any rate, he and a Pharisee named Nicodemus risked the chief priests' ire by asking Pilate to let them bury Jesus' body. Joseph was quite well-off and spent a small fortune preparing the body as for a royal burial and interring it in his own rock-hewn tomb. The men had to rush the job because both Passover and the Sabbath started at sunset.

The Sanhedrin remembered Jesus had predicted He would rise from death on the third day, so they asked Pilate to post a guard at the tomb. He did.

It was a bleak Sabbath for the Eleven. They spent it huddled in a house, expecting that at the first moment of sunset they would hear the heavy feet of soldiers at the door. But Saturday night fell, and nothing. They were awakened at dawn, however, by the women disciples wailing that Jesus' body had been stolen. Peter and John ran to the tomb and found it empty except for the burial cloths. This was astounding, since the ointments with which the body was wrapped included resins that, when hardened, would have cemented the cloths to the corpse like lead. It would have taken strange robbers to spend the time to painstakingly—and with marginal success—peel the grave clothes off the body and carefully fold them.

The guards were nowhere to be found. They had run to the chief priests with a wild story about an earthquake at the tomb and an angel who rolled the heavy stone from the mouth of the cave. The priest bribed them to say they fell asleep and the disciples stole the body, and the soldiers agreed because they knew the priests could have them executed for failing in a mission.

Some hours later, one of the women returned to the disciples' hideout claiming she had seen Jesus risen from the dead, and others said they had seen angels. The men ridiculed this nonsense, but then that evening two disciples ran in claiming to have met Jesus on the road northwest of town.

At that very moment Jesus actually walked into their locked apartment. He demonstrated that He was not a ghost by eating in front of them. He also showed them His nail wounds, the evidence He would carry into eternity that He had entered the depths of human pain and triumphed in it. Then He began to explain why He had to be killed and raised from the dead. Finally, He kept the first installment of His promise about the Spirit.

> Again Jesus said, "Peace be with you! As the Father has sent me, I am sending you." And with that he breathed on them and said, "Receive the Holy Spirit. If you forgive anyone his sins, they are forgiven; if you do not forgive them, they are not forgiven." (John 20:21-23)

The Spirit had empowered Jesus to do amazing miracles; it was even by the Spirit's power that the Father had raised Jesus from death. But the first power these men needed as ambassadors of the true King was the ability to forgive.

28

A Movement Explodes

◆

Acts 1:1–8:40, 9:32–11:30

Preparation

During the forty days after His return from death, Jesus appeared frequently to groups of His followers. He also appeared to His brother James; many of His friends and relatives found it difficult to believe He was the King during His former life, but seeing Him back from the dead sure convinced them. He would appear and disappear like a ghost, but He was too solidly physical to seem like anything other than a live person.

He did not do what one might have expected: materialize in the high priest's office or the temple courts and demonstrate His resurrection beyond any doubt. That would have been coercion. If He'd done that, the leaders and people would have been forced to bow to Him even though their inner commitments were unchanged. They still would not love Him. If blatant power displays had not won the generations who saw Moses on Sinai and Elijah on Carmel, they would not win this granite-hearted bunch.

So instead, Jesus trained His followers to present the evidence about Him in such a way that it would invite a change of heart. Like the prophets before them, these apostles would be the King's friends sent to woo a maiden on His behalf. One day He would indeed come to claim His realm by force, but in the meantime His disciples would infiltrate enemy territory and seek recruits.

Then He vanished for the last time, warning His troops not to take action until the Spirit of God came on them to equip them for the job. They already had the Spirit's power to forgive; they still needed His power to testify.

For the next ten days, the 120 of Jesus' followers residing in Jerusalem spent their time almost constantly in prayer. The one thing we know they did was select a replacement for Judas in the Twelve. If there had been twelve tribes of Israel with twelve patriarchs, the group reasoned, there had to be twelve apostles to lead the new Israel.

The other way they probably passed that time was in dealing with unfinished business among them, and between them and God—putting that power of forgiveness into practice. Jesus had shown them how it was done. On the eve of His betrayal, three times Peter had denied he knew the rabbi. So during one of His post-Resurrection appearances, Jesus drew Peter aside and asked him three times, "Do you love Me?" Peter, no longer the macho freedom fighter who had sworn to stick by Jesus to the death, three times replied that, yes, he loved Jesus to the best of his human ability, but not perfectly. In no way perfectly. Yet each time Jesus reaffirmed His confidence in Peter by commissioning him, "Feed My lambs."

Peter certainly didn't deserve to be trusted as head of the team, but Jesus' forgiveness had the ability to transform anyone who let it touch him or her. Jesus' trust *made* Peter trustworthy.

Perhaps it was like that for the rest of the 120, as Simon the Zealot and Matthew the tax collector let supernatural forgiveness weld together men who could not naturally love each other. Jesus' brothers were welcomed into the community they had ridiculed. Everyone forgot the old debates about which of them would be the greatest in the Kingdom. And at least one of the Sons of Thunder, John, became an impassioned proponent of brotherly love and unity.

Pentecost

At any rate, ten days after Jesus' final disappearance came the Jewish Feast of Weeks. It had originally celebrated the beginning of the wheat harvest, but of late it had come to commemorate God's covenants. Greek-speaking Jews called the day Pentecost because it was fifty days after the Passover Sabbath (*pente koste* = fiftieth day). On this feast day, the biblical historian Luke tells us redundantly for emphasis that the 120 followers of Jesus "were all together in one place" (Acts 2:1). They were together spiritually as well as physically, for the power of forgiveness had done its work.

Into that place of unity, the Spirit of God burst as wind and fire. The power of testimony came upon the believers, and they began to proclaim the news about Jesus in the dozens of languages of the known world. At Babel God had confused human languages so as to crush the threat of unified evil; now He gave a token that He was beginning to reverse that process. A true unity of those filled with His Spirit would reknit for good what God had unraveled to prevent evil.

A hundred and twenty people shouting in different languages at the top of their lungs attracted attention. Pentecost had brought to Jerusalem pilgrims from everywhere Babylon and Greece had scattered Jews, and these pilgrims were astonished to hear amid the gibberish that someone was declaring wonders about God in their own obscure local dialects.

A crowd gathered, some snickering that the babblers were drunk. Eventually Peter made himself heard in Greek over the tumult. Jesus had said that the Spirit's power to drive out demons was evidence that the Kingdom was in Israel's midst (Matthew 12:28). Now Peter announced that this display was nothing other than the fulfillment of Joel's prophecy of the Day of the Lord:

"I will pour out my Spirit on all people.
Your sons and daughters will prophesy,
   your young men will see visions,
   your old men will dream dreams." (Acts 2:17)

Then Peter went on to explain how David had predicted that the Son of David would be recognized by His resurrection from death. The supernatural languages were evidence that Israel should believe the apostles' testimony that Jesus had in fact risen and was the long-awaited King. Peter pleaded with his audience to be baptized as a public sign that they were turning their allegiance to Jesus the King. This, Peter told them, was their only hope of survival.

About three thousand people took up Peter's offer. Most of them were just visiting for the feast, and within days they carried their news and their revolutionized lives home to all parts of Europe and the Middle East.

The Assembly in Jerusalem
Those who remained in Jerusalem carried on the apostles' custom of living as one big spiritual family. They ate, prayed, and learned together daily, and took responsibility to see that all of their group were adequately fed and housed. The richness of unity with God and each other was so satisfying that many thought nothing of selling their possessions to provide for the rest. All Jerusalem held them in awe because of the power and love in their midst.

First, Peter healed a cripple on the front steps of the temple and announced to the amazed onlookers that this was a sign that the man they had crucified as a criminal was in fact "the author of life," the rightful King, and the Prophet Moses had predicted. The Sadducees were irate. For one thing, they didn't believe resurrection was possible, and these apostles were claiming it had happened. Moreover, they were saying it had happened to a criminal the Sanhedrin had condemned just months before. Peter was accusing them of killing the Messiah; if the people believed that, how would they feel about their leaders?

Finally, it was ominously close to blasphemy for Peter to say of Jesus things like, "Salvation is found in no one else, for there is no other name under heaven given to men by which we must be saved" (Acts 4:12). To a Jew, the one name by which one might be saved from anything was the unpronounceable Name of God.

But the whole city had seen Peter heal the beggar, so the Sanhedrin could do no more than threaten him. This hostility only roused the little community of believers to aggressive praying for God to enable them to proclaim Jesus with even more boldness.

Awe

The next event that gave the citizens of Jerusalem pause was the sudden death of two members of the new sect. There was no hint of foul play; the couple dropped dead in public for lying to Peter (and God) about money they had promised to give for the community's poor. Members were free to keep their possessions if they chose to do so, but lying to the Holy Spirit brought instant death. With God so palpably in their midst, deceit was impossible.

That incident put an end to all but serious converts joining the community. People would carry their sick relatives into the streets when Peter passed, hoping his shadow would fall on them and heal them. But they wouldn't undergo baptism just for thrills and free food. It was too dangerous.

Some in the Sanhedrin wanted to stamp out the new sect by executing the apostles. Peter refused to yield to their threats, and he would certainly have gone the way of Jesus had not Gamaliel, the leading Pharisee on the council, intervened. Gamaliel reasoned that if the sect was merely of human origin it would be a flash in the pan like every other cultic movement in the past two hundred years. But if it was from God, then nothing could or should stop it. The rest of the Sanhedrin couldn't fight that logic, so the apostles went back to talking about Jesus both in the temple and in private homes.

The Hellenists

The Twelve might have gone on indefinitely with their little Jewish community in Jerusalem. Except for their unconventional ideas about Jesus, they were scrupulously observant Jews. Nobody could find fault with them. They were content to pray and teach among their fellow Jews in Jerusalem, enjoying the goodwill of their neighbors.

But God had other plans. So He let this ground-laying party go on for a few years, then brought it crashing down.

His instrument was the Hellenists—Jewish followers of Jesus whose primary language was Greek rather than Aramaic/Hebrew (*Hellas* is the Greek name for Greece). The Hebraists and the Hellenists were two distinct Jewish groups in Jerusalem, and soon they became two factions in the community of Jesus. The apostles were all Hebraists, so to keep peace they urged their Hellenist brethren to choose leaders from among themselves. The apostles would still take responsibility for teaching, but the Hellenist leaders would see to it that their people's needs were not overlooked.

At least one of the Hellenist leaders soon began showing the same signs of divine power as the apostles. But this man, Stephen, was not one to sit quietly in the temple week after week. Many Jews believed that the age of the Messiah would displace the age of the Law of Moses. Moreover, God had said repeatedly through the prophets that He was not bound to a building. So Stephen reasoned that if Jesus had come, then the age of the Law was past and the whole temple system might as well be dispensed with. Stephen hadn't quite worked out how Jesus' death had fulfilled the sacrificial system, but he had a gut feeling that there was no point to the system anymore.

When he said this to the other Jews in his synagogue, however, he met with fury. Nobody but the Sanhedrin much minded these guys claiming Jesus had risen from the dead and was the Messiah. But when they started speaking against the temple and the Law, they were coming against sacred cows. Stephen was dragged before the Sanhedrin, and when he called them stiff-necked murderers, the mob stoned him to death.

The Community's Walls Expand

This lynching triggered a general uprising of traditional Jews against the followers of Jesus. All of the Hellenist and most of the Hebraist believers had to flee Jerusalem; the apostles managed to stay because of their impeccable reputations. But this flight, which appeared to be the community's destruction, was actually a godsend. Jesus had told the apostles, "You will be my witnesses in Jerusalem, *and in all Judea and Samaria, and to the ends of the earth*" (Acts 1:8, emphasis added). The community had been too comfortable to venture out on the next stage of its assignment, but now it had no choice.

Once again the Hellenists led the mission. Philip, another Hellenist leader, had great success proclaiming Jesus in Samaria, especially since he backed up his claims with the apostolic signs of healing and casting out demons. Even so, Philip acknowledged the apostles' authority to approve his ministry. After all, these new believers were not Jews, the chosen people, but the traditionally hated cultic Samaritans. So Peter and John came and inspected the situation, decided it was in line with what Jesus had taught them, and gave the Samaritan believers their blessing. As public proof that the Samaritans were full members of the community, God gave them the Pentecost signs of the Holy Spirit's presence.

From Samaria, Philip went on to bring the news of Jesus to a black man sympathetic to Judaism—yet another radical move for a religious group that had come to define itself by its ethnic purity. Philip finally settled in Caesarea, the seat of

Roman government in Judea and hence a largely Gentile city. Proclaiming the good news in that region kept him busy for the next twenty years.

To the Gentiles

But God knew that if a Hellenist launched the mission to the Gentiles, the Hebraists would never accept it. So He gave Peter a vision and nearly drove him to Caesarea to tell a prominent Roman military man about Jesus. This man had long been praying to and serving the Jewish God, but to the Jews he was still a dirty pagan. Peter broke with deeply ingrained taboos by actually living and eating with this man's household, in addition to welcoming them into the community of Jesus.

The signs of Pentecost fell on them when they committed themselves to Jesus, so what could Peter do? This was his defense when the Hebraists back in Jerusalem demanded an explanation. And after hearing his story, they had to admit he was right. As incredible as it seemed, they had to admit that God wanted even the "inferior" races in His Kingdom.

It was a good thing they admitted this, for the Hellenists were launching full steam ahead into Gentile territory. When the persecution drove them from Jerusalem, some of them had settled in Antioch, the third-largest city in the empire and the capital of Syria. Before long, crowds of Antiochene Gentiles were dedicating themselves to this Savior called Jesus Christos. With no Jewish background, *Christos* (Messiah) meant nothing to them as a title (the Oiled One?), so they treated it as a last name. Unbelievers in Antioch soon nicknamed them *Christianoi*, followers of this guy Christos.

If Philip's work in Samaria had been radical for the Hebraists, this new Gentile community in Antioch was off the page. The half million residents of Antioch were a cosmopolitan bunch, and people in such large trading centers tended to assemble their own approaches to spirituality from the smorgasbord of available religious options. A little Greek philosophy, a little Persian dualism, a little from the ancestral cult, a little Judaism, or maybe one of the other newer, fashionable cults. Antioch's priestesses of Daphne were famed ritual prostitutes. There was no telling what the pagans of Antioch might do with the teachings of Christ.

Accordingly, the apostles sent one of their trusted leaders, Barnabas, to inspect the Antiochene work. Barnabas was so impressed that he not only conveyed his approval to Jerusalem but decided to settle in Antioch. People were converting right and left; there wasn't enough leadership to keep up with them. Eventually, Barnabas thought of a fellow Hebraist believer who would be an ideal partner in slapping this Gentile community into shape. His name was Saul.

29

The Adventures of Paul

◆

Acts 9:1-31, 12:1–14:27

Saul

When Stephen was raising the hair on the back of Jewish necks in Jerusalem, Saul was a student of Gamaliel, passionately attached to the Law, and already influential among the young rabbis. The Law asserted that anyone hanged on a tree (which included crucifixion) was under God's curse (Deuteronomy 21:23). According to this logic, it seemed that Jesus could not be the Messiah, and anyone who said He was, was blaspheming. This reasoning led to Stephen's stoning, a deed in which Saul played some leadership role. After that, he got himself appointed as a leader in stamping out the Jesus-blasphemy, arresting and executing dozens of believers.

Having all but exterminated the plague in Jerusalem, Saul took an official delegation to nip it in the bud in Damascus. (See map, page 363.) But somewhere along the 150-mile trip northward, a flash of light knocked him to the ground. He heard a voice: "Saul, Saul, why do you persecute Me?" The voice identified Itself as Jesus.

Saul's clever reasoning was undone. Blinded and shattered, he let himself be taken to Damascus, where he fasted for three days. He groped to make sense of his world. If the voice was Jesus, then Jesus was indeed the Messiah. If Jesus was the Messiah, then somehow the curse of crucifixion had been overcome. But why would the Messiah deliberately let Himself bear a curse? Moreover, if the Messiah had come, then was the age of the Law over? But how could one live without the Law?

After three days of this, a believer named Ananias arrived at Saul's lodging to lay hands on Saul. Jesus had appeared to Ananias in a vision and ordered him to restore Saul's sight and impart the Holy Spirit to him. Nothing short of a vision would have moved Ananias to approach Christian enemy number one, and even so Ananias argued with Jesus about the wisdom of this move.

But Jesus insisted that this persecutor would become one of His chief ambassadors: "I will show him how much he must suffer for my name" (Acts 9:16). Not a very encouraging promise, perhaps, but by this time Saul was a broken man, ready for anything.

Saul in Action

The first thing Saul did after recovering his strength was make the rounds of the synagogues proclaiming Jesus as the Son of God. This claim from the man notorious for leading the Jerusalem persecution was electrifying. First electrifying, then infuriating for those who tried to refute him. For Saul knew the Jewish Scriptures backward and forward, and could argue Jesus' messiahship from any passage his opponents chose. He did this for more than two years in Damascus and the surrounding district of Arabia until the Jews were at last so enraged that they plotted to kill him. His followers had to smuggle him out of the city.

Next he traveled to Jerusalem, where the believers who remembered their martyred friends would have nothing to do with him. Eventually Barnabas saw the potential in Saul and convinced the apostles to accept him. Once part of the community, Saul launched his confrontational persuasion tactics in the synagogues until murder plots started surfacing again. Again Saul was smuggled out of town, and this time the community told him to go back to his hometown of Tarsus and lie low. He was still too much the same arrogant hothead he had always been, and he needed his rough edges smoothed before he could accomplish anything useful. This training period went on for years until Barnabas arrived to invite him to Antioch.

Antioch's Leadership Team
The believers in Jerusalem were organized under the leadership of the twelve apostles plus some "elders." This was a natural system since synagogues were run by teams of elders. It was unheard of to have one man in charge.

Antioch seems to have adopted a similar team approach; at one point we read of five men called "prophets and teachers" making certain decisions for the citywide believing community. As in Jerusalem, much of their teaching, worship, and practice of life in Christ probably went on in homes and workplaces, but in some way the small cells were linked under their leadership team. Barnabas was a member—perhaps the most prominent one—of the Antiochene team. Saul became the fifth member when Barnabas brought him in to assist in teaching the Jewish Scriptures, the truths about Christ, and the lifestyle of a believer.

When Saul had been in Antioch for some months, some prophets arrived from Jerusalem. Prophets evidently functioned as official emissaries from the apostles, as well as bearers of messages from God. Like the prophets of Israel, they spoke God's current word to the community on matters about the present and the future. But because the Holy Spirit now inhabited every believer, these New-Covenant prophets no longer bore the sole responsibility for hearing from God. Antioch's leadership team included prophets (Barnabas and/or Saul may have served that function), but Jerusalem's prophets seem to have served alongside the leadership.

At any rate, one of the Jerusalem prophets, Agabus, told the Antiochene community that the empire was about to undergo famine. Judea was particularly at risk. The Antiochenes decided to show their love for their Judean brethren by sending aid. As Jews who had lived in Jerusalem, Barnabas and Saul were the natural choices for emissaries. (As it turned out, famine hit various parts of the empire successively during this decade. Judea suffered severely in AD 46 and 47.)

Barnabas and Saul seized this chance to report to the Jerusalem leadership on the work in Antioch. Everyone agreed that it was crucial to prevent two distinct branches of the faith from developing: a Jewish one based in Jerusalem and a Gentile one based in Antioch. So they came to an agreement about the essentials of their message, "the good news," or "gospel" as they called it. They also agreed that while there was only one community and one message of Christ, the Antiochene team (especially Saul) would be responsible for getting the message to the Gentiles, while the Jerusalem team (headed by Peter) would take responsibility for the Jews, particularly in and around Palestine.

An Apostolic Team

This idea of getting the message to the Gentiles burned in the hearts of the Antiochene group. Their approach to strategic planning was to spend extended periods of time fasting, praying, and worshiping God. In the midst of one such session, one or more of the prophets received instructions from the Holy Spirit. Barnabas and Saul were to be set apart for a new task: to take a mobile team westward into areas where the gospel had never been proclaimed.

The two of them set out with Barnabas's cousin John Mark. Their plan was to go to cities as the Holy Spirit led and to find a synagogue in each one. Up to this point, the gospel had been most successful among Gentiles who either had fully converted to Judaism or sympathized with Jewish beliefs but had not yet undergone the rites of conversion. Also, God had laid down a principle that the truth must be offered to the chosen race first before it was proclaimed among the nations. The Jews still deserved a chance to take up their ancient assignment to be lights to the Gentiles.

Saul had the rare privilege of being a Jew born with Roman citizenship. His family must have had some standing in his hometown to have won that right. As a citizen, he had a Roman name as well as his Jewish one. His Roman surname was Paulus, and when he left Antioch to proclaim Christ to the Gentiles, he decided to use that name rather than one that advertised his Jewishness. One of his basic principles of ministry was to adapt to the culture he wanted to reach in every way possible. He wouldn't compromise his morals, of course, but in nonessentials like food, clothing, customs, and even his name he was committed to "going native" in order not to obscure his message.

A curious shift occurred as Barnabas, Paul, and Mark traveled from city to city. When they left Antioch, Barnabas was the ranking team member. But it soon became clear that Paul was the more gifted spokesman and that God was choosing to work more miracles of power through Paul than Barnabas. Without debate, Paul became the senior partner.

Moreover, during this trip the biblical account shifts from calling the partners "prophets" or "teachers" to labeling them "apostles." Paul and Barnabas began to realize God had given them a commission parallel to the Twelve's. They were apostles to the Gentiles. No one would challenge the Twelve's special status, since they had actually been with Jesus, but Paul and Barnabas were now serving as "sent ones" with apostolic authority and even the signs of power—blinding a sorcerer and healing a lame man—to back it up.

So the local team in Antioch had spawned something new: a mobile apostolic team for spreading the gospel to places it had never touched. The threesome journeyed to the island of Cyprus, then sailed to the coast of Asia Minor. Young Mark had had enough of the grueling missionary lifestyle by that time and took a boat to Jerusalem. But Paul and Barnabas hiked inland to and around the region of Phrygian Galatia.

Every Sabbath they would visit a synagogue, and as learned Jews from Jerusalem they would naturally be invited to speak on the passage of Scripture for the day. Invariably Paul would use the passage as a springboard to announce the Messiah. He consistently won over Gentile converts and sympathizers, but the Jews were usually furious and ran the team out of town. However, the expulsion normally didn't take place until a tiny new community of believers had been established.

Homeward Bound

After planting seeds in seven towns, the pair retraced their steps to visit each cell group. Along with impressing on the new disciples the basic truths they needed to remember, the team had a word of tough encouragement: "We must go through many hardships to enter the kingdom of God" (Acts 14:22). It was not going to be easy to follow Christ in towns where the community of faith numbered maybe a dozen, where the Gentiles scorned people who accepted only one God, and where the Jews viewed the new sect as a wicked heresy.

In each city, Paul and Barnabas selected a few of the most responsible new believers to serve as elders. It wasn't ideal to put raw recruits in charge of a platoon, but there weren't any alternatives. And these people had the Holy Spirit just like every other disciple, so the apostles trusted Him to mature the new plants however He chose.

What with the snail's pace of ancient travel and the time needed to establish new cells, this trip probably took a couple of years. But sometime in AD 48, the mobile team arrived back in Antioch, flush with victory, to report to their home community. There they stayed for probably more than a year.

No doubt they needed the rest. Road life in the ancient world was not first class. A very rich man might rent a carriage, but exactly two means of travel were available to anyone else: a ship by sea, or one's two feet by land. (Horses were extremely hard to ride since stirrups and real saddles had not yet been invented.)

The Roman roads were pretty good and relatively safe; at least there were no pillaging armies, although bandits were inevitable. And about every twenty-two miles was an inn.

But twenty-two miles a day is a stiff pace on foot. If the road was hilly, the weather wet or muddy, or the morning start delayed, Paul and Barnabas no doubt camped in the open. Heat or illness could weaken them; snow could block a mountain pass; hail, flooding, and wild animals could be life-threatening. The road across Asia Minor (modern Turkey) crosses a plateau that averages 3,000 feet of elevation, and is twice that in some sections. Temperatures rise and plummet dramatically.

Furthermore, the inns were not exactly the Ritz. Most were bare courtyards surrounded by rooms. Baggage and animals shared the courtyard with livestock drivers, who slept around dried dung fires. If Paul and Barnabas were low on funds, they would probably have slept with them. If they had more money, they could rent a bed in a room along with several strangers who snored, or who might steal their possessions while they slept. There was also the inevitable colony of bedbugs.

If a traveler wanted food from a local peasant, he had to pay for it. Paul was trained as a leather worker, but it took time to ply the trade. Yet Paul preferred to avoid mooching off the people he was introducing to Christ, so the team probably spent stretches of time working to earn money to finance the next leg of their trip.

With land travel so slow and hazardous, one might think people would have traveled by sea whenever possible. But because ships of the day were at the mercy of prevailing winds, east-to-west sailing was exasperatingly slow. Paul preferred to walk west and sail east. Further, passenger ships were rare, and cargo ships took passengers only when they had room. Paul and Barnabas would have to find one going in their direction, haggle with the owner over the fee, then wait until the captain had judged both winds and omens to be favorable. (Sailors were even more superstitious than landsmen.)

On board, passengers took turns cooking their own food in the galley after the crew was fed; the captain generously furnished water. A stray splash or rough seas might mean no fire for the evening. There was no way to refrigerate meat, so ships planned to dock at least every few nights. But if a storm or long voyage delayed docking, only grain would be edible.

Few ships had cabins, so passengers lived on deck with only the sail for shade and shelter. Experienced travelers brought tents for nights when the ship docked at a port with no inn.

Shipwreck and damage were common. Violent storms made winter sailing suicidal, but even in spring and fall sailing was a risk. Yet Paul was willing to take it. In the course of his life, in addition to trudging about 1,795 miles overland on missionary journeys, he also logged about 1,290 miles by sea.

In a letter some years later, Paul mentioned that an illness first brought him to preach in Galatia (Galatians 4:13). This may have been a preexisting condition, but weeks of exposure, hunger, thirst, sea sickness, and hard hiking might drop even a strong man in his tracks.

30

Breaking the Culture Barrier

◆

Acts 15:1–16:5, Galatians

A Matter of Principle

The community at Antioch was no doubt honored to receive such a visitor as the Apostle Peter. And Peter was as pleased with the work in Antioch as Paul and Barnabas knew he would be. The leadership team had done an amazing job of translating the gospel into terms Gentiles could understand (lacking Jewish background on terms like *Messiah* and *Kingdom of God*) without distorting the essential message. The Way of Jesus had not degenerated into one more Greek cult that promised immortality through contact with the divine.

And Peter, who had received a vision from Christ repealing the *kosher* laws, was quite comfortable socializing with Gentile believers. If Jesus Himself said so, then the long-standing Jewish prejudice against filthy pagans was null and void.

But then a delegation arrived claiming the authority of James, the ranking member of Jerusalem's leadership team. These visitors bore a new policy: One could not belong to the people of God unless one adhered to all of the traditions of Jewish law, including circumcision. One had to be a Jew to be a disciple of Jesus.

Further, they told Peter privately that his behavior in Antioch was threatening efforts to spread the gospel back home. The apostles had been enjoying great favor among their Jewish kinsmen because they were known to be faithful observers of the Law. Peter was undercutting that reputation by openly flouting the *kosher* laws. Would he please rein in his own freedom for the sake of reaching the Jews?

Certainly Peter would do that, and immediately he withdrew from sharing meals with Gentiles. Under pressure from the delegation, the rest of the Jewish believers in Antioch followed suit. Even Barnabas. But not Paul. He was incensed.

Peter may have been the chief apostle, but in Paul's eyes he was just a brother and not above reproof. And since his fault was public and influencing many, his reproof had to be public, too. For by bowing to Jewish scruples—even in order to draw them to Christ—Peter was compromising an essential point of the gospel and endangering efforts to reach Gentiles. Peter's withdrawal implied that Gentiles were second-class believers. It suggested that Peter supported the delegation's whole position about having to become a Jew in order to be a child of God.

Faith or Religious Rules

Barnabas and the rest hadn't thought through the implications of this position, but Paul had been thinking about the Law for a long time. Look, he said, if you won't even eat with these Gentiles, you're pretty much saying that they're not part of the family. Therefore, you're saying that something other than committing one's life to Christ is necessary to join God's family. You're saying we need two saviors: Christ plus the rules.

But we've already admitted that keeping the Law never got us anywhere. We could never keep it well enough to satisfy God. That was why Christ died: to take the place of us lawbreakers. And we died with Him, so the Jewish Law no longer applies to us as dead people. We live with His life now, obeying God by the power of the Spirit within us. By all means, let's pursue the moral character to which the Spirit draws us—love, joy, self-control. But the ritual laws of circumcision and diet are irrelevant. At best they don't make us more like Jesus, and at worst they divide the community and deny that Christ's mercy alone is sufficient.

What got to Paul was that Peter and the rest already knew all this. They were just afraid to come out and say that belief in and commitment to Christ alone, not keeping the rules of a religious culture, were what God required. And they were afraid because part of them cared more about what people thought than what God thought.

But the part of them that really cared about God was stung by Paul's rebuke. Peter, Barnabas, and the other Antiochenes immediately saw the truth. However, the delegation did not. Hot debates got nowhere, so at last it was decided to send Paul and Barnabas to Jerusalem to sort the issue out.

Conference at Jerusalem

Not just the leadership team, but most or all of the Jerusalem community gathered to weigh a matter with such huge implications. The bulk of public opinion leaned toward the Law party. But Paul's accounts of the miracles God had done among the Gentiles were powerful, and Peter redeemed himself by siding with Paul. He reminded the assembly of the incident with the Roman soldier and concluded his speech with a question, Why put a yoke on the Gentiles that we have never been able to bear? Both we and they are saved by Christ's unearned work in our lives. Period.

When James—a man known to be zealous in observing the Law—was convinced, his influence swayed the assembly to consensus. James proposed that the council circulate a letter to avoid any confusion or misrepresentation. That letter would free the Gentiles from Jewish rules but would ask them to avoid three practices that Jews found especially difficult to tolerate. Paul himself didn't see anything immoral in two of the practices (eating meat used in pagan sacrifices or meat from which the blood had not been fully drained), but he agreed that Gentile believers could go that far in restraining their freedom for love of their Jewish brethren. The third requirement—avoiding sexual immorality—Paul agreed was a moral absolute, not a cultural preference.

This landmark conference gave the transcultural Christian community two bedrock principles. First, the religious rules of one group, no matter how hallowed by time, must not hinder another group's freedom to serve Christ by the Spirit. But second, it may sometimes be entirely appropriate for a group to voluntarily limit its freedom out of love for another group.

Paul on the Move Again
The Jerusalem community dispatched two of their own prophets to accompany Paul and Barnabas in delivering the letter to Antioch. Paul got on so well with one of those prophets, Silas, that a few months later he invited Silas to join him as a new partner. Paul and Barnabas had been planning to revisit the communities they had founded, but a disagreement told them it was time to part ways. So now there were two apostolic teams sent out from Antioch: Barnabas and his nephew Mark; and Paul and Silas.

We know little about Barnabas's movements during the following years, but a great deal about Paul's. First he revisited each of his plantings to see if knowing Christ was having the desired effect upon the people's lives. Considering that the fledgling communities had had no one but the Holy Spirit to nurture them for at least eighteen months, it was remarkable how healthy they were.

In one town Paul found a teenage believer eager to join the traveling team. As an uncircumcised half-Jew, Timothy had faced identity crises all his life—he was fully welcome among neither Jews nor Gentiles. Now for the first time he belonged to someone—Jesus—and despite his shyness he longed to leave his hometown behind to serve his new Master. Paul was glad to have him. But in order to solve Timothy's neither-fish-nor-fowl problem, Paul circumcised him. For Paul the rite no longer had a major spiritual significance, but he was all for anything that would dissolve social barriers to the gospel. If Timothy would be more effective as a full Jew, fine. Circumcising Gentiles, of course, was another matter.

Letter to Galatia

At some point during these years—perhaps even before the Jerusalem council—Paul had to hit the Judaism issue head on in Timothy's hometown and the other Galatian communities. The same sorts of legalists who misled Peter in Antioch were confusing Gentile believers in Galatia. (See map, page 362.) These "Judaizers" even questioned whether Paul was an apostle at all.

Paul was of course furious when he heard that his fledgling Galatian charges were being told to adhere to Jewish religious rules. In a scathing letter he defended his apostleship, rebuked the Galatians for listening to hogwash, and laid down the essence of his view of the gospel. The Spirit of God is active in your lives (he told the Galatians) because you believed in Christ, not because you kept religious rules. Christ bore the lawbreaker's curse for you, so that you could live freely by the Spirit. Therefore, the Spirit will continue to work in you, making you more loving, as you actively yield to the Spirit's influence and say no to the impulses of your selfish nature. Persistently obeying the Spirit will accomplish what nitpicking about rules cannot possibly do.

He continued, "As for those agitators [urging circumcision], I wish they would go the whole way and emasculate themselves!" (Galatians 5:12). Paul was on most matters incredibly humble and gentle, but like Jesus, he pulled no punches with people who corrupted the essentials of God's message.

More than any other man of his day, Paul understood what God had been doing ever since Eden. God had chosen a people not to huddle together in their cultural superiority, but to be a lamp in the blackness of paganism. He'd had a purpose in separating Israel geographically, ethnically, and culturally; He had to protect a group long enough for some basic concepts (one God, holiness, the Messiah) to take root. Now the time had come to scatter the people of God, to send them—equipped with the message of Christ and with the Holy Spirit—into the streets and the nations. Just as Jesus had sought out the sick over the healthy, the rough over the nice people, so Paul was committed to the Gentiles with all their unpleasant habits and funny accents. And he wasn't interested in adapting them to the religious culture he found comfortable. He was interested in renovating their hearts.

C·H·A·P·T·E·R

31

Strategic Bases

◆

Acts 16:6–19:41, 1 and 2 Thessalonians

Macedonia

Paul's mission strategy was a combination of shrewd planning and careful listening to the Holy Spirit. For some weeks Paul, Silas, and Timothy plodded uncertainly across Asia Minor as the Spirit kept saying, "Not here" and "Not that way." Well, which way do You want us to go then? At last, word came in a vision: Macedonia.

So they sailed for the rugged land north of Greece and a few days later found themselves in the Roman colony of Philippi. (See map, page 362.) "Roman colony" meant that the town was wall-to-wall Italian war veterans thoroughly bigoted against Jews. There wasn't even a synagogue in town, only a spot outside the gates where a few women gathered to pray.

That was good enough for Paul. He found the prayer spot, and it wasn't long before one of the gathering, a wealthy businesswoman named Lydia, believed the message and invited the team to stay in her home. Her entire extensive household followed her lead. Overnight Philippi had a Christian community.

281

The biblical account of how the gospel spread from Jerusalem to Rome is called The Acts of the Apostles. It is the second of a two-volume history by a doctor named Luke. (The Gospel of Luke is his first volume; it recounts the work of God from just before Jesus' birth to His resurrection. The Acts picks up the story at that point.)

Luke focused on Paul's work because he was a colleague and sometime companion of Paul. He may have been from Antioch, or perhaps the seaport of Troas, or even Philippi. At any rate, at the point where he describes the sea voyage from Troas to Macedonia, Luke begins to speak of "we" instead of "they." He was an eyewitness to the events at Philippi as well as later events in his book, and it was probably through watching Paul that Luke came to appreciate how the Holy Spirit operated.

In fact, Acts could equally be called "The Acts of the Holy Spirit." Luke's first volume described how Jesus fulfilled His mission to proclaim good news to the poor and freedom for the captives; his second recounted how the Holy Spirit picked up that job after Jesus' departure and fulfilled it through ordinary people.

But could Paul really be called ordinary? When he was in Philippi, a lynch mob, an arrest on a charge of anti-Roman proselytizing, a merciless flogging, and a miraculous escape from prison were all in a day's work. Hounded out of that town, the team hiked another hundred miles to Thessalonica, the capital of Macedonia, where another mob attacked them after a mere three weeks. (See map, page 362.) The seedling community smuggled the team fifty miles away, but some Thessalonian Jews pursued them until Paul had to flee Macedonia entirely.

Greece
Paul sailed south to Athens while Silas and Timothy stayed in Berea to solidify the work there as best they could. To pass the time, Paul talked about Christ with anybody who would lis-

ten, but made little headway. Beautiful Athens held a mystique won five centuries earlier by a generation of brilliant poets, artists, philosophers, and statesmen. But now Athens's laurels were faded: the best philosophy students sought other universities; the best artists worked elsewhere. Yet second-rate scholars abounded, and what they lacked in creative thinking they more than made up for in pride. They could tell in a minute that Paul lacked the genteel accents of a cultured gentleman, and that his doctrines were backwater notions far from the fashionable views of educated men. On the whole, they were much less concerned with whether his ideas were true than with whether they were "in."

Silas and Timothy arrived eventually, but Paul was more concerned about the Macedonian newborns than with Athenian snobs. It was a lot to expect of people who had known Christ for bare weeks to withstand contempt and even outright violence from their neighbors. Paul grieved to think his seedlings might have collapsed under pressure. So he immediately dispatched Timothy to check on the Thessalonian community and Silas to visit Philippi. He himself set off down the Greek peninsula to Corinth. (See map, page 362.)

Corinth was Greece's political and economic hub, as it commanded both the land route through Greece and the sea route from Italy to anywhere east. Its population of some 250,000 free persons plus 400,000 slaves included every nationality in the known world crowded into a few bustling square miles. The temple of Aphrodite attracted tourists and sailors to its sacred prostitutes, who catered to any taste. In fact, the general tenor of the town prompted a Greek slang term: to "Corinthianize" meant "to practice sexual immorality."

Paul was overjoyed to meet some Jewish believers in Corinth. Priscilla and Aquila had left Rome a year or so earlier when Emperor Claudius expelled all Jews from that city because of riots instigated by someone named "Chrestus." At least, that was the way the Romans saw it. It's not unlikely that Jewish followers of Christ had reached Rome and caused the same tumult Stephen had raised in Jerusalem and Paul in nearly every city he visited. But the Romans could make nothing of this Jewish dispute; all they cared about was public order.

At any rate, here in Corinth were a couple of seasoned troops for Paul to ally with. Amazingly, they were leatherworkers just as he was—a perfect match. For a while the new team supported themselves making tents and other leather goods. Their business was an ideal forum for exposing customers and neighbors to Christ, and they could spend their Sabbaths discussing Jesus in the synagogue.

Letters to Thessalonica
Eventually, Silas and Timothy returned from Macedonia with good news and money. The good news was that both Thessalonica and Philippi were standing firm against bitter hostility. The money came from Philippi; the Philippian community wanted to be full partners with Paul in the work of spreading the gospel. They knew their main task was to attract their neighbors to Christ by the way they lived. Paul carried the message across cultural and geographical lines, converted whoever was ready to respond, and moved on; then the local group would continue to expand in its sphere of influence. That was the standard strategy. But the Philippians also wanted to support Paul's work with prayer and money. They were his first planting to think of that.

Paul must have been overjoyed to receive this financial gift. For one thing, it meant that the Philippian group was healthy enough to be caring about God's wider purposes, not just personal needs. For another, it meant Paul could devote himself full time to talking about Christ instead of spending long hours at leatherworking.

He may well have sent Silas back to Philippi with a thank-you note, but if he did, it no longer exists. We do, however, have two letters Paul sent to Thessalonica about this time; Timothy played courier for the next six months or so.

Those letters gush with Paul's pride over his spiritual children and his longing to see them again. Evidently, news of the Thessalonians' tough faith in the face of suffering had spread in unexpected directions around the empire, for Thessalonica was a busy seaport. In a world full of cults, this group stood out for its love and commitment despite the odds.

The letters also stress the model Paul tried to set. In 1 Thessalonians 2 he wrote, "We are not trying to please men but God" (verse 4); "We could have been a burden to you, but we were gentle among you" (verses 6-7); "We loved you so much that we were delighted to share with you not only the gospel of God but our lives as well" (verse 8); and "We worked night and day in order not to be a burden to anyone" (verse 9). Such attitudes, along with the courage to face persecution, would give the Thessalonian believers credibility among their skeptical neighbors. Paul knew preaching like his could not touch those leathery hearts, but the changed life of a kinsman or coworker would gain Christ a hearing. So "how to live in order to please God" (1 Thessalonians 4:1)—an ethical, loving lifestyle—was his theme.

What undergirded that lifestyle was the hope that set the believers apart from the pagans around them. Their response to a loved one's death, for instance, could be confidence rather than despairing grief because they knew Jesus' promises about the future. Some unknown day, Jesus would return for His own, the dead ones would be raised to life, and all believers would be caught up to be with Jesus forever. God's people need never say permanent goodbyes. This certainty of resurrection could enable the Thessalonians to resist futile sensuality, face martyrdom calmly, and handle tragedy in ways that would make the pagans take notice.

In his second letter, Paul also responded to some prophecy or letter that was supposed to have come from him. Paul was reputedly saying that the Day of the Lord—the day of Jesus' return—had already come. No, said Paul, that would not happen until "the man of lawlessness" appeared, proclaimed himself God, and convinced many by working miracles. Paul's comments about this man of lawlessness (an evil world leader?) seem cryptic because in his letter he was simply alluding to things he'd said at length in person.

That's the hardest thing about interpreting the letters in the Bible. They were written to specific groups in specific situations, and all we have in each case is a small slice of an ongoing two-way discussion. It's like listening to part of one side of a telephone conversation and trying to figure out what's going on.

Legal Precedent

Compared to his stops in other towns up to this point, Paul spent an unusually long time in Corinth: a year and a half. Perhaps his (or God's) reasoning was that Corinth should become the kind of base for regional outreach that Antioch was in Syria. Trading hubs like those made ideal bases because people and information flowed through them so rapidly.

Paul's success in drawing key members of the Jewish community to Christ (including an important synagogue official and a wealthy Gentile sympathizer) made him a stench in the Jews' nostrils, but they were unable to stage the kind of lynch mob that had been so effective in Thessalonica. Plan B was to bring charges against Paul in the Roman court. Freedom of religion was not an automatic right; a religion had to be explicitly authorized to be legal. Judaism was legal, and the Way of Jesus had always been seen as a Jewish sect. However, the Corinthian Jews insisted it was not Judaism at all, and therefore was not legal.

But to the Roman governor it seemed that both Paul and his accusers were Jews, and their argument had to do with Jewish doctrines. In refusing to try the case, he unknowingly set a precedent. For almost a decade more—a crucial period— the messengers of Christ had a precious legal umbrella. Had Gallio ruled against Paul, Christianity might have become immediately outlawed throughout the empire while it was still possibly too young to survive statewide persecution. A decade later, the fire would be too big to stamp out.

Personal Business

To say that Paul protested imposing Jewish rules on Gentiles is not to say that he himself turned his back on the customs he grew up with. Toward the end of his stay in Corinth, he made a vow as an act of thanksgiving and devotion to God (as prescribed in Numbers 6:1-21). The vow required that he visit Jerusalem to offer a sacrifice in the temple—Paul evidently saw nothing wrong with such Jewish rites. So he spent the spring and summer of AD 52 sailing to Jerusalem, visiting his friends in Antioch, hiking across Asia Minor with stops at the communities he'd planted, and finally arriving in Ephesus perhaps as winter was shutting down travel for the year.

Ephesus

Ephesus promised to be another strategic base for outreach, like Antioch and Corinth. It was the queen of the rich Roman province of Asia. Through her port passed goods from China and the eastern provinces bound for Italy. Wide avenues, huge public buildings and squares, and luxurious private homes were all designed to impress tourists. A hundred local aristocrats owned most of the land around Ephesus and controlled the city government. However, the strength of the city was its large class of merchants, businessmen, and craftsmen. These people might be barely better fed than day laborers, nearly as wealthy as aristocrats, or somewhere in between, but none of them had any say in the government unless he was a "client" of one of the ruling hundred.

The business/working class tended to be politically dissatisfied and interested in any kind of new religion, so it was a fertile field for the messengers of Christ. Back in the spring, Paul had left Priscilla and Aquila in Ephesus on his way east, and by the time he returned in the fall, they were already hard at work with their leather business as a base for contacting their target group. They had met a sophisticated Egyptian Jew who had learned some distorted version of the gospel in his hometown of Alexandria (where one of the empire's premier universities was always churning out the latest in esoteric philosophy). Once Priscilla and Aquila set him straight, Apollos turned out to be a gifted spokesman. He eventually moved on to Corinth to assist in teaching believers and debating unbelieving Jews.

A City in Turmoil

Paul spent three months appealing to the Ephesian Jews until their hostility drove him to shift his base from the synagogue to a lecture hall. He spent the normal working hours making tents with his partners, and the siesta time of 11:00 a.m. to 4:00 p.m. teaching about Christ. He attracted a great following among the working class for his teaching, backing it up by miraculous healings and exorcisms. Ephesus was a hotbed of the occult, and Paul's miracle-working was just what many Ephesians needed to draw their attention. Supernatural power was something they took seriously. New converts burned a small fortune (more than two hundred years' wages for a laborer) in books of sorcery, and news about Christ spread throughout the metropolis and the surrounding area.

In fact, Paul's team was so successful during its two-year stay in this strategic city that its efforts rocked the local economy. In a fragile system like Ephesus, this nearly spelled political disaster. Here's how it went:

Nearly every man in the business/working class belonged to a club with other men in his profession. Although these were social clubs, not political parties, Rome sometimes outlawed them because they encouraged sedition. The shipwrights or the weavers often rioted when they felt their interests threatened, for there was no peaceful, legal means of petitioning the government. Now one day a silversmith named Demetrius decided that his business was slumping because people weren't buying as many silver shrines of

Artemis as they used to. He blamed the decline on Paul, who claimed the goddess Artemis was no goddess at all. Demetrius got the men of his club stirred up about this, and soon others in related trades joined them.

The issue wasn't just silverworking; it was a matter of civic pride that touched the number one industry: tourism. Of the dozens of gaudy temples in Ephesus, the greatest was dedicated to Artemis. It was the biggest tourist attraction in half the empire: resplendent with 127 marble pillars inlaid with gold; crammed with works by the world's leading artists; mobbed with sightseers, especially during the May fertility festival. Idolatry was big business, and Paul's preaching threatened it.

As happens in an already discontented ghetto, it took almost no time for a riot to erupt. Crowds chanted "Great is Artemis of the Ephesians!" in the streets, and one of Paul's team members was identified, seized, and carried bodily into the open-air theater. Paul wanted to address the mob, but he had a friend or two among the city's ruling aristocrats, and they begged him not to enter the theater. In the end, one of the top city officials managed to silence the crowd, but only with threats of Roman intervention. This was no idle warning; Rome was known to suppress riots ruthlessly.

Lynching was averted, but Paul knew he had reached the end of his welcome in Ephesus. The end of his job as well. He and his team had launched a fine, healthy community; it could carry on spreading the gospel to neighbors and coworkers, while the mobile team moved on to untouched ground.

32

Crisis in Corinth

◆

Acts 20:1-3, 1 and 2 Corinthians

Bad news

If Paul had had nothing else to do in Ephesus but make a living and nurture former occultists in the ways of Jesus, he would have had his hands full. But he was also keeping tabs on affairs in the other cities he'd worked in. Most of his seedlings were apparently flourishing, despite hostile soil. But the Corinthian group became a nuisance during his last year in Ephesus.

First came news that a member of the community had a sexual alliance with his father's wife (presumably not his mother). Paul wrote to Corinth with instructions not to associate with someone like that; blatant incest of a kind that shocked even pagans brought disgrace on the people of God.

Sometime later a believer named Chloe visited Paul in Ephesus and brought more discouraging news. The Corinthian group was splitting into factions, each of which claimed some prominent Christian leader as its authority. Several of the factions expressed contempt for Paul and his messages telling them what to do. Then three Corinthians brought

292 / CRISIS IN CORINTH

Paul a letter from the whole community. This letter was full
of questions about various issues, but the messengers also
reported that the incest was continuing, and class snobbery
and other cancers were infecting the church. In response to
these ills, Paul dictated a second and very long letter—the one
we call 1 Corinthians.

Corinth may have had a reputation for loose morals, but
it was also known for money and intellectual pride. It was rich
in commerce and prostitution, and its upper classes tended to
have pretensions of philosophy. Predictably, wealth, loose
morals, and intellectual pride lay at the root of the troubles in
the Corinthian church.

Wisdom and Foolishness
Paul tackled the pride first. The anti-Paul factions apparently
regarded him as an inferior apostle compared to Peter and
Apollos. That both of these men were honorable apostles Paul
agreed,[1] but the Corinthians entirely misunderstood what that
job implied. To them, an apostle held the community's highest rank, with the people deciding who was and who wasn't
one. The criteria included an air of authority, talent at public
speaking, philosophical sophistication, and an impressive
appearance. Paul's sin was that he lacked stage presence.

He scoffed at this attitude. First of all, God turned up His
nose at sophistication; He had always deliberately chosen the
weak and foolish to fulfill His plan so that nobody would try
to take credit. Anybody who thought his brains or talents were
earning a place in God's front office needed to go back to
sweeping floors.

Second, Paul deliberately avoided using a slick presenta-
tion to attract converts. He wanted people to commit themselves because they witnessed the power of the Holy Spirit in
their midst and fell in love with the crucified Christ, not
because Paul's performance wowed them.

It wasn't that God's truth was so simple that any fool
could understand it. It was that the kind of wisdom necessary

to understand it was not intellectual. IQ made no difference. God's truth required the wisdom of humility. Apostleship wasn't some grand rank that one could lord over everybody else. It meant one had to excel at unselfish service, refuse to compare himself to others, take no interest in a pecking order, and accept weakness, dishonor, hunger, homelessness, and slander. In God's upside-down system, the ranking office was to be "scum of the earth" (1 Corinthians 4:13). When the Corinthians understood that, they would be ready to be taught some of God's "sophisticated" truths.

Discipline

Next, Paul explained his views on handling immorality. These people who were so proud of their religious knowledge were still unmoved by a case of open incest. Paul repeated that they should expel the offender from their group until he stopped his offense. This wasn't a matter of a besetting sin that someone was struggling against and occasionally giving in to. It was a coolly chosen lifestyle. The community needed to withdraw its spiritual protection so that Satan could have free access to inflict the natural consequences of flagrant evil. The Corinthians would actually be doing the man a favor, since suffering might be the only thing that would bring him to his senses.

Furthermore, excising the cancer would keep it from infecting others in the group. Paul clarified what he'd said about avoiding the immoral. He didn't mean avoiding immoral pagans; all pagans were immoral, and God's people were called to reach out to them. Rather, he meant avoiding believers (or those who claimed to believe) who practiced gross sin without a blush.

The community needed to be serious about exercising discipline. Paul was shocked that people had to take fellow believers to court to get justice because the community wouldn't even discipline swindlers. Paul wasn't encouraging a cult attitude where the group should correct every deviation from its norms. Almost always, God was the trainer and judge, not people. But in glaring cases like adultery, idolatry, theft, and slander, the community needed to step in.

Sex and Marriage
The fact is, Corinthian society made it hard to have healthy views on sex. Visiting prostitutes was standard recreation. Nobody thought twice about it. So Paul had to explain why God forbade something as apparently harmless and fun as extramarital sex.

Free sex isn't harmless, he said. Intercourse isn't just a physical act; it actually forges a powerful link between the partners. But a believer's body and spirit are united with Christ. The Holy Spirit permeates not just his spirit, but also his body. So to take that which belongs to God and join it to a prostitute makes real intimacy with Christ impossible. Physical acts have spiritual consequences. Paul's bottom line: "You are not your own; you were bought at a price. Therefore honor God with your body" (1 Corinthians 6:19-20).

However, side by side with those who regarded sex as morally neutral were some in Corinth who considered it base. Greeks considered spirit good and matter evil. Thus, according to them, the human spirit was divine but the body was corrupt. Some people concluded that spiritual persons could therefore do anything they liked with their bodies (the free-sex faction), while others concluded that spiritual persons should deny their bodies' desires, especially those for food and sex. These same two pagan points of view were apparently rife in the Corinthian community. Some people were evidently saying that believers should avoid not only sex outside marriage but also sex inside marriage, and even marriage itself. Since Paul was himself unmarried and celibate, they pointed to him as an example of the truly spiritual man. In reply, Paul explained why he recommended his own lifestyle to those who could handle it, but unhesitantly advised marriage to everyone else.

Rights and Responsibilities

Paul gave these judgments on sex and marriage in response to questions brought by his three visitors. Another question had to do with eating meat sacrificed to idols. Was it okay or not? The issue was important because it was hard to avoid such meat in Corinth. For one thing, nearly all dinner parties, trade association meetings, and other social occasions included some dedication to the patron deity of the gathering. Many parties and meetings were actually held in temples.

Furthermore, nearly all butchers (except Jewish ones) sold sacrificed meat; many were even attached to temples. When an animal was offered in a temple, a small portion was burnt for the god, the worshipers got some (they usually ate it right there in a dinner party), and the priests got the rest. What the priests couldn't use they sold to the butchers. Since only the best animals could be offered to the gods, the best meat was more than likely from a sacrifice.

So, in order to avoid idol meat, one would have to shop only at Jewish butchers (or Christian ones if there were any) and never attend any social occasions with pagans. For anyone whose livelihood depended in part on business dinners or trade association meetings, this was out of the question. For anyone who cared about social standing, it was absurd.

Some of the Corinthian Christians reasoned that since the idols were not real gods there was no reason to sabotage their businesses, their social standing, and their diets. These enlightened ones may have been the more wealthy and educated who were used to eating meat daily in ordinary, nonreligious situations. Knowledge was one of their great values—for instance, the knowledge that idols were nothing.

However, others found it difficult to shake the idea that the idols they had been worshiping all their lives were real, powerful entities who somehow contaminated the meat offered to them. Among this group were probably the poorer members of the community whose daily diet was vegetarian and who normally saw meat only in temple feasts. For them, the association between meat and idolatry was strong. This group couldn't help feeling that by eating meat offered to idols they were defiling themselves, and by attending parties in temples they were countenancing the worship there.

There was one other factor in this debate. In the Jerusalem decree, the apostles had all agreed that Gentiles need not be circumcised but must avoid sexual immorality and food sacrificed to idols. Paul did not mention this decree (to which he had agreed only a few years earlier) in his letter to Corinth, but some Corinthians may have been trying to enforce it.

It took Paul several pages to outline the principles behind eating or not eating idol meat. He wanted to leave his readers not just with a yes-or-no rule, but with standards they could apply widely.

First, love is more important than knowledge. Yes, idols are nothing and Paul usually wouldn't hesitate to eat idol meat. But if somebody doesn't know what we know, we shouldn't just sneer at that person. If he's a weak believer, one who is tempted to violate his conscience and imitate us, we should *voluntarily limit our freedom* out of love for him. (On the other hand, if he's a Pharisee who is tempted not to imitate, but to complain and judge, we should *refuse to give in* to his pressure.) Encouraging someone to violate his or her conscience is harmful.

Second, serving God is more important than exercising rights. As an apostle, Paul had the right to financial support from the people he converted and trained. But he voluntarily declined that right and worked to support himself so that money matters wouldn't keep people from coming to Christ. Paul was always ready to forgo his own preferences to draw someone to Jesus. He practiced Jewish culture among the Jews and Greek culture among the Greeks. He ate meat with the meat-eaters and vegetables with the vegetarians. Moral standards he would not sacrifice, but with social customs he was flexible.

Third, purity is more important than comfort, and self-deception is easy. In the midst of liberty, Paul exercised self-discipline so that he wouldn't be overtaken by addictions. In the unbridled pursuit of freedom, addiction becomes bondage. Paul lived constantly like an athlete in training, keeping his body and spirit in shape for serving God. He pointed to Israel's history as proof that sharing in idol feasts led easily to idolatry, loose sex, and coldness toward God. Those strong Corinthians who were so sure they could attend dinner parties at temples and not be tempted to share in the worship, drunkenness, and sex that accompanied them should think again. Were these knowledgeable ones really as strong as they thought? For if they crossed the line and dabbled in paganism, they had better be clear on the implications: they were worshiping demons.

Corporate Worship

Next, Paul addressed some questions about corporate worship. He scolded some women who were asserting their freedom in Christ by deliberately offending against the social customs of the day. Those women needed to show respect for their husbands and everybody else by covering their heads when the community gathered for worship, as was considered proper from one end of the empire to the other. There was no good reason for deliberately looking like a prostitute.

Paul also rebuked the rich members of the community for making a mockery of the Lord's Supper. At that time, believers commemorated Jesus' last meal with His disciples by eating a full meal together, the "love feast" (Jude 12). The meal was supposed to be like a potluck dinner, with each member bringing something to share. But in Corinth, the rich were arriving early with the fine meats and wines they were used to, and going ahead without the rest. The slaves and artisans arrived later when they had gotten off work. They had to make due with the scanty food they were able to bring.

When pagan aristocrats gave feasts, they usually invited their entire households. The slaves and servants received smaller portions and cheaper wine than the higher class guests. Evidently, the rich members of the church considered this appropriate in the love feast as well. Paul considered it sacrilege. The love feast was a holy celebration, a foretaste of the Kingdom wedding banquet, a profound sharing in the very blood and body Jesus offered for humankind. It resembled sitting down to dinner with God Himself; and like the meal Israel's elders shared to seal the Old Covenant, this meal bound those who ate it in union with each other and Christ. To treat it lightly was to spit in God's face, and Paul honestly attributed some of the illnesses and deaths among the Corinthians to this travesty.

Spiritual Gifts
Another knotty problem had to do with the way people treated abilities they received from the Holy Spirit. People with certain spectacular gifts were claiming higher status than those who lacked them. Those who had only "ordinary" abilities felt inferior. Paul came up with an analogy to explain what God was really doing.

The community of believers, he said, is like a human body. Each person is a limb or organ of the body. No organ is unnecessary, even those that seem to have less glorious functions (like livers cleaning impurities from the blood). God's Spirit works through each member to fulfill the function he or she is designed for.

When the Spirit enables someone to do something useful for the body, such as heal or prophesy, it is not so that the person can be exalted. It is so that a necessary job can get done. Bringing the presence of Christ to a dark world requires some supernatural activities. Each believer should do the activities he is equipped for without comparing himself to the rest. In the final analysis, everybody needs everybody else if the whole job is going to get done.

The Corinthians thought the ability to speak or pray in an unknown language was superior because it seemed so dramatic and obviously supernatural. Paul's criterion was different. A gift to long for was something like prophecy, the ability to speak words from God that strengthen the body. It was great to speak in unknown languages if it built you up in Christ (although you shouldn't disrupt community gatherings with it), but it was far better to build the whole group up. Love, not flashiness, was the standard by which to measure everything.

The Corinthians were so eager to show off their abilities in order to win status that worship gatherings were degenerating into bedlam. Paul urged the people to offer their gifts in turns, focusing on what would do the most good for the group.

Resurrection

The last big issue Paul addressed in this long letter was resurrection. Paul taught that when Christ returned, His people would be raised from death to live with Him forever. Some in Corinth were apparently denying that physical resurrection was possible or even desirable. After all, if bodies are nasty and corrupt, as most Greeks believed, wouldn't it be much more spiritual to be a disembodied immortal soul? And how could a body that gets sick and old be suitable for eternal life?

First of all, said Paul, if there's no resurrection, then Jesus wasn't resurrected either and we might as well be pagans. Physical resurrection is a cornerstone of the gospel.

Second, there's no need to dismiss resurrection because of crude ideas of what it would be like. It's not a matter of coming back to life in the body you had when you died—old or crippled. Like a seed that is buried in one physical form and sprouts into a startlingly different one, so we die in one form and will be raised in another: imperishable, glorious, a "spiritual body" (1 Corinthians 15:44).

Paul understood that death was the great terror behind every human fear. He wanted the Corinthians to understand that for them, death held no threat. So he wrote,

When the perishable has been clothed with the imperishable, and the mortal with immortality, then the saying that is written will come true: "Death has been swallowed up in victory."

"Where, O death, is your victory?

Where, O death, is your sting?" (1 Corinthians 15:54-55)

He who clung to the resurrected Christ could face anything.

Closing

Paul closed with some personal business. Years earlier, he had promised the apostles in Jerusalem that he would "continue to remember the poor" (Galatians 2:10). He had brought a contribution from the Gentile churches to the Jerusalem church during a famine, and the apostles wanted him to continue to do this. Jerusalem was a poor city; the Jews there were supported partly by contributions from Jews living abroad, but the followers of Jesus had no access to those funds. They needed help from their spiritual offspring, and Paul was glad to aid them.

Recently, Paul had decided to take up a collection among his communities in order to acknowledge the debt the Gentiles owed the mother community in Jerusalem, to show that these Gentiles were genuine believers, and to knit the Jewish and Gentile groups together. He planned to visit Corinth on his way from Ephesus to Macedonia, so he asked the Corinthians to have their contribution ready when he arrived. There was no set fee; it was between them and God what they wanted to give.

Ambassadors of Reconciliation

Paul dispatched this lengthy message and asked Timothy to drop in at Corinth on his way back from Macedonia to see how his letter was received. Timothy was rudely rebuffed, and when Paul himself visited Corinth briefly, the defiant factions humiliated him. Paul wrote a severe letter "out of great distress and anguish of heart" (2 Corinthians 2:4) and sent it with Titus, another of his young associates. This anguished letter is now lost.

Paul left Ephesus with the issue still unresolved, so, contrary to his former plan, he went to Macedonia to gather the contribution for Jerusalem while Corinth hopefully cooled down. There Titus met him with good news: the Corinthians had repented of their rebellion. Paul quickly sent Titus back with a fourth letter full of affection as well as a stern warning—the letter we call 2 Corinthians.

Not that there wasn't still tension. Paul's adversaries were still saying that by changing his itinerary, Paul proved that he couldn't be trusted. And they still hinted that he wasn't a genuine apostle and was probably pocketing the money he was supposedly gathering for the people in Jerusalem.

In response, Paul defended at length his trustworthiness and genuineness. But his defense was much less self-centered than Christ-centered. He exalted "the God of all comfort" who rescued his team from life-threatening pressures in Ephesus, the God who had commissioned and equipped Paul for his job and who continued to set the agenda and take care of Paul's needs. He wrote, "Not that we are competent in ourselves to claim anything for ourselves, but our competence comes from God" (2 Corinthians 3:5). Paul saw himself as a common clay pot holding a priceless treasure: the message of Christ, who transforms those who behold Him into glorious beings like Himself.

Paul wanted the Corinthians to taste his passion for Jesus and his mission. "Christ's love compels us," he wrote (2 Corinthians 5:14). If Jesus truly did die for humankind and was really raised from death, then there is no longer any need for people to devote their lives to self-seeking ends. On the contrary, it makes no sense to do anything other than serve Christ in relieved gratitude. All of the reasons for self-focus—fear of death, of failure, of rejection; craving for love, for security, for mattering in the universe—all have been rendered pointless by the Cross.

The hope of resurrection transfixed Paul and made him capable of anything:

Therefore we do not lose heart. Though outwardly we are wasting away, yet inwardly we are being renewed day by day. For our light and momentary troubles are achieving for us an eternal glory that far outweighs them all. So we fix our eyes not on what is seen, but on what is unseen. For what is seen is temporary, but what is unseen is eternal. (2 Corinthians 4:16-18)

Paul laid before the Corinthians all the things he had gladly endured for Christ: "beatings, imprisonments and riots . . . hard work, sleepless nights and hunger" (6:5). And he summarized his mission—indeed, the mission God had been on since Adam—in one word: reconciliation. "God was reconciling the world to himself in Christ, not counting men's sins against them. And he has committed to us the message of reconciliation. We are therefore Christ's ambassadors, as though God were making his appeal through us" (5:19-20).

The "we" he referred to were first of all the members of his apostolic team, and secondarily the members of local bases like Corinth. Reconciliation was a spiritual war. The Snake had blinded the minds of unbelievers (4:4). So how do you combat an Enemy who fights by blinding minds? What are the true marks of an apostle? An impressive appearance? Tough talking?

No. The world wages war with physical might and intimidation, or with glitz and image. We, said Paul, wage it with a spiritual power to demolish fortresses of the mind. We fight with prayer, truth, integrity. We capture thoughts and turn them to Christ. For we are out to defeat not people, but the Enemy who rules their hearts and minds.

It's a subtle war that has never made its generals look

impressive. Moses, Samuel, Elijah, Isaiah—all were great men of the Spirit who continually faced abuse because they refused to play the image game.

Was Paul's apostleship in doubt? He pointed to three credentials: first, the scores of people he had brought to Christ and established in communities such as Corinth; second, the miraculous signs that had first confirmed Peter's apostleship; and third, a litany of suffering for Christ. Paul boasted about his sufferings rather than his successes because he knew that everything he had accomplished was by the power of God. He delighted in his weakness because he had learned that when he was weak, much more than when he was confident in his strength, Christ could work powerfully through him.

To stir the Corinthians to jealousy, Paul also boasted of how generously the poor Macedonian communities were contributing to the Jerusalem fund. Paul didn't want to manipulate the Corinthians, but he knew that many of them were far wealthier than those in Philippi and Thessalonica, and he wanted them to learn the joy of giving without calculating a return. Giving had rewards the Corinthians had never imagined. It was an area of Christlikeness they had not tasted. And if there was any doubt about Paul's integrity, he assured his readers that representatives from each contributing community would accompany him and the gift to Jerusalem.

Paul in Corinth

Titus and two other well-respected believers carried this letter to Corinth, so that when Paul and the delegation to Jerusalem arrived, the Corinthians would be ready to receive them. Paul didn't want the Corinthians to look unprepared, selfish, or in disarray in front of brothers they had never met. Titus's mission was apparently successful, for Paul's group stayed three months in Corinth until some Jews plotted to kill him and forced him to leave.

NOTE

1. There seem to have been more people recognized as apostles than just Paul and the Twelve. Paul includes Apollos with him and Peter in 1 Corinthians 3:1–4:13, where he calls them "us apostles" (4:9). Barnabas, Epaphroditus, Silas, and Timothy also receive the title (Acts 14:1-4; Philippians 2:25—translated "messenger" in NIV; 1 Thessalonians 1:1, 2:6-7). Then there were men Paul called "super-apostles" or "false apostles" (2 Corinthians 11:5,13), men whom the Corinthians considered apostles but who were not sent from God.

The term may have had a fluid meaning; the Twelve certainly held an authority in the international community that Epaphroditus or Timothy did not.

33

Paul's Manifesto

◆

Romans

A Letter of Introduction

Even as Paul was heading east to Jerusalem, his thoughts were already turning westward. It was AD 57; Paul had been apostling for a decade, and he felt his work in the eastern half of the empire was fulfilled. He had planted strategic bases from which central Asia Minor, western Asia Minor, Macedonia, and Greece could be reached. (See map, page 362.) Local leaders were equipped to spearhead internal care and outreach. So Paul was looking to a region that had never heard the gospel: Spain, the farthest end of the empire.

On the way to Spain, Paul hoped to satisfy a longing to visit Rome. Although legally a citizen, Paul had never seen the famed imperial capital. A stay there would be a chance to meet members of the sizable network of home-based communities of believers already flourishing in Rome. Paul hoped that the Roman believers would help provide funds and a base of operations for his mission to Spain.

However, Paul had met only a few of the hundreds of

believers then living in Rome. Also, he could not journey westward until he finished his errand in Jerusalem. So during his three-month sojourn in Corinth in the spring of 57, he dictated a long letter introducing himself to the Roman communities. It turned out to be his greatest treatise on his view of the gospel.

Rome

The first followers of Jesus in Rome were probably Jews. Business, religious pilgrimage, and pleasure were constantly carrying Jews back and forth between Rome, Jerusalem, Antioch, and other cities. There may even have been Roman Jews among the first Pentecost converts. Priscilla and Aquila had belonged to the Roman community of believers before Paul met them in Corinth.

All Jews were expelled from Rome in AD 49 because of the riots caused by "Chrestus." But a few years later they were back, and by 57 there were also a substantial number of Gentile believers in Rome. Predictably, the multiethnic composition of the communities of Jesus was causing some tension.

At that time, Paul's understanding of the gospel was only one of many circulating around the empire. Only a very few of the Roman believers had ever heard from Paul what he believed. Others had presumably heard rumors of his ideas, probably with certain distortions. But like believers everywhere, the Romans were working out a view of the gospel more or less on their own, with the Holy Spirit and the Old Testament to guide them. Some approached their relationship with Jesus from an orthodox Jewish point of view, others from an idolatrous past, and others from one of the many Jewish sects with various interpretations of the Old Testament and Jewish tradition.

Consequently, Paul decided that the best way to introduce himself was to explain carefully what he actually believed. This would clear up any confusing rumors and surface any crucial disagreements. His readers would get a chance to chew on his ideas and even discard some of their false ones before they saw him in person. When they read how he handled some of the personal issues they were facing, they would get to evaluate what they thought of him as an apostle. After all, they were not automatically obliged to recognize his authority. He had been appointed by nobody but God, and unless the Holy Spirit showed them who he was, they had no reason to back him.

The Righteousness of God

Paul chose as his theme *the righteousness of God*. Righteousness was an old biblical concept: the state of being in right covenant relationship with someone, legally in the right, or declared "not guilty." The gospel, said Paul, reveals how a person can be restored to a reconciled, intimate, covenant relationship with God. It tells how one can become God's loyal subject, adopted child, spouse, and friend.

Paul laid out his explanation carefully, with his eye on both Gentile and Jewish believers in Rome. First he defined why both Jews and Gentiles had broken relationships with God. On the one hand, by choosing the delusion of idolatry over gratitude to their Creator, the pagans had mired themselves in sexual perversion, greed, murder, and every other vice. It was a fair portrait of life on any street of Corinth or Rome. On the other hand, by trusting in their performance of religious duties, the Jews had entangled themselves in a subtler trap: pride. They thought themselves better than the pagans because they not only abstained from debauchery but also lived the lifestyle prescribed by Moses.

Now to Paul, there was nothing wrong with living according to the Law of Moses. It was a cultural form given by God to shape a nation, and it had its advantages. But if one kept the outward customs without letting the Holy Spirit produce the inner transformation that the Law really required, then the Jewish lifestyle was pointless. Worshiping once a week, performing certain rites, and eating the right foods just were not the essence of a right relationship with God. You could recognize a real friend of God by that inner transformation, what Moses called a circumcised heart (Deuteronomy 30:6, Romans 2:29).

Here was the Jewish mistake. The Jews thought the proper grateful response to God's love was keeping rules. But the response God wanted went much deeper.

So the Law had served its primary purpose: It was an objective standard by which one could see plainly that both Jew and Gentile were falling short. With that fact clear, God had provided a way to restore the broken relationship. Jesus had borne the full weight of human evil, so there were no outstanding debts for a person who chose to accept Jesus' payment. By swearing allegiance to Jesus, one changed sides in the war between God and Satan. Adam had chosen Satan's side, so his children were all born into rebellion. But when a person changed sides by choosing Jesus, he received the same standing with God that Jesus had: son and friend.

Jews might balk. Surely, they thought, the rules of Judaism were still necessary! But Paul pointed out that Abraham had been declared righteous without keeping any of the Law of Moses, even circumcision. Abraham simply bet his life that God was trustworthy. Religious customs were beside the point.

Living by the Spirit
Okay, so God is happy when we bet our lives on Christ rather than on a religious system. Does that mean we can do whatever we want? No, Paul insisted. Remember the slime the pagans live in. They're in bondage to all sorts of addictions and delusions. Doing whatever you want turns out to be a worse prison than obeying God. You can choose evil freely once, even twice, but before you know it, evil has wrapped its tentacles around you and you've lost the power to say no.

Furthermore, consider what it means to bet your life on Christ. The public ceremony by which a person declared his allegiance to Jesus was baptism. It was like a funeral: a public declaration that someone was dead. In this case, one was joining Christ in His death. Symbolically, baptism was death by drowning—death to one's past evil, self-centered life. When one came up out of that water, one was choosing to be joined to Christ in His resurrection, choosing to pursue freedom from one's addictions, compulsions, and other slaveries. Not freedom to do whatever one wanted (that was a fast route back to bondage), but freedom to serve the God of life.

Under the Old Covenant, the only way ordinary people could serve God was by keeping the Law by their own effort. A few prophets and leaders had the power of the Spirit for service, but they were rare. The trouble was, the Law set that inner standard: not only must we not steal, but we must not even covet. And the natural rebelliousness of humans responded by going crazy with covetousness. People who really wanted to please God could manage the external rules flawlessly—they could be model religious persons—but they'd shipwreck every time on those inner attitudes. They were utterly enslaved to covetousness, or pride, or anger.

Thank God, said Paul, that Christ's death made possible not only a restored relationship, but also the process of inner transformation. Friends of God are able to have God's Spirit actually live inside of them. The Spirit's power is constantly available to help them choose what God wants; all they must do is to set their minds and wills on that choice, to make a moment-by-moment choice to be united with, directed toward, and impelled by the Spirit of God. In the beginning it can be a gut-wrenching choice, but bondage slowly releases its claws with each decision. It's not just that the Spirit adds that extra bit of grit that was lacking in the willpower of believers; it's that the Spirit makes what was utterly impossible fully possible (though not necessarily easy).

Paul couldn't get over the honor of the relationship with God that the Spirit made possible. He was overwhelmed that he could call the Lord of the universe *Abba*—Papa. When the

Kingdom appeared in its fullness, Paul looked forward to a share in it alongside his Brother Jesus. He longed, he groaned with the cosmos to be freed from bondage to decay. The hope of resurrection gripped him. And more than resurrection: the goal of the Spirit's work in God's children was nothing less than to make them like the Son of God in perfect moral beauty.

God's Faithfulness

At the end of chapter 8, Paul's letter crescendos in a rhapsody about how confident his readers can be that God will love them faithfully to the end. Then he takes a sharp turn and talks about the Jews for three chapters. Why? Because from all he has said so far, one could get the distinct impression that God has in fact abandoned them. And if them, why not us?

So Paul struggled to explain the plan behind God's sovereign choices. Throughout history, God had been making apparently arbitrary choices to befriend one individual or group and to reject another. He chose Abraham over the rest of the world, Isaac over Ishmael, Jacob over Esau. He raised up a pharaoh for the express purpose of humiliating him. The point of the choosing was never mere favoritism. On one hand, God has the right to do whatever He likes with what He made. But beyond that, His choosing has a loving purpose: to continually mold a people who could become the seed of the community of Christ. His eye was always on the nations lost in darkness.

God hadn't broken His promise to Israel. That promise had always belonged to those in ethnic Israel who really believed in Him. There had always been a true Israel within Israel, a remnant who clung to God while the rest wandered. That remnant persisted in Paul's day, and God still stuck by His promises to them.

The trouble with most of Paul's fellow Jews, he continued, was that they thought covenant keeping was a matter of living a Jewish lifestyle. Because they didn't see that a relationship with God required nothing but a passionate trust, they didn't grasp that the Law was meant simply to prepare them for Christ. Therefore, they didn't recognize Him when He came. God didn't reject them; they simply refused to respond when He virtually shouted His truth to them.

But even so, God's promise to Israel was not void. Paul and other believers like him were proof that a faithful remnant still lived to inherit the promise. They inherited it not because of their ethnicity or their devotion to Jewish customs, but because of God's free kindness. And as for the many Jews who had rejected Christ, God was bringing good even out of that. For if most Jews had recognized Jesus as Messiah in Paul's day, the people of God would have been overwhelmingly Jewish and it would have been much harder for Gentiles to retain their Gentile culture while becoming believers. The gospel would have had a much harder time penetrating Gentile society if it had retained unnecessary Jewish trappings. So amazingly, Jewish unbelief inadvertently opened the gospel to pagans. But Paul warned Gentile believers not to look down on the Jews. He looked to a day when Jewish unbelief would have served its purpose, and God would turn that race's heart.

Living Sacrifices

So much for God's supposed promise breaking. Paul concluded his discourse by outlining how one should live in light of God's mercy. If the externals of Jewish Law weren't the standard, what exactly were the qualities that the Holy Spirit wanted to instill in God's people?

Paul's list is lengthy, but it boils down to what Jesus said: the commandments are summed up in a sacrificial, open hearted, wildly generous and joyful love for friend and enemy alike. Such love included mundane duties like obeying the civil government and maintaining sexual and emotional discipline. It also included working out the tensions of a diverse community. The Roman network included believers with sundry convictions about whether one should be vegetarian, keep Sabbaths and holy days, abstain from wine, and so on.

Paul's counsel was much like what he told the Corinthians: Know what you personally can and can't handle. Know what God's written Word says about moral standards. Based on these facts, form your own convictions. Don't look down on the weak, but let love for them limit your freedom. Don't judge those who disagree with you or impose your standards on them.

It was a heavy letter for an introduction. And Paul was straightforward about his agenda—his hope that the Romans would be his partners in ministry. He also begged their prayers for protection on his trip to Jerusalem. Something told him that trouble awaited him there.

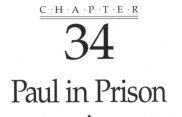

34

Paul in Prison

◆

Acts 20:4–28:31, Ephesians, Philippians,
Colossians, Philemon

Arrest in Jerusalem

Paul was an international pariah among the Jews. That spring
of AD 57 he fled Corinth because they were trying to murder
him. On his way east, he visited with the elders of the Ephesian community to say goodbye; he expected never to see
them again because of trouble awaiting him in Jerusalem. Each
time his ship docked at a port where disciples of Jesus lived,
the Holy Spirit would warn them of danger in Jerusalem, and
they would beg Paul not to go. But Paul insisted the Spirit
wanted him to go, even if it meant death.

The elders of the Jerusalem community greeted Paul's
Gentile delegation warmly. However much they appreciated
the money, though, they were more concerned with how
Paul's arrival would affect their work. It was rumored in the
community that Paul was teaching Jews not to keep the Law.
This was probably false—he had said only that keeping the
Law's external rituals did not affect their standing with God.
Unless they were trying to reach Gentiles, Paul didn't mind

their cultural preferences. But Paul's own freedom to ignore the Law had undoubtedly affected Jewish believers who knew him. In any case, the Jerusalem elders asked Paul to finance an expensive sacrificial rite for some men, as a sign that he was still a practicing Jew.

Paul was glad to do that. But one day some Jews who had seen Paul in Ephesus noticed him in the temple. They incited a riot, accusing Paul of bringing unclean Gentiles into the sacred temple precincts. The penalty for that was death. Only the intervention of the Roman troop commander saved Paul from a lynching.

The commander granted Paul's request to address the crowd, and they listened with fascination as he described his encounter with Jesus on the Damascus road. But when he got to the part where Jesus sent him to the Gentiles, they went wild. The commander had no idea what was going on, so he had Paul dragged off for questioning. He tried to get the Sanhedrin to make a coherent charge, but Paul threw the Jewish council into confusion by saying, "My brothers, I am a Pharisee, the son of a Pharisee. I stand on trial because of my hope in the resurrection of the dead" (Acts 23:6). The Pharisees on the council began to defend Paul staunchly (they had a long-standing dispute with the Sadducees about resurrection). The dispute degenerated into a brawl, and the commander was obliged to have Paul carried out to keep the Sadducees and Pharisees from tearing him apart between them.

The next day Paul's nephew informed the commander of a Jewish plot to assassinate Paul, so the commander had this perplexing but obviously important prisoner moved to the Roman governor's headquarters in Caesarea.

Waiting in Caesarea

Governor Felix was the first former slave ever to become governor of a Roman province. His brother was an imperial toady. Felix kept Paul under house arrest for two years without settling his case. He didn't want to release Paul, even though he knew the charges were absurd, because he feared making the Sanhedrin upset. Also, he was hoping Paul would offer him a bribe. But he wouldn't condemn Paul to death because something about his message scared and fascinated Felix. Occasionally the governor would send for Paul to hear him talk about Jesus, but statements about self-control and judgment for wrongdoers made Felix too uncomfortable to actually face what he feared was true.

When Felix's brother finally fell from favor in AD 59 and could no longer protect him, Felix was recalled to Rome for mishandling riots, overusing violence, and other acts of incompetence and corruption. Because he couldn't afford to make the Jews any madder than they already were, he left Paul in prison.

Three days after Felix's replacement arrived in the province, representatives of the Sanhedrin arrived to press charges against Paul and request that he be transferred to Jerusalem for trial. But Paul, knowing that a trial in Jerusalem meant death and that God wanted him to testify in Rome, appealed for trial before Caesar. It was his right as a Roman citizen, so Governor Festus agreed.

To Rome

Sailing westward was tedious because the prevailing winds blew eastward and rudders hadn't been invented yet. It was already October before Paul, two companions, and his guard reached Crete. Sailing in autumn was hazardous bordering on insane, and Paul prophesied trouble, but the harbor into which the ship had limped was unsuitable for wintering over. When a gentle south wind blew in, the pilot thought he had a prime chance of reaching a better harbor. Suddenly a northeaster swept through and enveloped the ship in a two-week-long virtual hurricane. The crew threw the cargo overboard and rationed the food—nothing helped. At last Paul coolly added a second prophecy that everyone would survive because his God wanted him to testify before Caesar.

A few days later the crew was able to ram the ship aground on the island of Malta. There Paul further amazed his guards by sustaining no ill effect from the deadly bite of a viper, and by healing many sick Maltans by laying his hands on them and praying for them. In response, the Maltans entertained Paul and the other men generously all winter. But Paul's guard took the first ship that left harbor the next March, and in a few weeks Paul was under house arrest in Rome. The first thing Paul did was contact the local Jewish leaders to give them their chance at accepting Jesus as their Messiah. As usual, few heeded him, but he now felt free to turn to the Gentiles. For two years Paul worked at full steam while under arrest in a house he had to rent with contributions from friends.

Letter to Philippi

Under house arrest, Paul had to pay rent and buy food. But the believers in Rome were very likely reluctant to support a missionary accused of an imperial crime. It was not illegal to be a disciple of Jesus, but it was dangerous to be associated with enemies of the state, so prudent people kept at arms' length from someone Rome suspected of agitation and treason.

The believers in Philippi had chimed in with financial support when he was planting the community in Thessalonica (Philippians 4:16) and again in Corinth. They were Paul's most loyal financial supporters. At some point, however, they lost track of him, perhaps after he set off for Jerusalem with their gift for the poor. So, when they heard that Paul was in financial straits, they dispatched one of their members, Epaphroditus, to bring Paul some cash and take care of him while he was under arrest. But Epaphroditus became severely ill, so Paul felt he should send him back to Philippi to finish recovering. He sent Epaphroditus with a letter explaining the unexpected return, thanking the Philippians for their gift, informing them about his circumstances, and exhorting them to respond to their none-too-pleasant situation in a way befitting servants of Christ.

Partners

The way these friends were always there when Paul needed them, always eager to support him with prayer and money, always avidly serving Christ in their own sphere as Paul was in his—all this told Paul they understood what partnership or community was supposed to be about. The affection between them and Paul had deep roots born of time and shared commitments.

Paul reassured them that his imprisonment was actually advancing the gospel because as soldiers took shifts guarding him, they were forced to observe the community of Christ in action. By now the whole imperial guard had heard the gospel. Likewise, Paul urged the Philippians to use their shaky situation to the best advantage. If the hyperpatriotic Roman colonists of Philippi made life rough for followers of an obscure Jewish cult, their very response would make the pagans sit up and take notice.

The attitude that would grab attention most would be that selfless, humble unity that was possible only among those who were truly letting the Holy Spirit change them into being like Jesus. Only people who understood that Jesus had emptied Himself of His rights for the sake of the humans He loved could "Do nothing out of selfish ambition or vain conceit, but in humility consider others better than yourselves" (Philippians 2:3). Paul wasn't urging people to be doormats before a few strong-willed leaders, but to exercise the same tough-minded unselfishness Jesus displayed. When unbelievers saw a group of people free of complaining and arguing, that would be positive proof that Christ was more than just another god.

Joy

Another attitude that would attract the pagans was joy. How many of those hard-bitten colonists knew joy? But the people of God had every reason to rejoice because they could release their anxieties to One who had the love and power to take care of His own. In frank prayer born of genuine trust, God's people could find peace in the midst of both danger and the daily grind of life's hassles.

Paul added a warning against listening to the circumcision party, who urged believers to substitute rules for relationship. Paul assured the Philippians that his years of flawlessly obeying religious rules had never given him anything of value. All of his self-powered achievements were worthless "compared to the surpassing greatness of knowing Christ Jesus my Lord, for whose sake I have lost all things" (3:8). Paul didn't even mind sharing Jesus' suffering and death because that enabled him to taste Jesus' resurrection.

In fact, as much as Paul deeply appreciated his friends' gift, he wanted them to know that he valued it more as a love token than as survival funds. Life was tough in Philippi for someone who allied with Jesus, and Paul hoped to set an example of contentment in the face of hardship. He wrote, "I know what it is to be in need, and I know what it is to have plenty. I have learned the secret of being content in any and every situation, whether well fed or hungry, whether living in plenty or in want. I can do everything through him who gives me strength" (4:12-13). Strong words from a man who could have been a prosperous rabbi, but who had chosen prison, lean living, even shipwreck and imminent execution.

Crisis in Colosse

Sometime during his imprisonment in either Caesarea or Rome, Paul received a visitor from the believing community in the town of Colosse. Colosse was a small cosmopolitan city in Asia, less than a hundred miles from Ephesus. Originally known for its wool industry, the town had declined considerably and had been surpassed by Laodicea, ten miles to the west, and Hierapolis, twelve miles to the northwest.

The community at Colosse was probably planted by Epaphras, one of Paul's converts at Ephesus. Paul had never been to Colosse, but Epaphras apparently felt that the town fell under Paul's apostolic jurisdiction. At any rate, when trouble brewed, Epaphras sought Paul's advice.

The gospel flourished in Colosse until some false teachers arrived and confused the young believers by mixing ideas from pagan cults with the gospel. Unable to combat this cancer alone, Epaphras appealed to Paul for help. Paul did the only thing he could: write a letter to help the Colossian believers see the truth.

First, the false teachers were claiming that Christ was less than God, on the level of a created angel. Against this doctrine, Paul stressed that Jesus "is the image of the invisible God. . . . For by him all things were created. . . . For God was pleased to have all his fullness dwell in him" (Colossians 1:15-19).

Second, the teachers said true enlightenment required knowledge of certain secrets. Paul countered that the only secret anybody needed to know was God's plan to place Christ's life in anybody who welcomed it, Gentiles included.

Third, the troublemakers were teaching believers to practice ascetic rules about food, sex, and an amalgam of Jewish ritual: "Do not handle! Do not taste! Do not touch!" (2:21), they said. Those rules had something to do with the worship of angels, or spirit beings—perhaps rituals and physical self-denial put a person in harmony with or appeased the spiritual forces. In Greek culture, it was commonly believed that the material world was essentially evil, or at best indifferent. Therefore, the body was evil and had to be controlled. Also, between the pure divine essence and base matter there supposedly lay a host of spiritual powers who ruled the world. Religion was largely aimed at pleasing those powers.

Against these ideas, Paul insisted that the only thing necessary for intimacy with God was commitment to the crucified and resurrected Jesus. On the cross, Jesus defeated all the anti-God spirit beings, so the Colossians had nothing to fear from them. As for rules to control the body, they appeared to be wise and spiritual, but in fact they failed to affect what really counted: lust, greed, and selfishness in the heart.

The real key to holy living, said Paul, is to set your mind on the agenda and activities of God's Kingdom. Instead of worrying about external rules, invest your energy in putting to death real evil in yourself: lust and sexual immorality, evil desires and greed, malice and lying and slander. Invest in seeking Christlike qualities, such as compassion, forgiveness, and peace. Paul seemed to think these were attainable qualities (maybe not overnight) for people filled with Christ, in love with Christ, drawing on Christ's power.

Paul did lay down a few rules; they had to do with how to run a household. They were remarkably progressive rules in that strict, hierarchical society: Not only should wives submit to husbands, but husbands should love their wives and not be harsh with them. Not only should children obey their parents, but fathers should take care not to embitter their children. Not only should slaves obey and work diligently, but masters should be fair. Compared to the practice in most pagan homes where wives, children, and slaves were mere property, this was progressive thinking.

A lifestyle that fit the society but treated everyone with dignity was important for two reasons. First, it encouraged harmony in the community. But second, it made the gospel attractive to outsiders. Paul commissioned the Colossians not only to pray for his ministry, but also to keep reaching out to their pagan neighbors: "Be wise in the way you act toward outsiders; make the most of every opportunity. Let your conversation be always full of grace, seasoned with salt, so that you may know how to answer everyone" (4:5-6).

A Personal Intervention

One of Paul's team members, Tychicus, carried this letter from Rome (or Caesarea) to Colosse. With him went a new believer named Onesimus. This Onesimus was a slave of another Colossian believer, Philemon. Onesimus had apparently stolen something from Philemon, then run away—crimes punishable by death. However, somehow he had found his way to Paul and, under his influence, become a follower of Jesus.

Onesimus preferred staying with Paul, rather than returning to Colosse to face his master. But Paul wanted to give
Philemon the chance to do something Godlike. So he sent
Onesimus back with a letter for Philemon, asking him to do
what God had done: free Onesimus from slavery and accept
him as family rather than as a servant.

How could Philemon say no? He owed Paul his own life
(a fact that Paul did not blush to point out), and Onesimus was
a brother now. God Himself had freed Philemon from slavery
and an unpayable debt; could he hold Onesimus to the letter
of the law? Paul didn't bother to attack slavery as an immoral
institution on humanistic grounds. He merely laid the situation out in plain colors and let Philemon judge for himself: is
it even conceivable for one child of God to treat another as
unforgivable or inferior? (Of course, if Onesimus began to take
advantage of Philemon, the Colossian community would have
to deal with that.)

Letter to Ephesus

Yet a fourth biblical letter dates from Paul's time in prison (no
doubt he wrote dozens of letters since he could not travel).
This one reads more formally than Paul's often ironic and
blunt personal notes. Although addressed to the community
in Ephesus, Paul writes as though many of his readers are
strangers to him (he says he's *heard* of their faith, not seen it).
Probably this letter was meant to circulate among communities throughout Asia, many of which Paul had never visited.
In almost musical phrases, it sketched the glorious place
believers have in God's eternal purposes, and the lives they
should live in light of their identity.

Ever since He conceived the idea of creation, God had one
overarching plan: "to bring all things in heaven and on earth
together under one head, even Christ" (Ephesians 1:10). His
idea was not a rigid hierarchy, but a choreographed dance
with the Son of God as center and leader—the Source from

whom would flow the patterns and rhythms of relationships.

But some of God's spirit creatures had followed the Snake in rebellion, and had ensnared men and women into their corruption. Instead of a grand ball, there was war. Hostility against God and man devoured souls.

Yet God was not thwarted. All along, His plan had been to teach His creatures—especially those without bodies who inhabited the heavens—something about Him they could never otherwise understand. They knew His power and holiness, but certain areas of His wisdom eluded them. Above all, love was a mystery. (It may even have been their incomprehension of love that inspired the rebels' contempt for their Maker.)

The cosmos watched as God painstakingly groomed a family generation after generation: Seth, Noah, Shem, Abraham, Isaac, Jacob . . . Jesus. The line had survived by a hairsbreadth more than once. But when the time was ripe, the King invaded earth to begin reversing the process of hostility. First He reconciled humans to God by taking their penalty upon Himself. Then He reconciled these freed ones to each other by dissolving the barriers between them. Even pagans, who throughout the time of the Old Covenant had seemed hopelessly sunk in moral slime, were now welcomed into God's family. In His agony, Christ had embraced all their evil to Himself, neutralized it, and changed former children of evil to children of glory.

The dance was born: Christ had united warring factions into one body, one community, with Himself as its head. The spirit beings who well knew human hearts must have gaped. Who would have thought Christ could weld such selfish renegades together?

This, said Paul, is the primary reason the community exists on earth: "His [God's] intent was that now, through the church, the manifold wisdom of God should be made known to the rulers and authorities in the heavenly realms" (3:10).

Precisely because it is humanly impossible, the united Body of Christ parades God's wisdom.

Therefore, Paul went on, it is crucial that we live up to our noble calling. Not only is the pagan world looking on to judge Christ by the quality of *our* love and unity (John 13:35, 17:23), but so are the heavenly beings. Our reason for existence is not only to be ambassadors of reconciliation, drawing unbelievers to Christ through the quality of our lives; it is also to display God's greatness to the universe through that same quality of living. God has raised us from the sludge and made us joint heirs of Christ's wealth—how should we respond?

We should seek to live as reconciled people through the power of God's Spirit at work within us. Humility, harmony, and forgiveness don't come naturally; we have to be actively dependent upon God to produce them in us. Paul prayed that God "may strengthen you with power through his Spirit in your inner being . . . that you, being rooted and established in love, may have power . . . to grasp . . . the love of Christ" (3:16-18). Paul knew that only a person who was experiencing Christ's love and the Spirit's activity would have what it takes to live as a reconciler.

To Paul, this "unity of the Spirit" (4:3) was not uniformity—in which everyone thinks the same thoughts, lives the same lifestyle, does the same things, enjoys the same things. Nor did he describe it as a tight system where subordinates mutely obey orders from on high. Paul saw it as a body, a living organism in which each part had function and responsibility. God gave the community certain people whose job was to equip the rest to do their jobs. The body wouldn't work as long as some members were mature but the rest were infants living off their leaders and believing whatever new ideas drifted by. Paul's vision was for each member to be mature and connected to Christ on his or her own, drawing strength from Him to do his or her unique tasks, and interconnected with other believers like the cells of a body or the members of a team. As in an orchestra, wide diversity would weave together in harmony. Christ Himself would be the conductor.

The cultural expressions of the body might vary greatly, but certain core values would be constant: integrity, honesty, healthy ways of handling anger, no obscene language or bitterness. Family order was essential because it mirrored the dance; in fact, the relationship of husband and wife was supposed to echo the love union between Christ and the community of believers. Paul had an astounding view of sacrificial love within marriage, and his view of social relationships in general exploded the authoritarian norms of the day: "Submit to one another out of reverence for Christ" (5:21).

Paul closed this letter in a way unusual for him: with an open reference to the war. Usually he preferred only to allude to the cosmic conflict, and to focus his readers' attention on their earthly job of living lives that would attract unbelievers to Christ. But this time he felt it necessary to stress that his readers were not in a struggle against the Roman authorities, malicious neighbors, or irritating relatives. Rather, they were engaged in a violent wrestling match with evil spiritual beings. Those beings were committed to corrupting love and mutual submission in the body. They would use every trick to encourage domination, manipulation, selfishness, and hostility. The defense against such deception, said Paul, was to armor oneself with Christ's nature: His truth, righteousness, salvation, faith, a solid understanding of the gospel, and God's written Word.

These became offensive weapons when employed in prayer. In giving humans the freedom to make real choices in their world, God had actually committed Himself not to do certain things unless humans invited Him. The rebel spirits thought God weak for yielding some of His authority to paltry humans. That He loved the dust-creatures enough to become one with them was inconceivable.

But God's joke was this: He would not esteem the traitors even so much as to defeat them with His ungloved power. He had vanquished them decisively through the humiliation of the Cross, and now He was handling the cleanup through the prayers and love works of this very community of humans.

C·H·A·P·T·E·R

35

Farewells

◆

1 and 2 Timothy, Titus

Nero's Pogrom

Luke's book of Acts ended with Paul spending two years in Rome under house arrest, awaiting trial. What happened then? Was Paul convicted of anti-Roman agitation and executed? Or was he acquitted and allowed to pursue his plans, either westward to Spain or back east to his current communities?

We don't know. Tradition has it that he was acquitted in AD 62 but rearrested and executed two to five years later in a general persecution of Christians. In AD 64, a fire broke out in Rome, raged for five days, completely consumed three of the city's fourteen districts (including the imperial palace), and ravaged seven others. Emperor Nero worked overtime to help the homeless, but rumors flew that he had arranged arson in order to rebuild the city to his taste. (It was true that the reconstruction he financed was far more elegantly planned than the old irregular blocks of tenements, but the new approach was partly aimed at fire prevention.)

As the whispers grew louder, Nero became desperate for

scapegoats. He fastened on a controversial sect: the Christians. Some said they were cannibals (they supposedly ate somebody's flesh and blood in a secret rite). They were certainly atheists and antisocial, for they refused to worship the Roman gods or participate in public functions, calling them debauched and idolatrous.

So the Christians were charged with arson, and anyone fingered as a member of the sect was rounded up. "A huge crowd" of those who admitted being followers of Christ were convicted, as a Roman writer put it a few decades later, "not so much of arson as of hatred of the human race." Antihumanists.

Nero had perverse tastes in fun. He opened his gardens for the mass executions. Believers were crucified, sewn in animal skins and hunted by dogs, doused in pitch and lighted, raped in reenactments of Greek myths. Even the jaded Roman populace thought Nero was going too far. Nonetheless, sporadic arrests and killings continued for several years.

Paul may have been one of the early casualties, or he may have been imprisoned and killed as late as AD 68. Rome is the only city that claimed to hold Paul's tomb in the early centuries after his death, so it's a safe guess that he was tried and executed there. But all we know for sure is that three more of his letters survived to be included in the New Testament. They seem to date from the last years of his life, whenever that was, and they share certain themes in common.

First Timothy
At some point late in his career, Paul sent Timothy to handle some problems in Ephesus while he himself continued on to Macedonia. When he realized that he would not soon get back to Ephesus, he dispatched a note to Timothy with his instructions in black and white. This letter would be read aloud to the community and would remove all doubt that Paul's authority lay behind what Timothy was trying to accomplish.

Timothy's main assignment was to silence certain leaders

who were teaching falsehood, and to make sure that qualified people were in leadership roles. The troublesome teachers were provoking useless controversy by inventing doctrines that had nothing to do with the essence of the gospel.

That essence, for Paul, was simple: "Christ Jesus came into the world to save sinners—of whom I am the worst" (1 Timothy 1:15). In all his years of passionately serving Christ, Paul had never lost his amazement that God had shown so much kindness, and even honor, to someone who had actually murdered His people. Wide-eyed gratitude had always shielded Paul from pride, and he wanted to set that example before the leaders in Ephesus, especially Timothy.

Beyond that example, Paul had specific criteria for assessing candidates for leadership in the community. Integrity, proven ability to govern one's own family, and experience in serving Christ figured prominently. Several times Paul repeated that an overfondness for money was something to watch out for.

He also had instructions for what should happen in community gatherings. Believers should pray for the pagan civil authorities (which, despite his own experiences in prison, Paul viewed as a gift from God). Disputes should be reconciled before the group gathered to pray. Women should dress modestly, gaining their self-esteem not from being the best dressed but from the quality of their service to others. They should also not compete with the men for control.

The community should take responsibility to care for widows who were truly in need. In fact, one of the things that impressed pagans the most about the followers of Christ was the way they took care of poor members. But Paul insisted that the group as a whole should not have to support elderly people who had family, for it was first the family's responsibility to care for its own. Also, there was no sponging off the community; those on support had to be too old to work and known for their past service. Paul counseled younger widows not to make vows of chastity because eventually they might want to get married. As happy as Paul was in the single life, he was ever practical.

Paul encouraged Timothy to believe the prophecies spoken over him years earlier, and not to let anyone look down on him for being barely thirty years old. Love, faithfulness, and God's commission were his qualifications for leadership, not age. (Timothy seems to have been persistently inclined to self-doubt.) Paul viewed Timothy as his son in a special way, and he pulled out all the stops to offer the support of an affectionate coach.

Titus

Titus, another of Paul's longtime team members, was probably not much older than Timothy but had a tougher personality. At some point Paul worked briefly in Crete and then left Titus to remain as his representative until another team member could replace him.

Crete was no easy assignment. The laziness, wickedness, and dishonesty of its people were proverbial, even among pagans. When Apollos and a lawyer named Zenas happened to be passing through Crete, Paul asked them to carry a letter to Titus so that, like Timothy, he would have his authorization from Paul in writing. His instructions were much like those Timothy received: evaluating the character of potential leaders; silencing factions who had unethical motives, and who were threatening to seriously sidetrack the group; teaching and modeling a lifestyle consistent with a believer's mission in the world. "Doing what is good" became a refrain in this letter sent to a community who apparently found this a challenge.

Second Timothy

Paul's second letter to Timothy was the farewell of a man who knew he was about to die. He was no longer under house arrest, but sat chained in a cold, damp dungeon somewhere in the bowels of Rome. One of his friends even had trouble finding out where he was being kept. He was lonely—some colleagues had deserted him, others were away on assignment, and only Luke remained. Paul wrote to Timothy partly to ask him to come and be with him during his last days. Of Timothy, Paul had told the Philippians, "I have no one else like him" (Philippians 2:20). He wanted his favorite son with him.

Personal desires never completely overshadowed Paul's sense of ministry, however. Many of the original apostles were dead, and all were aging. It was time to pass the baton to the next generation—people like Titus and Timothy and the leaders in local communities. Paul's chief concern was that this generation understand the gospel accurately and thoroughly, and that they pass it on the same way to those who came after them. There were so many teachers traveling from town to town with concoctions of the gospel and pagan mysticism. Paul had devoted his life to keeping the gospel pure—not so that it could be set in concrete, but so that it would remain unencumbered by cultural trappings or outright falsehood. A Jewish gospel or a Greek gospel would be impotent to renew lives in Spain or Africa.

Likewise, just as they had to keep the message pure, so the upcoming generation had to keep their lives pure. Corruption would be forever licking at leaders' heels, and many would give in. Paul charged Timothy to set an example with his own life, and not to shrink from confronting other leaders to keep them from dragging whole communities down with them. (Paul had confronted even Peter when the gospel was at stake.) On the other hand, quarreling and resentment were absolutely to be avoided. Confrontation did not mean mudslinging.

Paul did not hide his personal pain from his friend, but he didn't want Timothy to be discouraged by it. Yes, it hurt that everyone deserted him at his trial. But that didn't matter because "the Lord stood at my side and gave me strength, so that through me the message might be fully proclaimed and all the Gentiles might hear of it" (2 Timothy 4:17). Even trial and martyrdom could be used for God's agenda. Let the pagans watch how a believer handles suffering and death; let them wonder at his joy and hope; let them ask where this hope came from. He would tell them this:

> I have fought the good fight, I have finished the race, I have kept the faith. Now there is in store for me the crown of righteousness, which the Lord, the righteous Judge, will award to me on that day. (2 Timothy 4:7-8)

36

International Mail

◆

Hebrews, James, 1 and 2 Peter, Jude

A Message to Jewish Believers

Paul was not the only servant of Christ sending letters around the Mediterranean world. The Bible includes eight other letters that the early believers accepted as authoritative from God. Three were written by the Apostle John; two by the Apostle Peter; one each by James and Jude, two brothers of Jesus; and one by an unknown author.

The latter bears only the title, "To Hebrews." It was apparently sent to a single community of Jewish believers living somewhere in the Roman Empire. Its author was someone with stature in the international network and a personal bond with his readers: perhaps Paul, Apollos, or Barnabas.

These Hebrew believers were facing two temptations to cool their passion for Jesus the Messiah. On one hand, they were still strongly attached to their Jewish ethnic identity and to the religious traditions of their people. They wanted to continue keeping the ceremonial laws, the festivals, the food laws, and so on. In many ways, they felt more akin to other Jews than to Gentile followers of Christ.

At the same time, they were facing persecution to abandon their commitment to Jesus. The pressure may have been coming from unbelieving Jews, who viewed them as traitors to God and true Judaism, and followers of a blasphemer. It was normal for Jews who announced faith in Jesus to be expelled from their synagogues, have their children barred from synagogue schools, and lose their jobs in areas controlled by Jews. Stresses like these may have begun to cause these Hebrew believers to reconsider their pledge to Christ.

Or, the tension may have been coming from the secular authorities. By AD 60, Rome was beginning to distinguish between Christianity and Judaism. The latter was a legal religion, but the former—if it was not just a Jewish sect—was not. As Judaism and Christianity diverged, it was becoming necessary for Hebrew believers to throw in their lot either with the people of Christ or with the Jews. To remain a Jew would mean security; to identify with Christ would mean legal and social limbo. The writer to the Hebrews observed that his readers had not yet had to shed their blood because of allegiance to Jesus, but we know that a scant four years later this was no longer true.

No matter what the precise source of their conflict, one thing was certain: Serving Jesus Christ was costing these Hebrew believers more than they were comfortable paying. Their apostolic friend faced them with this burning question: Is Jesus worth it all? Then he proceeded to persuade them that the answer was yes.

His message was that the way of Christ is better than any alternative—particularly Judaism. Jesus is greater than the angels, greater than Moses, a greater priest than Aaron, a greater sacrifice than those offered in the temple. He totally understands our weaknesses because He experienced life as a man; He learned what it feels like to obey God amid terrible suffering. Yet He is a priest in the line not of Levi but of Melchizedek, whose name means "king of righteousness." David had foreseen the coming of an eternal Priest-King in his line and had written, "You are a priest forever, in the order of Melchizedek" (Psalm 110:4). This Priest offered one perfect Sacrifice once for all humans, for all time. Therefore, the butchering of animals day after futile day was obsolete. It was a picture to explain what Jesus would do, but now it was passé and would soon fade away.

The writer wanted his Hebrew comrades to understand how suffering fits into the life of God's people. "It was fitting," he wrote, "that God . . . should make the author of their salvation perfect through suffering" (Hebrews 2:10) because pain is the hallmark of life after Eden. The writer goes on, "Since the children have flesh and blood, he too shared in their humanity so that by his death he might destroy him who holds the power of death—that is, the devil—and free those who all their lives were held in slavery by their fear of death" (2:14-15).

So death need hold no terror for His servants. They can follow the example of God's people in every generation who have endured anguish with clear-eyed hope because they were convinced that God was telling them the truth—even with no material evidence to back it up. Noah built a land-locked boat and kept faith in it for half a year; Abraham went to his grave with only one son and a square yard of land; Isaac, Jacob, and Joseph bet their lives on a Kingdom they never saw; Moses gave up princedom; Rahab risked her neck for a God she'd only heard of. Generations of faithful Jews had faced death because they refused to settle for the easy compromise. Could this generation do less?

The choice was stark. Jesus' death had gained access for believers to the very throne room of God. They had the full rights of sons and daughters to stand before the Father and tell Him anything. But if they retreated from this offer out of fear of what unbelievers might do, there was no other hope available to them. To know that Jesus was the Son of God, and to reject Him for self-protection, was to choose death.

To the writer of this letter, Jesus fulfilled the Old Covenant in every minute detail. His last illustration summed up his point. Under the Old Covenant, the blood of a sin offering was brought to God's throne in the temple, but the body was burned outside the camp or city because it was corrupt—stained with the evil of the people for whom it substituted. Therefore, "Jesus also suffered outside the city gate to make the people holy through his own blood. Let us, then, go to him outside the camp, bearing the disgrace he bore. For here we do not have an enduring city, but we are looking for the city that is to come" (13:12-13). The holy city of Ezekiel's vision. A new Jerusalem. The Kingdom of God.

James
The letter to the Hebrews is written in more elegant Greek than any other New Testament book. It is also the New Testament's finest overall commentary on the Old. Clearly, its author was a man of remarkable learning and culture.

The little letter of James, by contrast, is the plain talk of a Jew who probably knew little of the world outside Palestine. The author identifies himself simply as "James, a servant of God and of the Lord Jesus Christ" (James 1:1). Of the three followers of Jesus named James (the English equivalent of Jacob), this one was probably the eldest of Jesus' four brothers. However, he based his authority not on physical kinship to Jesus, but on having been forgiven by Him.

During Jesus' earthly lifetime, James thought He was a bit crazy. But when Jesus appeared to him after the Resurrection, James changed his mind. He became a leader of the Jerusalem community; Paul even called him a "pillar" of that team. James's judgment of the Gentile question carried the day at the first Jerusalem council.

James was known as "James the Just" by the people of Jerusalem, both followers of Christ and others. He was scrupulous in observing the Law and had a reputation for holiness and asceticism. However, the Jewish historian Josephus recorded that James was stoned by the Jews in AD 62 for violating the Law.

James did try to make the way of Christ more appealing to Jews by encouraging Jewish believers to keep the Law and avoid eating with Gentiles. But there is no evidence that he claimed the Law was necessary for pleasing God, and he supported outreach to Gentiles that did not bind them to the Law. He was eager to compromise on purely cultural issues, but he utterly refused to compromise with pagan morals.

Because of its very Jewish flavor, James's letter has caused Gentile believers some confusion. It barely mentions Jesus at all, and never His death and resurrection. Some readers have felt it contradicts Paul's teaching that one cannot do anything to earn God's favor. But in fact, James shows no sign of ever having read Paul's letters to the Romans or Galatians. He simply uses some of the same words differently.

James may have written as early as AD 45, before Paul began planting communities and before there were many Gentile believers. Or, he may have written as late as from AD 55 to 60, when Paul's teachings were being widely discussed, misquoted, and misconstrued. Either way, it seems that James was trying to correct a distortion of the gospel. A lot of people had responded to the news that they could enter the Kingdom of God just by believing that Jesus was King and God. But some of the people got the idea that being born into God's family was all there was to it, that believing in Jesus was just a mental agreement to a set of ideas.

James wanted to counter this notion that one could remain a spiritual baby forever. To him, "believing" or "faith" was not just a mental assent. It was the kind of active trust that moved Abraham to tie his son to an altar, that prompted Rahab to put her life on the line. Even demons believe intellectually, said James. Real faith can be seen in actions like caring for the poor and avoiding moral corruption.

James was writing to people who he assumed knew the gospel, so he didn't rhapsodize on mystical union with Christ or the meaning of the Crucifixion. Instead, he got down and practical about how to live in light of the gospel.

He called his readers to a tested, mature commitment.

James was blunt. Don't blame God when you are tempted to do evil; blame the slime in your soul and deal with it. Don't call yourself the community of God and then treat well-dressed people better than shabby ones. Don't claim to be a teacher of the gospel when you can't control your mouth. Don't imagine you're wise if envy and ambition are poisoning your heart. Don't just read the Bible; do what it says.

James may have been committed to the outward rules of the Law, but he was no legalist. He understood human psychology surprisingly well. The reason you have conflicts with people, he said, is not because of them. It's because you have desires in your heart, and you want to make people fulfill them. Your desires aren't met because (1) you refuse to depend on God for them, or (2) they are selfish. James's solution: First, just decide that God is in charge, and you are not. Second, stop listening to what you know is demonic deception. Third, go to God with your desires, trusting that He'll welcome you. Stop pretending and face the damage that your self-centeredness is doing. Grieve over it. When you really want God more than your selfish desires, He will be able to change your heart and satisfy your longings.

First Peter

We know much less about Peter's activities than Paul's because he didn't have a friend like Luke following him around taking notes. Tradition has it that Barnabas's nephew Mark took notes on Peter's memories of Jesus, and that those notes became the basis of the Gospel of Mark. But what Peter did after the book of Acts leaves him in Jerusalem around AD 50 is unknown.

Early sources are unanimous that he died in Rome under Nero's persecution, either in the pogrom immediately after the fire, or a year or two later. He had evidently been in Rome for some time nurturing the communities there.

Of the two surviving letters of Peter, the first says Peter

wrote it (along with Paul's former colleague Silas) from "Babylon" (5:13). Early believers sometimes used that name to symbolize the ultimate corrupt pagan city, so Peter may have been referring to Rome. Alternatively, he may have been in literal Babylon (which at that time was a small town on the Euphrates River) or in an Egyptian military outpost by that name.

He sent this letter to believers in several provinces of Asia Minor. They were suffering the usual harassment by pagan neighbors and the normal hassles of life, and Peter wanted to help them live up to their calling in the midst of the stress. He addressed them as "aliens and strangers in the world" (1 Peter 2:11)—citizens of another Kingdom who should not be surprised that the people of this planet find them confusing, unnerving, even threatening. He also named them "a chosen people, a royal priesthood, a holy nation, a people belonging to God" (2:9). Their mission: to praise their Master not only with their lips but also with their lives.

He wrote, "Live such good lives among the pagans that, though they accuse you of doing wrong, they may see your good deeds and glorify God on the day he visits us" (2:12). How does a pagan glorify God? By turning away from his rebellion and toward Christ. The behavior of a royal priest draws unbelievers to God. So, in 3:15 he tells his readers to "always be prepared to give an answer to everyone who asks you to give the reason for the hope that you have. But do this with gentleness and respect." Don't be alarmed if a coworker or a city official ridicules or interrogates you. See it as an opportunity to offer life to that person. A royal priest is ready with the words of the gospel as well as the deeds.

Like Paul, Peter saw daily life as an ideal chance to make Christ attractive. A slave who did excellent work and endured abuse without bitterness would stand out in the crowd. A wife who glowed with inner contentment would make a pagan husband take notice. A husband who treated his wife with respect would be noteworthy. A community where the leaders were not in it for the money or the prestige,

and where the young respected instruction from the old—
that would be something for the pagans to think twice about.

Second Peter

In his first letter, Peter dealt with how to respond to persecution from outside the community. In his second, he addressed
the other main problem that plagued the body: fraudulent
teachers distorting the gospel for their own gain. Peter was
evidently furious when he dictated this letter, for it rings with
comments like, "These men are springs without water and
mists driven by a storm. Blackest darkness is reserved for
them" (2 Peter 2:17)!

The community to which Peter wrote was being thrown
into confusion by men who distorted the gospel so badly that
they could even justify drunken orgies in broad daylight. They
may have been forerunners of the full-blown cults of the next
century who said nothing a spiritual person did with the body
mattered. They preyed upon people who had just converted to
Christ from paganism and were struggling to give up wild sex
and drinking. According to Peter, the false teachers "promise
them freedom, while they themselves are slaves of depravity—
for a man is a slave to whatever has mastered him" (2:19).

Also, the charlatans were claiming to have some secret
knowledge beyond the gospel that one needed to know in
order to be secure about one's life after death. Against this
notion, Peter insisted that God had already given believers
"everything we need for life and godliness through our
knowledge of him" (1:3). It is knowing Jesus personally and
intimately, not knowing some esoteric body of information,
that enables a person to live the spiritual life.

Finally, the false teachers were ridiculing the idea that Jesus
would ever return and usher in the end of the earth as we know
it. It had been decades since His departure, and a lot of believers were getting impatient. They hadn't expected to live their
whole lives waiting. But Peter said that God's slowness allowed
more people to have a chance to respond to His invitation.

It was indeed looking like the whole first generation of believers might die out before Christ's return. That was not at all what Peter and his colleagues had expected thirty years earlier when they ate and talked with the resurrected Jesus. They expected the end of the world any day. But in looking back, Peter understood that Jesus had said nothing that guaranteed He would return within Peter's lifetime, or even within the century. Like Abraham, Peter and his readers had to keep looking forward with unproven hope.

Jude

Much like his brother, Jude called himself "a servant of Jesus Christ," but he also emphasized that he was "a brother of James" (Jude 1). He knew he was too obscure to claim authority on his own; he preferred to claim kinship with a leader in the Jerusalem community rather than with Jesus Himself. After all, every one of his readers could claim to be a brother of Jesus in the only way that really counted.

Jude's letter is a short warning about frauds similar to those Peter denounced. Disagreement about precise understandings of the gospel was one thing—there was plenty of room in the body for that. But these men were claiming that God's free forgiveness meant they could commit any immorality they wanted and not fear God's anger. Paul had been accused of teaching that, and he had strongly denied it. Jude pulled out all the stops in condemning such an idea, which was a slap in God's face. As Paul had told the Romans, what person who really loved God enough to receive His grace would want to enslave himself to activities that grieved God?

One odd practice both Peter and Jude warned against was slandering spirit beings, even evil ones. It's hard to imagine why so many false teachers were mocking demons, and one might wonder what was wrong with doing so. But respect, even for evil beings, seems to be a value in God's Kingdom. Rudeness and contempt are devilish characteristics, even when directed against the Devil himself.

37

The View from Heaven

◆

1, 2, and 3 John; Revelation

John

The other apostles were all dead by AD 90, but the Apostle John remained—the last living man who had been intimate friends with Jesus during His life on earth. The Romans had leveled Jerusalem and burned its temple to the ground back in AD 70 to stamp out a Jewish revolt. That was the end of the Jerusalem community. Its members were now scattered. John ended up in Ephesus, where the believers received him with honor bordering on awe.

After all, John had been Jesus' closest friend. Furthermore, in his late sixties John had become something of a visionary prophet, somewhat like Daniel. In his youth Jesus had dubbed him a "son of thunder" because of his temper. Now that intensity was channeled into a passion for his Lord and a talent for piercing to the core of an issue. His demeanor would have been alarming had he not placed such a high value on gentleness and love.

Ephesus and environs had been Paul's assignment during his lifetime, but now John took responsibility for believers in every town for a hundred miles around. It was probably for them that he wrote his Gospel during the years around AD 85. And when a clique of pseudo-Christians began to wreak confusion in the area, John's response was a letter that circulated among the communities under his care.

Ultrapluralism

Asia was a cultural melting pot. Greeks, Egyptians, Syrians, and Persians had immigrated over the generations and mixed their customs with whatever ancient ways still lingered. Few people thought it necessary to hold one school of thought rigorously. They thought there were many roads to truth, and a person took what he liked from each—a pinch of Plato, a dash of Persian dualism, and one's ancestral cult for tradition's sake.

In this environment, Jews and Christians were considered narrow-minded and even atheistic for paying homage to just one God. Most people acknowledged hundreds and favored several. Some hedged their bets by joining one or more "mystery" cults—groups with secret rites of initiation that promised encounters with the divine and bliss in the afterlife. There were sects that mixed Judaism with Plato or astrology or secret revelation. Thus, it was inevitable that someone would try to add the teachings of Jesus to a Greek-Persian-occult casserole and challenge the apostles' gospel.

Fifty years after John's death these semi-Christian hybrids were as common, various, and thorny as roses. The seeds were planted in John's lifetime. The full-blown systems are labeled Gnostic (from the Greek *gnosis*, meaning "knowledge") because they all offered some secret knowledge by which a person could be saved. This knowledge was not available through study, but only through revelation from some higher spiritual plane. It was basically self-knowledge; one recognized the divine spark that was the true self.

Most Gnostics believed in a divine redeemer who would bring the knowledge of the true self. Some identified that redeemer with Jesus; others did not. Those who did talk of

"Christ" were not thinking of the Jewish King, but of a sort of spirit who had "emanated" from "the divine Absolute." Some believed Jesus was the Christ but only appeared to have a flesh-and-blood body during His time on earth. (They thought matter was too corrupt for a pure spirit being to take on.) Others said the Christ-spirit descended upon Jesus at His baptism and departed just before His death.

Evidently, some men with views like these joined the communities of Asia for a time and provoked strife. They eventually withdrew in anger when they failed to persuade the majority, but the believers were upset. They were asking questions like, "What's the truth about Jesus and 'the Christ'?" "How can you tell a real child of God from a fake one?" "How can I tell if I'm really a child of God?" John's first letter answers those questions.

First John
John's style seems repetitive to readers accustomed to step-by-step logic. He writes in a spiral, cycling through the same basic ideas deeper and deeper, from every angle. The ideas of *knowledge* and *confidence* recur over and over, as John emphasizes what believers know and how they can be confident that they know it. John himself was confident that his readers really did have a relationship with God, and he didn't want them to worry about it. But he also didn't want them to be led astray by people who claimed they needed something different.

There are three basic tests, John told his readers, to know if they are really children of God. First, genuine children of God walk in the light of moral truth. They're not sinless—maybe they lapse into selfish behavior regularly—but they're at war with the self-centered side of their nature. They're seeking every possible strengthening of the Holy Spirit and making every choice they can for purity rather than corruption. They don't tell themselves their behavior doesn't matter just because they've been "saved." And when they catch themselves doing wrong, they're quick to admit it to God and fervent in asking

God to change them. They want to be like God, who is the perfection of moral purity. Obeying God is a joy to them, not a
teeth-gritting duty. They're glad when God shines a spotlight
on the areas where they tend to lie to themselves. And they
don't gloss over their actions with excuses. They regularly take
a hard look at their lives and call the slime what it is.

Second, real children of God love the rest of the family.
"Love each other" was Jesus' paramount command, so people
who want to obey God will make this instruction a priority.
Jealousy, hatred, and indifference will be fading traits in
people who have God active in their lives. And John's notion
of love was not mere sentiment. He had in mind deeds like
taking care of brothers and sisters with material needs, and
laying down one's very life for them. "Dear children," he said,
"let us not love with words or tongue but with actions and in
truth" (1 John 3:18).

Third, people who truly know God hang on to the certainty that Jesus was the Christ who was born, lived, and died
in a human body. John stresses that he himself had actually
heard, seen, and touched the eternal One who came from God.
Anyone who bent the truth about Jesus to make Him less than
fully God and fully human didn't really know God at all, for
one could not know the Father without knowing the Son.

Believing the truth about Jesus, obeying His commands,
and loving other believers were for John the three interwoven
strands of belonging to God. One could not obey without
believing, and to obey and to love were aspects of each other.

John had just one final request: "Dear children, keep yourselves from idols" (5:21). Or, as he put it earlier, "Do not love the
world" (2:15). John was not telling the Asians to hold their
pagan neighbors in contempt. He was warning against the great
temptation that plagues the most seasoned believer: desiring
something in the world system more than God. It might be a
man's longing to feel really important through the work he
does, or a woman's yearning for a man who will truly cherish
her. It might be the lust for possessions, power, comfort, secu-

rity, or praise. Whatever it is, it becomes an idol and an addiction when a person pursues it as though it will give life. John's solution: Stop believing that those things give real life. Love the Father. Pursue *Him* with that unquenchable longing.

Hospitality

Love and truth figure prominently in John's first letter as key features of life with God. In his next two letters, he shows how to apply them in a balanced way to two practical situations.

The Romans knew that a prosperous, united empire needed a way for people to travel safely. So they invested a lot of money and effort in building roads and guarding them from bandits. The stone highways were smooth and wide enough for soldiers to get to trouble spots quickly. And while robbers and wild animals were not eliminated in lonely areas, they were curbed enough to let civilians travel with some security.

And civilians did travel. Not only merchants and government officials, but tourists, pilgrims, magicians, priests of every cult, and teachers of every imaginable doctrine walked or rode from Syria to Spain and back again. A teacher of grammar or philosophy would arrive in a town and try to attract paying students among the sons of local men. Religious missionaries sought adoration (and money) for their deities and doctrines. Among all these the ambassadors of Jesus Christ traveled, doing their best to stand out from the competition as messengers of truth.

There were inns every twenty-two miles or so along the Roman roads, but we've already seen that they were no place for respectable folk. Most people tried to stay with friends of friends when they traveled. And because the spread of the gospel depended on apostolic teams, hospitality was considered a key expression of Christlike love. Paul often stayed with converts when he visited a town. Likewise, he asked believers to house messengers and teachers, and to help them with provisions for the next leg of their journeys (Romans 15:23-24, 16:1-2; Titus 3:12-13).

But when it became known that believers would feed and house anyone who claimed to be a teacher of the gospel, unscrupulous people began to take advantage. *The Didache,* a manual for Syrian communities, gave guidelines for hospitality: an apostle may stay up to two days and may receive only provisions, not money, when he leaves; a person who wants to stay longer must work; and so on. John's communities in Asia were having similar problems, and he wrote 2 and 3 John to address them.

Love and Truth

Second John was sent to "the chosen lady and her children" (2 John 1). In the name of love, this lady was welcoming into her home some of the false teachers John combatted in his first letter. John reaffirmed to her the importance of loving other believers. But, he said, love ceases to be love when it loses sight of truth. To give aid and a forum to teachers who distort the gospel is to do harm to real believers. If you really want to show love for the people of God, wrote John, reject visitors who teach falsehood about Jesus.

John's third letter is addressed to a friend of John's named Gaius. Some of John's envoys had visited Gaius's community and had brought back glowing reports of Gaius's hospitality. This, wrote John, is living by love and truth. Now John was sending to Gaius's community an emissary named Demetrius. He respectfully asked Gaius to offer Demetrius the same kindness. (Third John is basically a letter of introduction letting Gaius know that Demetrius really did represent John. With so many impostors around, it was a good idea to send genuine emissaries with letters.)

John was especially concerned because someone prominent in Gaius's community—one "Diotrephes, who loves to be first"— had told the rest of the community to have nothing to do with John and his messengers. Diotrephes's doctrine may have been pure, but his arrogant, controlling attitude was far from the love and truth John expected. John warned Gaius that Diotrephes might try to have Gaius expelled from the community for housing a friend of John's, but Gaius was not to worry. John hoped to arrive in person soon to face Diotrephes.

Both of these little letters are snapshots of the kinds of hassles that sprout like weeds as soon as the people of God try to gather in community. It's easy to become frustrated when pettiness poisons the community. It would be nice to think that becoming God's children would immediately make men and women the loving people they should be. But it doesn't. John's response was not to throw up his hands in disgust, but to hang in with the Father's stubborn family and try to urge them on to maturity. His approach required strong doses of both love and truth.

Revelation
John wrote these three letters in the early AD 90s. For a while after Nero's death in AD 68, persecution of believers was a small-scale affair—a brawl here, a little job discrimination there, and malicious gossip nearly everywhere. The main thorns in the community's side were self-proclaimed teachers of divine truth.

But toward the end of his reign, Emperor Domitian began to lose his mind. Roman poets had always sung extravagant praises of their emperors, calling them gods incarnate in all sorts of flowery ways, but Domitian was the first to believe them. He liked to be addressed as "Our Lord and God." He decreed that anyone holding public office or testifying in court—effectively almost everyone—must offer a pinch of incense to the emperor's guardian spirit and declare "Caesar is Lord." People who refused to worship the emperor in this way might lose their jobs, their homes, even their lives.

For decades the slogan of God's people had been "Jesus is Lord." The gospel asserted that Jesus was King of the world and would come back soon to claim His domain. But the years had passed, and there was no sign of Him. Arrogant teachers were a cancer within the communities, and by this time claiming allegiance to Christ was growing more and more dangerous. Was it worth it? Was God really in control of events on earth?

Around AD 95, John went to the Roman penal colony on the island of Patmos, off the coast of Asia. He went either as a prisoner or as chaplain to the increasing scores of believers exiled there. One Sunday while praying, he received a spectacular series of visions with a single message: *Yes, I am still in control.* Under the inspiration of God, John wrote a letter to seven Asian communities urging them to stand firm in the face of the attacks assailing them. That letter, the book of Revelation, recounts John's glimpse into the spiritual realm. Like no other biblical book, it unveils the war between the Snake and the Lamb of God.

Seven Communities

John had been Jesus' dearest friend. But when the resurrected Lord appeared to him glowing with divine fire, John fainted, just as more than one prophet had done before him. Jesus picked him up and identified Himself in terms calculated to shake John's wavering comrades to attention: "Do not be afraid. [John was no doubt trembling with terror.] I am the First and the Last. I am the Living One; I was dead, and behold I am alive for ever and ever! And I hold the keys of death and Hades" (Revelation 1:17-18).

Jesus dictated brief notes to each of the seven communities to whom He wanted John to send this revelation. Each memo offered praise, criticism, or both; counsel; and a promise "to him who overcomes." The messages were blunt.

For instance, the Ephesian community was doing great at rejecting falsehood, but in the process had hardened into a tight, loveless orthodoxy. Jesus warned them that if they didn't regain their youthful passion for God, their group would soon shrivel and fade out of existence.

Believers in Smyrna were being denounced to the authorities by Jews who considered their beliefs blasphemy. Jesus reminded them of His own death and resurrection, and urged them to face martyrdom with confidence.

The imperial governor resided in Pergamum, Asia's political capital. He held the "right of the sword" to execute whomever he willed. But Jesus told the community in Pergamum that *He* held the sword that mattered. He commended them for not flinching under persecution, but rebuked them for tolerating certain members who still dabbled in paganism.

Some Thyatirans wanted to believe it was okay to share in the pagan practices that were so much a part of trade guilds in their town. It was tough to do business and avoid idolatry, and a so-called prophetess was winning fans by offering an easier way. Jesus praised the Thyatirans' love, faith, service, and perseverance, but warned them not to tolerate compromise with debauchery and idolatry.

Jesus had harsh words for the community in Sardis: "You have a reputation of being alive, but you are dead" (3:1). A glitzy public image meant nothing without the dynamic group life that came from active love.

Jesus had nothing but tender encouragement for the little embattled group in Philadelphia. But His final message to wealthy Laodicea pulled no punches. The community there deemed itself rich, but Jesus called it "wretched, pitiful, poor, blind, and naked." The city took pride in its banks, its industry in black textiles, and its famous eye ointment. Jesus counseled the Laodiceans to get gold, white robes, and eye salve from Him. Material comfort had made the Laodiceans lazy and self-satisfied. They had no passion for Jesus because they didn't feel any great need for Him. Jesus loved them too much to leave them in their complacency. He bared His heart to them, urging them to open their hearts to Him before it was too late.

Visions

After recording these jarring memos, John was treated to a tour of Heaven. He saw the Father enthroned, blazing like the fire of a thousand gems. Four bizarre angelic beings sang ceaseless praise, and twenty-four "elders" added their song to the Creator. A slain but living Lamb appeared and received a scroll. The worshipers sang a new song to the Lamb because He was acclaimed worthy to open the scroll and disclose its contents.

What did it all mean? John's readers would have had much less trouble than we at deciphering it, since apocalyptic (books of symbolic visions) was a familiar type of literature at that time. The symbolism of numbers and certain objects was fairly standard, somewhat like the symbolism of political cartoons today.

We are often forced to guess at the meaning of specific bits of John's visions. The gist of this one seems to be that by His death as a sacrifice for sin Jesus won the right to bring the contents of the scroll—perhaps a contract declaring God's plan for the fulfillment of history—into effect.

John watched as the myriad inhabitants of Heaven exulted that Jesus was bringing about the climax of history. But as Jesus broke each of the scroll's seven seals, John saw that the inhabitants of earth were not so ecstatic. Conquest, bloodshed, war, famine, and death accompanied the breaking of the first four seals. With the fifth, the souls of martyrs cried to be avenged. When the sixth broke, cataclysm swept the earth and sky, and all humankind cringed in terror of the Lamb. Angels appeared to mark the people of God who remained on earth—to protect them from the rending of land and sea—and a multitude sang praises to God from Heaven. Jesus broke the seventh seal, and Heaven hushed.

Then followed a cycle in which seven angels blew seven trumpets. A third of the land was burned, a third of the sea turned bloody, a third of the fresh water became poisonous, a third of the sky's light was darkened, a plague of demonic locusts rose from the abyss to plague men, and a third of earth's population died. One might have thought that such calamity would humble the surviving humans, but it did not. They clung stubbornly to their worship of the Snake and his deeds: murder, theft, witchcraft, debauchery. Partial destruction achieved nothing. One trumpet remained.

An angel appeared and swore that the martyrs would wait no longer for justice. Then John saw Jerusalem with its temple rebuilt but harassed by pagans for three and a half years, while two witnesses stood against the persecution. The witnesses were martyred but raised from death, and an earthquake ravaged Jerusalem, bringing survivors to their knees before God. The seventh angel sounded his trumpet, and a song burst forth in Heaven proclaiming the coming of God's Kingdom.

Then John saw war on earth between a woman and a Dragon—the children of Eve and the children of the Snake—and war in Heaven between God's angels and the Dragon's. He saw a beast with the Dragon's power to attack God's people, and another with snakish power to delude unbelievers with false religion. The persecution was terrible, but more terrible still was the bloodshed of those who fell before God's angels.

Seven angels struck the earth with seven horrific plagues. Babylon, symbolizing the great whore city of the earth, fell amid mourning and mocking. But the chorus of Heaven raised another song: the Whore is dead, long live the Bride of the Lamb, the people of God. The wedding feast of the Kingdom was at hand.

Jesus appeared as a white horseman leading the armies of Heaven against His foes. The Dragon and his human servants were crushed, and the martyrs came to life to reign with Christ for a thousand years. Then came a final battle and the Dragon's final defeat, and then all humanity faced judgment before the throne of their rightful King. Those who were found guilty of treason were destroyed; those found to be loyal subjects were welcomed to the Kingdom.

Finally John saw the Kingdom itself in symbols woven from throughout the Old Testament. A voice proclaimed,

"Now the dwelling of God is with men, and he will live with them. They will be his people, and God himself will be with them and be their God. He will wipe every tear from their eyes. There will be no more death or mourning or crying or pain, for the old order of things has passed away." (Revelation 21:3-4)

To read John's visions is to be overwhelmed by color, sound, weird creatures, and strange events. One can study the specifics for clues to the future, or one can stand back to behold the tapestry. Whatever the details, the essence is clear: God's people can expect terrible suffering as the Dragon escalates the war in the final days of his fury. But they must cling to hope, confident despite everything that God will triumph in the end. Beyond martyrdom lies a Kingdom that fulfills every longing of the prophets. In Eden God visited His children, but that intimacy was brief. In the wilderness, He dwelt with His people in a tent that could be approached only with blood sacrifice. For thirty years He lived among His people in a human body that became the ultimate sacrifice. But one day He will dwell with them as never before.

In his letter, John identified himself as "I, John, your brother and companion in the suffering and kingdom and patient endurance that are ours in Jesus" (1:9). Those words summarized for John the believer's life. Suffering now. The glorious Kingdom just on the horizon. And therefore, patient endurance.

"I am coming soon!" Jesus promises three times in the last chapter of Revelation. Two thousand years later, His people still wait. Yet, John wrote, to be envied are those who can look past the anguish of today and trust their God for the joy of tomorrow: "Whoever is thirsty, let him come; and whoever wishes, let him take the free gift of the water of life" (22:17).

And we say, along with John, "Amen. Come Lord Jesus."

Author

Karen Lee-Thorp has served NavPress as series editor for the LIFECHANGE Bible study series, compiler of *A Compact Guide to the Christian Life*, and small-group materials editor. She has also written a number of small-group discussion guides, including most of those for NavPress's various video products.

Karen holds a B.A. from Yale University, where she specialized in the history of the church in the world—from competition with paganism in the Roman Empire to the black church in South Africa.

Time line   Dates are approximate, based on *The NIV Study Bible*

2100 BC	2000	1900	1800	1700	1600	1500

◄ Creation, Adam, Noah

◄ Abraham

● Isaac

● Jacob

● Joseph

● Jacob's family settles in Egypt   1876 BC

● Moses

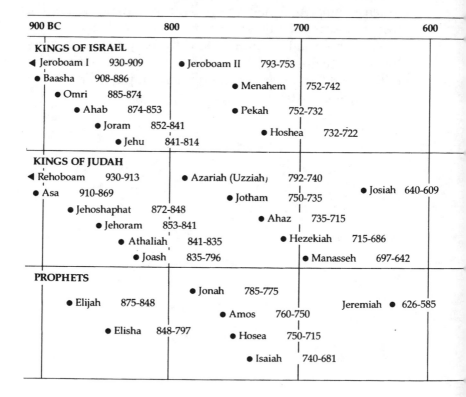

900 BC	800	700	600

KINGS OF ISRAEL

◄ Jeroboam I   930-909   ● Jeroboam II   793-753

● Baasha   908-886

● Menahem   752-742

● Omri   885-874

● Ahab   874-853   ● Pekah   752-732

● Joram   852-841

● Hoshea   732-722

● Jehu   841-814

KINGS OF JUDAH

◄ Rehoboam   930-913   ● Azariah (Uzziah)   792-740

● Asa   910-869   ● Jotham   750-735   ● Josiah   640-609

● Jehoshaphat   872-848

● Jehoram   853-841   ● Ahaz   735-715

● Athaliah   841-835   ● Hezekiah   715-686

● Joash   835-796   ● Manasseh   697-642

PROPHETS

● Jonah   785-775

● Elijah   875-848   Jeremiah ● 626-585

● Amos   760-750

● Elisha   848-797

● Hosea   750-715

● Isaiah   740-681

356

1500	1400	1300	1200	1100	1000	900 BC

● Moses leads Israel out of Egypt   1446 BC
  ● Joshua conquers Jericho   1406 BC

● Ruth marries Boaz
  about 1090

● Saul   1050

● David   1010

● Solomon
  970

Solomon dies; Israel and Judah split ● 930

● Period of Judges   1375-1050

Divided Kingdom   930-722 ●

600	500	400	300 BC

● Jehoiakim   609-598

● Zedekiah   597-586

● Obadiah   605-586

● Daniel   605-530

● Ezekiel   593-571

● Malachi   440-430

● Zechariah, Haggai   520-480

Time line   Dates are approximate, based on *The NIV Study Bible*

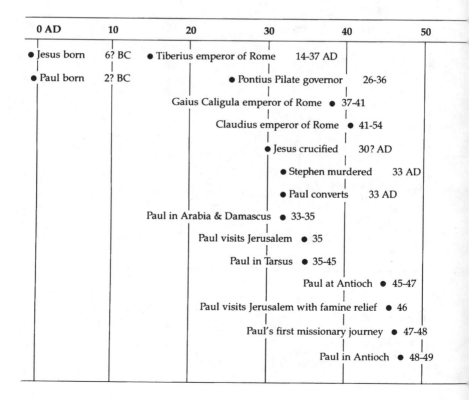

600 BC	500	400	300

◀ Assyria destroys Israel   722   ● Esther becomes queen of Persia   479

● Babylonian captivity   605-538   ● Ezra leads another return   458

● Babylonia takes first captives to exile, incl. Daniel   605

   ● Babylonia takes second captives to exile, incl. Ezekiel   597

      ● Jerusalem falls to Babylon   586   ● Nehemiah arrives in Jerusalem   446

         ● Cyrus lets Jews return to Judah   538

            ● Perian period   538-323

               ● Second temple completed   516

0 AD	10	20	30	40	50

● Jesus born   6? BC   ● Tiberius emperor of Rome   14-37 AD

● Paul born   2? BC   ● Pontius Pilate governor   26-36

                        Gaius Caligula emperor of Rome   ● 37-41

                           Claudius emperor of Rome   ● 41-54

                              ● Jesus crucified   30? AD

                                 ● Stephen murdered   33 AD

                                 ● Paul converts   33 AD

                     Paul in Arabia & Damascus   ● 33-35

                        Paul visits Jerusalem   ● 35

                        Paul in Tarsus   ● 35-45

                                 Paul at Antioch   ● 45-47

                     Paul visits Jerusalem with famine relief   ● 46

                              Paul's first missionary journey   ● 47-48

                                 Paul in Antioch   ● 48-49

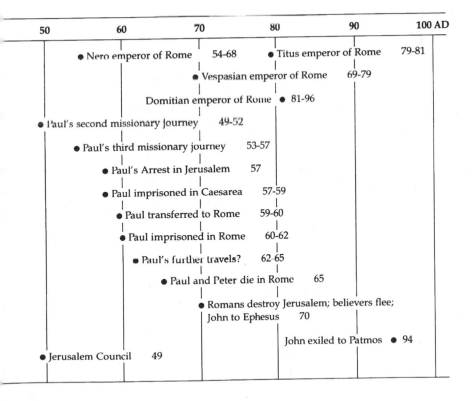

300	200	100	BC 0

● Alexander the Great conquers Persia, beginning of Greek empire   323

● Antiochus Epiphanes desecrates Jewish Temple,
as in Daniel's vision   167-164

Romans conquer Judea ● 63 BC

Herod the Great king of Judea ● 37-4 BC

Augustus Caesar first emperor of Roman Empire ● 27-14 BC

50	60	70	80	90	100 AD

● Nero emperor of Rome   54-68   ● Titus emperor of Rome   79-81

● Vespasian emperor of Rome   69-79

Domitian emperor of Rome ● 81-96

● Paul's second missionary journey   49-52

● Paul's third missionary journey   53-57

● Paul's Arrest in Jerusalem   57

● Paul imprisoned in Caesarea   57-59

● Paul transferred to Rome   59-60

● Paul imprisoned in Rome   60-62

● Paul's further travels?   62-65

● Paul and Peter die in Rome   65

● Romans destroy Jerusalem; believers flee;
John to Ephesus   70

John exiled to Patmos ● 94

● Jerusalem Council   49

359

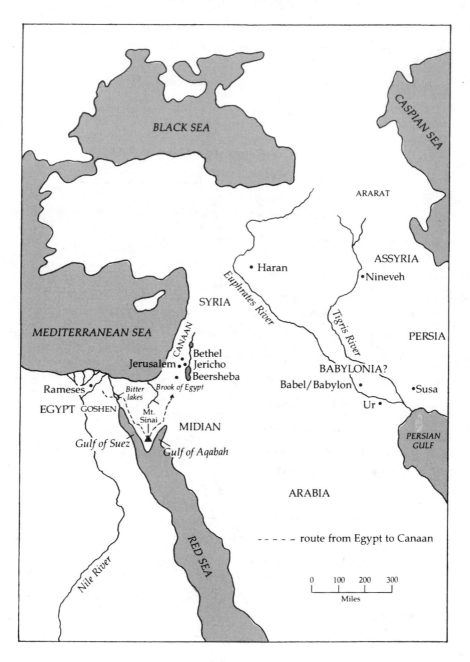

Map: Palestine, 2000–100 BC

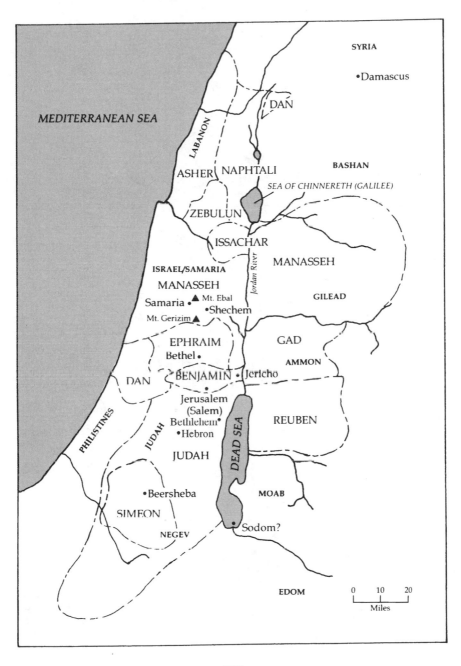

SYRIA

•Damascus

MEDITERRANEAN SEA

DAN

LABANON

ASHER NAPHTALI

BASHAN

SEA OF CHINNERETH (GALILEE)

ZEBULUN

ISSACHAR

MANASSEH

ISRAEL/SAMARIA

Jordan River

MANASSEH

Samaria • ▲ Mt. Ebal
•Shechem
Mt. Gerizim ▲

GILEAD

EPHRAIM
Bethel •

GAD

AMMON

DAN BENJAMIN • Jericho

•
Jerusalem
(Salem)
Bethlehem•
•Hebron

DEAD SEA

REUBEN

PHILISTINES

JUDAH

JUDAH

•Beersheba

MOAB

SIMEON

NEGEV

• Sodom?

EDOM

0   10   20
Miles

Map: The Roman Empire

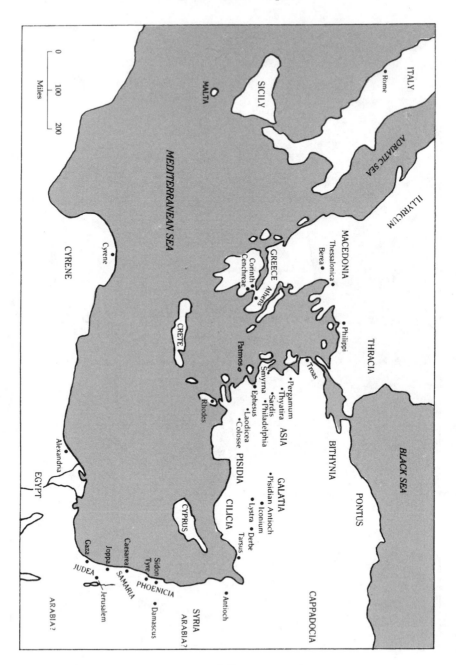

Map: Palestine Under the Romans

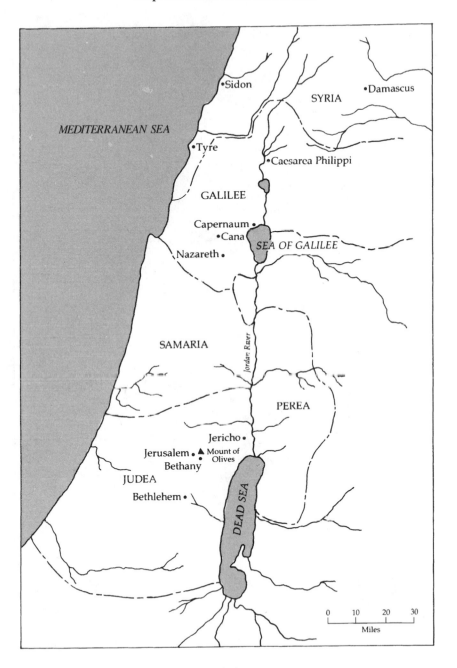

Map: Modern Times

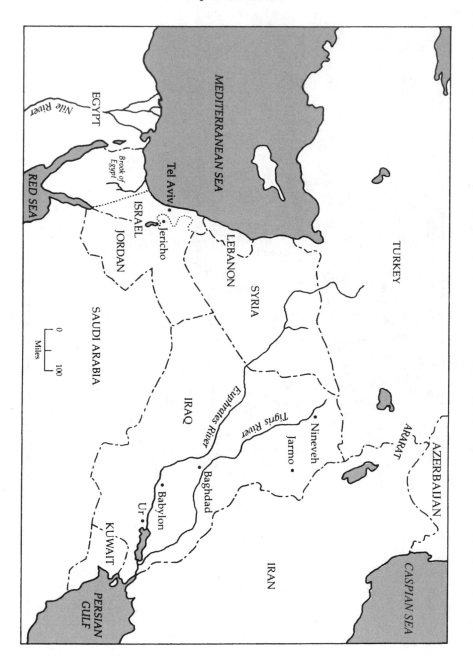

Index

220 · LEE

The Story of Stories
Lee-Thorp, Karen

DATE	ISSUED TO

220 · LEE

The Story of Stories
Lee-Thorp, Karen